D0389686

"An ambitious, original, and well-documented study that addresses some of the most interesting and important political-historical questions of our times."

—*Paul Hollander, author of* Political Pilgrims *and* The End of Commitment

"Jamie Glazov rolls over left-wing intellectual pretensions with a Mack truck that handles like a Porsche. He rounds them up—and when he's finished, there's nothing left."

—*Richard Perle, Assistant Secretary of Defense for the Reagan administration, now a fellow at the American Enterprise Institute*

"With compelling rigor Jamie Glazov exposes (once more) the reasons for the enduring appeal for the Left of hatred, violence, and intolerance as 'values' essential to the rise of a new world order. Marx, Ho, Fidel, Osama, and despots still-to-come can count on legions of recruits—the misfits, failures, and Fellow Travelers of the world—to rally to the cause. Truly a must-read for those who care about truth, the rule of law, and any hope of ultimate stability for humankind. The redefining work for twenty-first century readers of an eternal message."

—*Robert C. McFarlane, National Security Advisor to President Reagan, chairman and CEO of McFarlane Associates, Inc.*

"In years to come, this book will become a classic, not just for conservatives but for all Americans interested in the truth and how to combat a perfidious alliance."

—*Steven Emerson, author of* American Jihad: The Terrorists Living Amongst Us *and producer of the documentary* Jihad in America

"Jamie Glazov analyses with forensic skill how and why radical leftists come repeatedly to see virtue in the most murderous ruthlessness. Alas, his book will not be out of date for a long time."

—*Dr. Theodore Dalrymple, author of* Life at the Bottom: The Worldview that Makes the Underclass

"Any leftist who reads this, and has any honesty left in his mind, must recognize himself in this picture and, hopefully, be ashamed."

—*Vladimir Bukovsky, former leading Soviet dissident, author of* To Build a Castle *and* Judgement in Moscow

"A fascinating, illuminating, and extraordinarily insightful explanation of one of the most puzzling phenomena of our age: the alliance between the Left and the global jihad. This superbly enlightening book should be required reading for the American and European policymakers that are not utterly beholden to the Left, for most of them have yet to come to grips with the Islamic supremacist agenda and its totalitarian imperative—which Glazov ably exposes here."

—*Robert Spencer, author of the* New York Times *bestsellers* The Politically Incorrect Guide to Islam (and the Crusades) *and* The Truth about Muhammad

"Ferocious."

—*David Frum, National Review Online.*

"A must-read if America is going to survive the global war against Radical Islam."

—*Lieutenant General Thomas McInerney, USAF (Ret.)*

"*United in Hate* is a must-read for all Americans concerned with the future of America. Jamie Glazov's writing is eloquent and thought-provoking."

—*Brigitte Gabriel, a renowned terrorism expert and* New York Times *best-selling author. She is the founder of Actforamerica.org.*

"This fascinating and provocative encyclopedia of American leftism is a must for every American. It reads like a thriller. Dr. Glazov has become one of the West's most prolific and dynamic authorities on leftism. *United in Hate* helps us to understand the Left's heresies, and to restore America's patriotic unity."

—*Lieutenant General Ion Mihai Pacepa, the highest-ranking official to have defected from the Soviet bloc, whose latest book is* Programmed to Kill: Lee Harvey Oswald, the Soviet KGB, and the Kennedy Assassination

"This book should be required reading at every university, both in the West and in the East. Psychoanalysts, many of whom are in denial, and Left intellectuals everywhere, need to grapple with Glazov's information and point of view. His subject concerns the survival of the human race and the tragic bloodletting that has been done in the name of progressive, even salvational ideology. The book is hard to put down. Freud might say that Glazov is trying to strengthen Eros, the life force, in us and is doing monumental battle with Thanatos, the death instinct. In this work, Glazov has gone beyond Alice Miller and Eric Hoffer. I congratulate him and I strongly recommend the work."

—Dr. Phyllis Chesler, author of The Death of Feminism

"An informed, bracing, and scary wake-up call for anyone concerned with freedom."

—Brian C. Anderson, editor of City Journal and author of South Park Conservatives

"Through years of prattling about peace and human rights, the American Left was smitten by Joseph Stalin and turned an aggressively blind eye, obsessed by anti-anti-communism, as the Soviet Union slaughtered millions of innocents and enslaved tens of millions more. Now, as radical Islam kills and maims in the name of a hate ideology that condemns the Left's central pieties—intellectual, religious, and sexual freedom—it finds its strongest allies in the Left's redoubts: the academy, the media, and the Democratic Party. What explains this infatuation with evil? In United in Hate: The Left's Romance with Tyranny and Terror, Jamie Glazov provides a riveting, meticulously researched answer. A vital contribution on a subject that continues to vex."

—Andrew C. McCarthy, National Review legal affairs editor and best-selling author of Willful Blindness: A Memoir of the Jihad

"A pleasure to read. There is great satisfaction at seeing the dishonesty, hypocrisy, and deliberate distortions of the anti-American left exposed for what they are. Equally gratifying is to see the exposure of how the totalitarian Left, defeated in its ambition to establish communism in the West, has nihilistically embraced the most blood-soaked and bigoted varieties of Islamic jihadism in hopes that it will punish the West for its rejection of Marxism-Leninism."

—*John Earl Haynes, author of* In Denial: Historians, Communism, and Espionage

"Like many individuals who have fled tyranny, Jamie Glazov is justifiably outraged by the moral blindness of those who deprecate democratic values and norms. This passionate book is both deeply disturbing when it exposes the apologies and excuses offered by some American leftists for repressive regimes and policies and, like everything he writes, provocative."

—*Harvey Klehr, author of* In Denial: Historians, Communism, and Espionage

"Finally, someone has the courage and the bravery to fully expose a mystery which for years has baffled us. The truth is on the cover, but it takes someone like Dr. Glazov to make us see it."

—*Joan Lachkar, Affiliate Member for the New Center of Psychoanalysis, private practitioner in Los Angeles and author of* How to Talk to a Narcissist *and* The Psychopathology of Terrorism

UNITED IN HATE

UNITED IN HATE

THE LEFT'S ROMANCE WITH TYRANNY AND TERROR

by Jamie Glazov

WND BOOKS

UNITED IN HATE: The Left's Romance with Tyranny and Terror
A WND Books book
Published by WorldNetDaily
Los Angeles, CA
Copyright © 2009 by Jamie Glazov

Jacket design by Linda Daly

WND Books are distributed to the trade by:
Midpoint Trade Books
27 West 20th Street, Suite 1102
New York, NY 10011

WND Books are available at special discounts for bulk purchases. WND Books, Inc. also publishes books in electronic formats. For more information call (310) 961-4170 or visit www.wndbooks.com.

First Edition

ISBN 13-Digit: 9781935071600
ISBN 10-Digit: 1935071602
E-Book ISBN 13-Digit: 9781935071075
E-Book ISBN 10-Digit: 1935071076
Library of Congress Control Number: 2008940361

Printed in the United States of America

10 9 8 7 6 5 4 3 2 1

To my granddad, Gregory Rafalsky,
a doctor in the Soviet army,
Missing in Action, October 1941,
Vyazma-Smolensky region near Moscow.

TABLE OF CONTENTS

In his classic Homage to Catalonia (1938), George Orwell chronicled his own evolution during the Spanish Civil War from, essentially, a small-c communist to a social democrat. Having volunteered to fight to protect the elected leftist Spanish Republican government from being overthrown by Franco and Spain's fascists, Orwell by chance joined the militia of POUM, a far-left but anti-Stalinist party, rather than a Stalinist-backed unit. But the idealistic democratic and egalitarian values he saw among his POUM comrades in the front lines fighting the fascists soon came under assault from the cynical and totalitarian Stalinists. Orwell and his wife barely survived the murderous Stalinist purges in Barcelona. Badly wounded, he finally escaped to become, as a democratic socialist, the greatest chronicler of his time—in *Homage, Animal Farm, Nineteen Eighty-Four,* and other works—of the far Left's cynicism and devotion to tyranny.

All his life Orwell stood on the side of the poor and the oppressed and humanized their struggles in matchless prose. In doing so, he espoused values that, in economic terms at least, rightly bear the label "socialist" and would be regarded by most Americans today as decidedly on the left of the political spectrum.

But a key point we should all glean from Orwell's life and writings is that there are differences in appetite for central authority as well as differences in social and economic goals; people may agree on ends but not means, and vice versa. In this work, Dr. Glazov focuses his analysis on that part of the Left with a hearty appetite for authoritarianism, even tyranny, and distinguishes them from the politicians and activists on the Left who more closely resemble Orwell. A democratic socialist who devotes his life to the struggle for freedom and against totalitarianism can be a marvelous and valued colleague for others with the same goals although they may have strong disagreements between them about, say, the degree of income redistribution that is reasonable or the desired character of health care systems. And although George Orwell certainly criticized his own government and those of other democratic states when he felt they stumbled or wandered from their professed principles, he never lapsed into the habit of blaming the democracies first.

The Hitler-Stalin Pact of August 1939 that immediately enabled the German invasion of Poland and led to the outbreak of World War II fractured the Left in Europe and America along the lines Orwell had foreseen—having to do with the appetite for exercise of raw power. Leftists who were first and foremost totalitarians stayed with Stalin, even if that meant they had to be in league with Nazi Germany. Stalin had Trotsky assassinated and most socialists who could not stomach Stalin and Hitler split away to join the ranks of European democratic socialist and labor parties.

"In Old Moscow," to the tune of "My Darling Clementine" by American communist Walter Gourlay (party name Walter Cliff), wryly captures the spirit of those on the Left who felt betrayed by the Stalinists:

> "In Old Moscow, in the Kremlin, in the fall of thirty-nine
> Sat a Russian and a Prussian, writing out the Party Line.
>
> "Oh my darling, oh my darling, oh my darling Party Line
> Oh I never will desert you, 'cause I love this life of mine.
>
> "Leon Trotsky was a Nazi, oh we knew it for a fact
> Pravda said it, we all read it—before the Stalin-Hitler Pact.
>
> "Once a Nazi would be shot, see, that was then the Party Line
> Now a Nazi's hotsy-totsy, Trotsky's laying British mines.
>
> "Now the Nazis and Der Führer stand within the Party Line
> All the Russians love the Prussians—Volga boatmen sail the Rhine."

In the fascinating pages that follow, Jamie Glazov moves us forward some seventy years from the late 1930s to yet another battle for the soul of the Left in Western democracies. A number of the characters look similar to those of the thirties, at least in broad outline.

There are some Orwells: fighters for social justice; solid enemies of totalitarians of whatever stripe; reformers willing to criticize their own democratic—albeit flawed—governments; socially committed advocates of redistribution of society's wealth; men and women who live according to a strong sense of equality, but also fairness and justice.

Dr. Glazov's subject is not the Orwells but rather another group whom we might call the anti-Orwells: the twenty-first century equivalent of the Stalinists who embraced the notion of the Russians sitting with the Prussians a lifetime ago "writing out the Party Line." Historical analogies weaken if one attempts to use them predicatively, but the Nazi and the Stalinist cooperation of the late 1930s certainly cast some distinctive shadows on a number of current portraits.

Whose behavior today calls the Nazis and Stalinists of that era to mind?

Several candidates for modern Nazi equivalents emerge from Dr. Glazov's hard-hitting chapters; one of the most dramatic is the substantial parallel that emerges between the Nazis and today's extreme Islamists, both Shi'ite and Sunni.

Iranian President Ahmadinejad's calls for Israel to be "wiped from the face of the Earth" are certainly evocative of the Holocaust, as set out in *Mein Kampf* and then carried out. The Revolutionary Guard Corps is as close as we have seen to recreating Hitler's Brownshirts. Tehran's Evan Prison has been the killing field for thousands of Iranian reformers, trade union leaders, students, and journalists just as were similar locations in Hitler's Germany. A number of demands for regional domination by leading figures in the Tehran regime have more than a faint echo of the Thousand Year Reich about them.

The Sunni Islamists are tied to a powerful state in a different way. In his excellent work on al-Qaeda and 9/11, *The Looming Tower*, Lawrence Wright notes that, with just over one per cent of the world's Muslims, the Saudis control about ninety per cent of the world's Islamic institutions.

The Wahhabi doctrine they teach—murderous with regard to Shi'ites, Jews, homosexuals, and apostates and unremittingly repressive with regard to women—is essentially the same as al-Qaeda's. Both seek, differing only in tactics, to move us all toward a world-wide theocratic totalitarian dictatorship, the *caliphate*. The Wahhabi-al-Qaeda rivalry is lethal, but it is not a battle over values. It is essentially a bitter fight over who should be in charge of getting all of us under the Caliph's control.

In Tehran, Riyadh, or the al-Qaeda-Taliban strongholds of the Pakistani-Afghan border, the gender apartheid of Wahhabi/al-Qaeda and Khomeinist Islam is much in evidence. And although, as Dr. Glazov describes, in Indonesia, Morocco, and other locales within the Islamic world there are important movements to promote gender equality within the Islamic tradition, Wahhabi and Islamist influence in far too many places sanctions wife-beating, the stoning of women, "honor" killings on the flimsiest of charges, and genital mutilation. In domestic terms, women in Islamist societies today would see some 1930s parallels to aspects of their own lives in the way in which female German doctors, lawyers, teachers, and musicians were fired and told to stay in the home when the Nazis took power.

Islamist anti-Semitism is virulent, in part because of direct links between Nazism and the founders of the Islamist movement in the thirties and forties—such as Muslim Brotherhood founder Hassan al-Banna and the Grand Mufti of Jerusalem, Haj Amin al-Husseini; the latter was a collaborator with and adviser to Eichmann and Himmler in planning the Holocaust. In the fifties and sixties, Sayyid Qutb, the chief theorist of modern Islamism, put virulent anti-Semitism at the heart of that totalitarian doctrine.

If many aspects of Islamist behavior today echo that of the Nazis, who are our current Stalinists? Who are today's equivalent of those members of the Left in the West who embraced the Stalin-Hitler Pact and, at least until Hitler invaded Russia in 1941, happily consorted with their fellows on the totalitarian right, and made common cause against democracy and liberty? And why have a number of today's members of the far Left taken the path that they have instead of following the noble example of Orwell?

The answers to these haunting questions are the subject of this courageous and illuminating book.

R. James Woolsey
Venture Partner, VantagePoint
Director of Central Intelligence, 1993-95

Throughout the twentieth century, the Western Left supported one totalitarian killing machine after another. Prominent intellectuals from George Bernard Shaw to Bertolt Brecht to Susan Sontag venerated mass murderers such as Lenin, Stalin, Mao, Castro, and Ho Chi Minh, habitually excusing their atrocities while blaming America, and even the victims, for the crimes.

After 9/11, when the Islamist death cult made itself the West's new worst adversary, history repeated itself. The Left once again gave its affection to mass murderers and heaped its scorn on America and the West. The only difference this time around was that the Left's favorite murderers were waving not the red flag of proletarian revolution, but the black flag of Islamic jihad. As they did in the twentieth century, members of the political faith, like Jimmy Carter, Noam Chomsky, Michael Moore, and Tom Hayden, once again reached out to bloodthirsty tyrants bent on human destruction.

This book is dedicated to exploring the reasons why.

ACKNOWLEDGMENTS

I am most grateful and indebted to John Corrigan, Stephen Brown, John Perazzo, Robert Spencer, George Gabor, and Kenneth Levin, all of whom read the rough drafts of this book and provided numerous constructive criticisms, comments, and recommendations that greatly enhanced the work.

I owe deep thanks to David Horowitz. Thank you, David.

I am also grateful to my brother Grisha, my sister Elena, my brother-in-law Kevin Corrigan, and to their families for supporting me throughout the entire endeavor. To Ivan Wright, Anton Wright, Chris Wright, Robert Thompson, Dezembra Patsas, Natty Jackson, and Anna Atell, thank you for your friendship that sustained my perseverance.

I am indebted to Professor J.L. Granatstein, my academic mentor, who helped build the foundation that allowed me to take on this project.

I thank Lynne Rabinoff, my agent, for all her superb help in making the publication of this work possible. I am also grateful to Ami Naramor and Judy Abarbanel at WND Books for their hard work in paving the road for this book's publication. My adopted sister, Brigitte Gabriel, served as a providential godsend during a critical moment in terms of this book's future. The blessing you brought will not be forgotten, Brigitte.

To Latoya Lee, I cherish the love and caring you brought into my life while this book fertilized into reality. Thank you.

To my father and mother, Yuri and Marina Glazov, few words can express my appreciation for everything you have given me. Thank you, Papochka, for the example you set, and the upbringing and guidance you gave me. Mamochka, thank you for your priceless loving and intellectual nourishment. I am also extremely grateful for the indispensable help you gave me with this book.

Finally, to my mom's dad, Gregory Rafalsky:

In the fall of 1941, shortly after the Nazis invaded the Soviet Union, your daughter, my mother to be, was three years old and hospitalized in downtown Moscow for scarlet fever. One day, you came to say goodbye. As a medical doctor, you were scheduled to leave for the battlefront the next day. With her mother (my grandma) present as well, my mom was screeching with hysteria as you tried, with tears in your eyes and a stake in your heart, to say goodbye. As the family and staff were there to witness, your daughter was panting and crying with desperation, unable to catch her breath. Begging you not to leave, she pleaded that you wrap her up in a blanket and take her with you. You finally left, but ended up coming back to say goodbye again. And you did that ten times—all the while weeping with deep sorrow.

Because, like your daughter, you knew.

Before you finally left the hospital that day, a strange feeling possessed you and you requested that your daughter be immediately taken out of the hospital. Because you and your wife were doctors, you were permitted to have your child brought home that day.

That night, the Germans bombed that hospital into oblivion. No children survived.

You never came home. Your last postcard was dated October 31, 1941, from Vyasma, Smolensk.

My mom tells me that she spent her childhood years jumping up and down on her bed, imagining that she was looking far into the horizon and that, suddenly, you would appear there—smiling and finally coming home.

This book is for you.

"He's an impressive fellow, this guy. He really is. He's obviously smart as hell…. You'll find him an interesting man. I expected more of a firebrand. I don't think he has the slightest doubt about how he feels…about the American administration and the Zionist state. He comes across as more rational than I had expected…. He's actually, in a strange way, he's a rather attractive man, very smart, savvy, self-assured, good-looking in a strange way. He's very, very short but he's comfortable in his own skin."[1]

—Mike Wallace about Iranian president Mahmoud Ahmadinejad, who has called for the annihilation of Israel

Scarcely a day goes by when Islamic terrorism does not claim the lives of innocent civilians somewhere in the world. Doing nothing more than trying to earn a living, care for their families, and live in peace, these victims are by no means always situated in war zones; many are in regions that are ostensibly at peace. As anonymous in death as they were in life, these victims face savage murder on a regular basis by a loosely knit army of remorseless, modern-day barbarians whose every waking thought is devoted to beheading and otherwise mutilating impure "infidels" across the globe, and to creating a worldwide Islamic *caliphate* subordinate only to the deity in whose name it kills and oppresses.

Who remembers any longer the forty-two peace council participants a teenaged suicide bomber killed in Peshawar on March 2, 2008? Or the same number a *fedayeen* bomber murdered two days earlier in Swat, Pakistan, while attending a funeral? Let alone the fifty-six worshippers killed on December 21, 2007, when a terrorist carrying a bomb packed with nails detonated himself in a Kanaan mosque? The memory of the forty-plus people, including children, who lost their lives to bombs placed at a food stall and an amusement park on August 25, 2007, in Hyderabad, India, has also faded except among the grieving family members and friends left behind.

These are but a few of the many hundreds of terrorist attacks that have been carried out across the world in the post-9/11 era. Other attacks, of course, are more familiar to Westerners. For instance, there were the July 2005 coordinated bombings of London's public transport system, which killed fifty-two commuters and injured at least seven hundred; the Madrid railway bombings of March 2004, which killed 190 and wounded more than eighteen hundred; the May 2003 Casablanca bombings of a Jewish community center and a Spanish social club, killing forty-one people; and the October 2002 bombings on the Indonesian island of Bali, which took 202 lives.

Through luck and hard work, intelligence operatives around the world have foiled other Islamic terrorist plots seeking to cause even greater suffering, such as the infamous 1995 Operation Bojinka plot, whose aim was to simultaneously blow up, in mid-flight, twelve commercial airliners traveling between Asia and the United States.

It is difficult for most of us to imagine any American feeling the barest shred of affinity for the nihilistic monsters who plan and execute such deeds. Yet, as this book will demonstrate, the American Left has formed a tacit alliance with the radical Islamists responsible for these atrocities. These allies have pooled their efforts to oppose America's defensive war on terror.

The modern Left's core consists of the ideological descendents of the communist/progressive Left that wanted the West to lose the Cold War to the Soviet Union. Upon the foundation of their hatred for the United States, its members have forged their alliance with radical Islam, whose wellspring of anti-American hatred runs just as deep. In word and deed, both of these allies make it plain that they consider everything about Western civilization to be evil and unworthy of preservation; that they wish to see freedom and individual rights crushed by any means necessary, including violent revolution.

What else can explain former U.S. President Jimmy Carter's pilgrimage in April 2008 to Cairo and Damascus to meet with—and embrace—the leaders of the terrorist organization Hamas? What can explain his impulse to shake hands in solidarity with terrorists who have the blood of myriad Israelis—as well as Americans—on their hands? Carter met with Khaled Meshal, a Hamas leader suspected by Israeli authorities of being the mastermind of several high-profile terror attacks. The June 2006 abduction of Israeli soldier Gilad Schalit, for instance, was reportedly carried out at Meshal's behest. Meshal has habitually made clear that Israel's existence is intolerable and that the destruction of the Jewish state must be achieved through a relentless campaign of genocide. And the life force for that campaign is sealed in the Hamas charter—which states as its primary goal Israel's extinction. That is why, since Israel's withdrawal from Gaza in 2005 and the end of the so-called "occupation" there, Hamas and other Palestinian terrorist groups have launched over six thousand rockets and mortars into Israel.[2]

None of these realities could possibly have prevented Jimmy Carter from undertaking his Hamas odyssey; instead they served as the inspiration for it. After his meetings with Meshal and other Hamas figures, the ex-president emerged with the announcement that the terrorist organization was now ready to live in peace alongside Israel and that it would recognize the Jewish state. It didn't take long for Hamas to issue a clarification. To be sure, a curious and intentional misunderstanding had evidently occurred. Shortly after Carter's bizarre pronouncement, Hamas announced that its *raison d'etre* remained intact: the commitment to liquidate the Jewish state.[3]

In his eerie attempt to paint terrorists as peacekeepers and to blur their true genocidal campaign in the public eye, Carter, of course, was trapped in a self-imposed trance. He needed a smokescreen, some kind of temporary lie, to cloud the true and dark yearnings that had led him into the arms of America's, Israel's, and freedom's deadly sworn enemies. And these yearnings of Carter's were not new. Indeed, from the moment the terror organization scored its electoral victory in Gaza in January 2006, the ex-president became an avid supporter. He distinguished himself as one of the first figures to congratulate the terrorist group for its victory, meeting with its leaders in Ramallah, where his Carter Center has an office.[4]

When Hamas began its expected and blood-soaked purge in Gaza and fueled its rocket attacks against innocent civilians in Israel, Carter remained silent. And instead of denouncing Hamas, he embarked on a passionate one-man lobbying campaign on behalf of the terrorist group, urging the international community to launder money to Hamas through United Nations aid programs and then calling it "criminal" when the money for Hamas' genocidal program did not arrive.[5] All throughout, Carter has repeatedly declared Hamas to be an organization ready for peace. And in the process of uttering such falsehoods, he has sprinkled numerous pleas for the release of thousands of Palestinian terrorists in Israeli prisons who have Israeli blood on their hands.[6]

Carter's dalliance with Hamas crystallizes well the intentions that lurk in the heart of the Left. That dalliance makes clear why the radical Left behaved so morbidly a few years earlier at the sight of blue ink on an Arab finger: that image from the first free, post-Saddam Hussein election in Iraq that represented the most momentous change in the Middle East in recent times. And that extraordinary experiment in freedom on January, 30, 2005, much to the Left's dislike, was made possible by the American liberation of Iraq.

As Iraqis inhaled their first breaths of democracy, their neighbors caught the intoxicating scent of freedom as well. Inspired by the Iraqis' defiance of terrorism, the citizens of Lebanon decided that they, too, could take control of their lives. So they did what Eastern Europeans had done sixteen years earlier, repeating the miracle that brought an evil empire to a humiliating defeat: they took their courage to the streets—by the hundreds of thousands—in an overwhelming expression of people power. Lebanese of all ages shouted for their Syrian occupiers to evacuate their country. As Walid Jumblatt, a prominent Lebanese Druze leader, commented: "I was cynical about Iraq. But when I saw the Iraqi people voting three weeks ago, eight million of them, it was the start of a new Arab world. The Syrian people, the Egyptian people, all say that something is changing. The Berlin Wall has fallen. We can see it."[7]

The Arab Berlin Wall may not have fallen, but the first cracks had appeared in its ugly façade. Just as the Poles set off a chain reaction throughout Eastern Europe by overthrowing their communist regime in 1989, so the Iraqis triggered what appeared to be a domino effect throughout the Arab world in 2005. As the Lebanese protested loudly in their streets, the Syrians announced that they would leave Lebanon, and they actually began the first movements toward withdrawal. Shortly thereafter, in Egypt, President Hosni Mubarak promised the first real presidential election in his country's history. The Saudis, meanwhile, suddenly started mumbling about giving their women the right to vote.

Then, on October 15, 2005, another watershed: millions of Iraqis turned out to vote on their new constitution in a national referendum. Again, Iraqi voters risked their lives in the face of terrorist threats, handing the issuers of those threats yet another devastating defeat. Two months later, the Iraqis did it again. On December 15, 2005, an unprecedented eleven million defied the terrorists once more, coming out to cast their ballots in their nation's parliamentary elections—the third free vote within a year.

The Left, meanwhile, erupted in fury at the sight of these developments in Iraq. Leftists in all walks of life renewed their calls for American forces to cut and run. House Minority Leader Nancy Pelosi and Senator Ted Kennedy, Jimmy Carter's ideological soulmates, spearheaded the Left's effort, greeting the news of the successful election with calls for an immediate American withdrawal.[8] As author Ben Johnson noted, "just as one can see the light at the end of the tunnel, just as troop reductions might become a possibility, the Left continues to push for an immediate withdrawal that would snatch defeat from the jaws of victory, slaughter innocent Iraqis, and leave Americans more vulnerable than ever to an emboldened worldwide terrorist enemy."[9]

And a disturbing sight it was: in the third free election in one year, even the Sunni terrorists showed themselves to be more committed to a stable and democratic Iraq than the American Left. A terrorist group called the Iraqi Islamic Army, for instance, protected polls in Ramadi, while militants entered local neighborhoods to encourage Sunnis to vote—as indeed they did, in large numbers.[10]

During these developments, Naomi Klein, a columnist for *The Nation*, called on her leftist comrades to join hands with the Islamofascist terrorists headed by Shiite cleric Muqtada al-Sadr.[11] Similarly, George Galloway, British Member of Parliament and darling of the Left, repeatedly proclaimed—as in his debate with Christopher Hitchens at Baruch College in New York City in September 2005—his favorite themes: that the liberation of Iraq was a tragedy and that the most positive outcome would be the victory of the terrorists over U.S. forces.[12] He made sure his feelings of kindred affection for the Islamist enemy were no secret, unambiguously calling for a global Muslim-leftist alliance against America and its allies.[13] "Peace mom" Cindy Sheehan, serving as a poster child for the American Left, called the terrorists in Iraq "freedom fighters" and cheered for their victory.[14] Tom Hayden, meanwhile, wasn't content with simply cheering the terrorists on. Like Carter would travel to Damascus and Cairo to meet with Hamas in April 2008, the former American radical and eternal defeatist traveled to London in September 2005 to embrace Naomi Klein's hero, Muqtada al-Sadr.[15] Galloway engaged in his own fellow traveling, visiting Syria in November 2005, prostrating himself before its despot, and giving a speech at Damascus University in which he denounced America and Israel and extended his support to every possible enemy of the United States—from the terrorists in Iraq to Fidel Castro to Hugo Chávez.[16]

In these perturbing circumstances, the Left once again showed its true face. Western leftists witnessed Iraqis bravely choosing liberty and civilization over nihilism and despair; they watched the foundation for liberty and democracy being set in place; and they saw the possibility emerging that women, homosexuals, minorities, and all other citizens would be able to enjoy rights and freedoms in a land where there was once only terror, dictatorship, and death. Yet, in response to these inspiring and *truly* progressive developments, the Left only shrieked in hysterical protest.

The Left, of course, had tried passionately to prevent the liberation of Iraq in the first place—even though Iraqis were enduring the rule of a sadistic dictator who had built his despotism on the model of Joseph Stalin. In his effort to control Iraq and its population completely, Saddam Hussein perpetrated genocide against his own people, using chemical weapons against the Kurds and the Shiites. He launched war against Iran, using poison gas. He launched war against Kuwait. He sponsored and harbored Islamist terrorists and hinted at the possibility of arming them with WMDs. But when the United States embarked on the mission of freeing Iraqis and the world from this despot and the threat he represented, the Left erupted in ferocious protest. Its members organized mass "peace" demonstrations, waving pro-Saddam and pro-Islamist placards, and they joined with Islamist demonstrators in chanting *"Allahu akbar"* ("God is great")—the phrase shouted by Muslim suicide bombers before they blow themselves up along with innocent people.

On September 24, 2005, one hundred thousand demonstrators gathered in Washington, D.C., to jeer President Bush and demand the evacuation of American forces from Iraq. The demonstrators knew full well that if this happened, it would lead to a massive bloodbath, reminiscent of the carnage that followed the American withdrawal from Vietnam—which the Left had also promoted.[17] Tom Hayden represented the leftist disposition perfectly: having helped facilitate the communist takeover of Southeast Asia in an earlier era, he now set forth, in an *L.A. Times* op-ed piece, a plan for American surrender in Iraq.[18]

In the summer of 2006, while Iraq was working to make its new democratic structures a reality, Israel launched air strikes on Hezbollah targets in Lebanon and sent ground troops into the southern region of that nation to destroy the terrorist army's bases and weaponry—which included twelve thousand long-range rockets. The Israelis engaged in this defensive measure after a group of Hezbollah terrorists crossed into Israeli territory on July 12, murdering three Israeli soldiers and kidnapping two others. The largest terrorist army in the world then launched hundreds of rockets into Israeli cities and population centers in order to fulfil the sole reason for its existence: killing Jews.

Western leftists quickly reached out in solidarity to the terrorists of Hezbollah ("the Party of God"). *The Nation* led the way, excusing the terrorists, blaming the entire crisis on Israel, and offering solutions that would have robbed Israel of the ability to defend itself, while allowing its genocidal enemies every means of attaining their goal of a Final Solution in the Middle East.[19]

The Left's romance with Hezbollah was now totally out in the open, but it was nothing new.[20] In early May 2006, just a few weeks before Hezbollah's raid into Israel, MIT professor Noam Chomsky traveled to Lebanon to consummate a political love affair that had begun in the 1990s. Arriving in a southern suburb of Beirut, he entered the headquarters of Hezbollah and warmly embraced the terror organization's secretary general, Sheikh Hassan Nasrallah. It was a thrilling moment for the professor: finally, he had the honor of standing in the company of the criminals who had murdered 241 American servicemen at the Marine barracks in Lebanon in 1983 and, of course, untold numbers of Israeli citizens over many years— activities Chomsky had justified as "legitimate resistance" against an oppressor.[21] Having praised the terrorist organization throughout the 1990s, Chomsky could now put his complete seal of approval on Hezbollah in person. And he did: he gave his blessing to Nasrallah, praised his cause, and approved of his refusal to disarm.[22]

Hezbollah, like Hamas and President Ahmadinejad, is unambiguous in its yearning to annihilate Israel and all Jews, just as it is clear about waging war on America, whose "death" it has repeatedly called for.[23] Chomsky's Hezbollah odyssey, therefore, like Carter's Hamas sojourn that followed, constituted a simple and logical continuation of the Left's political pilgrimages of the twentieth century.

In my own daily life, I have witnessed myriad examples of this pathology. I observed with considerable curiosity how the leftists around me didn't trouble themselves to disguise their feelings about 9/11. I have known some of these leftists for years, and after the fall of the Soviet empire in 1989-91 many of them bitterly lamented to me that the "alternative to capitalism" was now gone. A significant number of them retreated into a silent and sullen shell.

Then came 9/11.

Almost overnight, these individuals underwent a miraculous transformation. A bright sparkle could once again be detected in their eyes, as their souls came out of a deep slumber. Never had I seen them so happy, so hopeful, and ready for another attempt at creating a glorious and *revolutionary* future. Without doubt, September 11 represented a personal vindication for them.

The images of innocent people jumping to their deaths from the Twin Towers evoked no sympathy from them. Instead, they saw only poetic justice in American commercial airplanes plunging into American buildings packed with people. For my leftist acquaintances, the jihadist terror war gave promise of succeeding in a project in which communism had failed: to obliterate the capitalist system itself. "The U.S. brought this on itself," they stated repeatedly.

The encounters I had were a microcosm of the Left's behavior on the national scene. In the blink of an eye after the Twin Towers went down, leftists were beating their breasts with repentance for their own government's supposed crimes and characterizing the tragedy that their nation had just suffered as a form of karmic justice. From Noam Chomsky to Norman Mailer, from Eric Foner to Susan Sontag, the Left used 9/11 to castigate America, informing the world that the three thousand innocent people who died in those attacks were merely collateral victims of the world's well-founded rebellion against the evil American empire.

The thesis was clear: When America bleeds, the victims are to blame, never the perpetrators. This is the paradigm of *the devil made them do it*, a central tenet of the progressive faith. So leftists joined in solidarity with the Muslims who danced in the streets after 9/11 — a Kodak moment for the Left everywhere.

The most notorious case was that of Professor Ward Churchill, the University of Colorado professor and imposter (he had falsely claimed to be part Cherokee in order to get his ethnic studies professorship). Churchill stepped forward to publicly reiterate his—and the Left's—world vision: he denounced his own nation as a genocidal empire, promoted America's terrorist enemies, excused 9/11 as a case of the "chickens coming home to roost," and called its victims "little Eichmanns inhabiting the sterile sanctuary of the twin towers." Grateful to the Islamist terrorists for attempting to destroy America's "global financial empire," he believed that the Americans who died on that horrible day deserved their deaths.

After 9/11, when the Bush administration set out to dislodge the Islamofascist Taliban in Afghanistan—and thus to disrupt al-Qaeda and minimize the chances of another 9/11—leftists protested furiously. Everything the Taliban represented was supposed to be anathema to the Left: the despotic intrusion of a theocracy into every sphere of human life, the brutal suppression of women, the torture and execution of homosexuals, the persecution of minorities. But the Left was unmoved. Instead, when American military action in Afghanistan liberated thirty-one million people from a Hitlerian nightmare and brought democracy to that tortured nation, leftists characterized President Bush as worse than the Taliban and the terrorists they harbored.

Billionaire and Democratic funder George Soros chipped in his own contribution helping to demonize Bush and to frustrate the war on the enemy that perpetrated 9/11.[24] When Bush made his statement, "Either you are for us or you are with the terrorists," in his address to Congress nine days after the attack, Soros, among others, did all he could to twist the meaning of Bush's pronouncement. In perceiving the nature of the global Islamofascist threat, the president had simply meant that governments (i.e. Iran, Afghanistan, Libya, etc.) that aided and abetted terrorists would be held to account. But Soros distorted the essence of Bush's theme, weaving it in such a way as to paint the president as being not only divisive, but a Nazi. In the fall of 2003, Soros affirmed that Bush's statement proved that the president was pursuing a "supremacist ideology" reminiscent of the Nazis. "It conjures up memories," Soros said, "of Nazi slogans on the walls, like *Der Feind Hört mit* ('The Enemy is Listening')."[25] None of this, of course, was based in any reality, but this did not matter to Soros, who views the term "war on terror" as a false metaphor and believes that it should be repudiated—so that it will not be fought.[26]

The Left's support of America's totalitarian enemies in all these contexts would be only a curiosity if the Left had no real influence. The tragedy, however, is that the Left has shaped much of the cultural and political consciousness of our time. The Left's agenda mattered immensely during the Vietnam War: even former North Vietnamese officials have admitted that the antiwar movement in America can take credit for communism's victory in South Vietnam and, therefore, for the tragic bloodbath that followed.

In the present context, the Left succeeded in making the United States vulnerable to 9/11. President Clinton, for instance, had many opportunities to either capture or kill bin Laden, but he refused to act.[27] Testimony about the "Able Danger" counter-intelligence program, furthermore, revealed that U.S. government agents knew of terrorist ringleader Mohammed Atta and his al-Qaeda connection two years before 9/11, but that Clinton-era policies forbade these intelligence officials from passing along their information to the FBI.

Another crucial instance occurred when, shortly before 9/11, FBI agents in Minneapolis identified Zacarias Moussaoui as having terrorist connections (Moussaoui was the so-called "twentieth hijacker" of 9/11) and applied for a search warrant to get access to his computer. Had the FBI agents been allowed to do so, two of the 9/11 hijackers would have been identified, along with the Hamburg cell that planned the operation. It is quite possible that the 9/11 attacks could have been prevented. But FBI headquarters in Washington, D.C., decided there was not enough evidence to request the search warrant, given the wall the Left had demanded between criminal and intelligence investigations—the wall that Attorney General Janet Reno had helped fortify in July 1995. And to this day, the Democratic Party and the Left have done everything in their power to sow defeat for America in Iraq.[28]

This leftist choice to support tyranny over freedom has always shocked and mystified me. My reaction is deeply personal: I come from a family of Soviet dissidents who fought for freedom under communism. My father, Yuri Glazov, was one of the dissidents who signed the "Letter of Twelve" in 1968. This petition denounced Soviet human rights abuses and stood up for prisoners of conscience. My mother, Marina Glazov, actively typed and circulated *samizdat*—underground political literature. Through these courageous efforts, my parents put their lives on the line. In the early 1970s, we faced the imminent arrest of my father. However, the temporarily relaxed conditions brought about by the Nixon-Brezhnev *détente* made it possible for us to leave the Soviet Union, thereby escaping doom at the hands of communist despotism.

We settled in America in 1972; I was five and a half years old. I will never forget the awe I felt at experiencing my first taste of freedom, even as a young boy who wasn't completely sure what it was. I will forever remember how ecstatic my parents were to get their hands on books they had dreamed of reading all their lives. They now also had time to read them, for they were liberated not only from tyranny, but also from the draining experience of standing in lines for hours just to buy basic foods to feed our family.

My father could also now, for the first time, speak out without fear in defense of Soviet citizens who were languishing in the Gulag and in psychiatric hospitals for their political and religious beliefs. For the first time, we lived without the dread to which I had been accustomed throughout my young life.

While we were cherishing our newfound freedom, we encountered a strange species: intellectuals in the universities who hated my parents for the story they had to tell. For the first time in their lives, my father and mother confronted an intelligentsia that was hostile to them. Back in Russia, dissident intellectuals risked their lives when they pronounced one word of truth about the horrible history of their country under communist rule. In America, most of the intellectuals who surrounded us scoffed at the importance of real intellectual freedom and dismissed my parents' experience; they demonized their own society, wished for its defeat, and supported the communist enemy that muzzled free speech and tortured millions of human beings.

As a very young boy, I learned that these intellectuals were "leftists." I remember witnessing how they tried to prevent my parents from drawing attention to the mass crimes of communism and to the brave souls who were fighting for freedom—people like Aleksandr Solzhenitsyn, Vladimir Bukovsky, Andrei Sakharov, Anatoly Shcharansky, Aleksandr Ginzburg, and many others. While my family agonized about the relatives and friends we had left behind, and as we kept the memory of their suffering alive in our hearts, our leftist "friends" reprimanded us for our views, instructing us to see America—our personal liberator—as the evil entity in the Cold War. They wanted us to dedicate our lives—as they had done—to the victory of the West's totalitarian adversaries.

When I am confronted with the Left's current romance with militant Islam, I therefore see something very familiar. But while its embrace of totalitarianism during the Cold War was always evident for those with eyes to see, the Left in those days was able to mask from many people its true allegiance, through the pretense of being on the side of "social justice," "equality," and the "progressive" agenda. Today the Left has torn off its own mask. Leftists have gleefully joined hands with those who kidnap innocent people off Iraqi streets and chop their heads off, or who strap bombs around their waists and blow themselves up next to women, children, and infants in baby carriages.

September 11 crystallized this whole picture for me, clarifying impressions that have been in my mind ever since I was a little Soviet *émigré* boy arriving in the United States. For me, 9/11 was utterly incomprehensible. The Twin Towers represented success, innovation, prosperity, inclusiveness, diversity, pluralism, and everything else for which a society ought to strive. I thought of all the effort that went into building those amazing towers, those precious symbols of human progress and ingenuity. And yet, someone wanted them destroyed. Someone preferred the shambles of Ground Zero to the human prosperity and hope of New York's financial center.

As I observed the Left celebrating 9/11, I wanted, once and for all, to get to the bottom of this phenomenon. What was this pernicious mindset that depicted the symbol of the world's most precious entities as worthless and ugly? Why did it seek to ally itself with totalitarian and death-worshipping forces? Why did it yearn to force historical blindness upon the world, and to wipe out the memory of the hundreds of millions of people who have suffered under totalitarianism?

I set out to write a book on the impulses that stimulate the radical mind and that have led to its love affair with radical Islam. The pages ahead are the product of that mission.

PART I

THE BELIEVER

CHAPTER ONE

The Roots of Denial

"Nothing is easier than self-deceit.
For what each man wishes, that he also believes to be true."

—Demosthenes

Τ*he story of the Left's love affair* with despotism begins with an examination of the core values and characteristics of members of this political faith. We will label the subject of this examination "the believer," and the ingredients that constitute the believer's psychological makeup will be referred to as "the believer's diagnosis."

In labeling the believer and exposing his true agenda, this study will hit the Left's rawest nerve. The Left habitually attempts to distance itself from its own history and to obfuscate any straightforward analysis of its political motives, goals, and allegiances. In so doing, the Left intentionally blurs its own complicity in the greatest crimes of the twentieth century.

The Left's indignation over David Horowitz's database—DiscoverTheNetworks.org: A Guide to the Political Left—is typical of this phenomenon. Launched in February 2005, DiscoverTheNetworks became the first Web site to define the Left comprehensively and map out its networks of individuals, organizations, and financial supporters.[1] Within hours of the Web site's first appearance on the Internet—before there had even been time to read a fraction of the site's content, which includes thousands of files—leftists lashed out in fury.

A typical assault came from author Kurt Nimmo, who called the new database a "smear portal" and alleged that it unjustifiably lumped together too many disparate people and forces, especially leftists with Islamist terrorists.[2] Nimmo made this charge even though DiscoverTheNetworks does not point to any organizational links between leftists and Islamist terrorists, but simply catalogues the support that leftists have given to terrorists—as exemplified by Michael Moore's praising the insurgents in Fallujah and promoting their victory over an imperialist United States.[3]

DiscoverTheNetworks makes it clear that it does not imply the existence of any formal "alliance" between radical Islam and the Left, but simply demonstrates, in its profiles of individuals (Moore, Noam Chomsky, Ward Churchill, et al.) and organizations (National Lawyers Guild, International ANSWER, Code Pink, et al.), that the radical Left consistently takes the side of Islamist terrorists in their jihad against the United States.

The absurd irony in Nimmo's condemning the implication of a leftist-Islamist alliance is that he himself is a leftist who supports and affiliates himself with Islamist terrorists (especially terrorists in Iraq's Sunni triangle).[4] Nimmo's logic clearly exemplifies the Left's traditional dismissal of any criticism aimed against it. Dedicating their lives to erasing individuality—including their own—and becoming part of a group from whose party line they cannot waver, these individuals nonetheless react with moral indignation when they are classified as being members of that group.

This tactic is part of the Left's desperate attempt to avoid an honest dialogue about its own historical record. Rather than confront the bloodbath that its ideas have spawned, the Left finds it far safer to engage in historical amnesia and outright Gulag denial.

But there is one sense in which we do have to be careful not to paint with too broad a brush. It is the hard and radical Left—the Left that reached out to tyranny and now reaches out to terror, motivated by the Marxist dream of destroying the world as it is and building a utopia on its ashes—that has shaped and represented the modern progressive movement. But this Left has nothing to do with genuine liberals. During the Cold War, people like Harry Truman and Walter Reuther were prominent in the Democratic Party—and they were liberals who genuinely opposed adversarial despotisms. But such liberals now make up a very small group of people who hold no influence within the Left's ranks. As a result, broadening the boundaries of what we label as "the Left" robs the term of any real meaning and, more tragic still, erases the memory of the millions of victims who were sacrificed for leftist ideals.[5]

In dissecting the leftist pathology, our mission begins with the task of illuminating the main ingredients of the believer's political outlook. We consider it a given that not *all* believers are identical, and that not *every* believer will share every characteristic listed. There is, after all, no mentally ill person whose illness has been engendered by *exactly* the same dynamics as have afflicted a similarly ailing person. But there are indubitably mental illnesses that stem from common sources and predispose their victims to similar dispositions and behaviors.

The bottom line is this: while dynamics and extremes vary, *every* believer will fit, to one degree or another, "the believer's diagnosis." This is particularly true for those legions of believers who today wish for the victory of Islamist terror over the United States.

CHAPTER TWO

The Believer's Diagnosis

"Everything that exists deserves to perish."

—Karl Marx, invoking a dictum of Goethe's devil
in *The Eighteenth Brumaire of Louis Napoléon*

In the eyes of Joseph E. Davies, who served for several years as the American ambassador to the Soviet Union before the Second World War, no human being merited greater respect than Joseph Stalin. The ambassador spent much time reflecting on why he believed the Soviet dictator deserved the world's—and his own people's—heartfelt veneration. He finally realized that the answer had always been staring him square in the face: it was that Stalin's "brown eye is exceedingly wise and gentle. A child would like to sit on his lap and a dog would sidle up to him."[1] Leading French intellectual Jean-Paul Sartre discovered a similar truth about his own secular deity, Fidel Castro. "Castro," he noted, "is at the same time the island, the men, the cattle, and the earth. He is the whole island."[2] Father Daniel Berrigan, meanwhile, contended that Hanoi's prime minister Pham Van Dong was an individual "in whom complexity dwells, in whom daily issues of life and death resound; a face of great intelligence, and yet also of great reserves of compassion...he had dared to be a humanist in an inhuman time."[3]

The objects of all this adoration, of course, were despotic mass murderers. One crucial question, therefore, surfaces: what exactly inspires a person, and an entire mass movement, to deify a monstrous tyrant as a father-god who transcends the singular and encompasses, as Sartre put it, all the people and their land? The answer to this question helps illuminate the contemporary Left's romance with Islamist jihadists, just as it helps crystallize the Left's alliance with the most vicious totalitarians of the twentieth century.

The believer's totalitarian journey begins with an acute sense of alienation from his own society—an alienation to which he is, himself, completely blind. In denial about the character flaws that prevent him from bonding with his own people, the believer has convinced himself that there is something profoundly wrong with his society—and that it can be fixed without any negative trade-offs. He fantasizes about building a perfect society where he will, finally, fit in. As Eric Hoffer noted in his classic *The True Believer*, "people with a sense of fulfillment think it is a good world and would like to conserve it as it is, while the frustrated favor radical change."[4]

A key ingredient of this paradigm is that the believer has failed to rise to the challenges of secular modernity; he has not established real and lasting interpersonal relationships or internalized any values that help him find meaning in life. Suffering from a spiritual emptiness, of which he himself is not cognizant, the believer forces non-spiritual solutions onto his spiritual problems. He exacerbates this dysfunction by trying to satisfy his every material need, which the great benefits of modernity and capitalism allow—but the more luxuries he manages to acquire, the more desperate he becomes. We saw this with the counterculture leftists of the sixties and seventies, and we see it with the radical leftists of today. Convinced that it is incumbent upon society, and not him, to imbue his life with purpose, the believer becomes indignant; he scapegoats his society—and ends up despising and rejecting it.[5]

Just like religious folk, the believer espouses a faith, but his is a secular one. He too searches for personal redemption—but of an earthly variety. The progressive faith, therefore, is a secular religion. And this is why socialism's dynamics constitute a mutated carbon copy of Judeo-Christian imagery. Socialism's secular utopian vision includes a fall from an ideal collective brotherhood, followed by a journey through a valley of oppression and injustice, and then ultimately a road toward redemption.[6]

In rejecting his own society, the believer spurns the values of democracy and individual freedom, which are anathema to him, since he has miserably failed to cope with both the challenges they pose and the possibilities they offer. Tortured by his personal alienation, which is accompanied by feelings of self-loathing, the believer craves a fairy-tale world where no individuality exists, and where human estrangement is thus impossible. The believer fantasizes about how his own individuality and self will be submerged within the collective whole. Hoffer illuminates this yearning, noting that a mass movement:

> appeals not to those intent on bolstering and advancing a cherished self, but to those who crave to be rid of an unwanted self. A mass movement attracts and holds a following not because it can satisfy the desire for self-advancement, but because it can satisfy the passion for self-renunciation. People who see their lives as irremediably spoiled cannot find a worthwhile purpose in self-advancement. They look on self-interest as something tainted and evil; something unclean and unlucky…. Their innermost craving is for a new life—a rebirth—or, failing this, a chance to acquire new elements of pride, confidence, a sense of purpose and worth by an identification with a holy cause. An active mass movement offers them opportunities for both.[7]

As history has tragically recorded, this "holy cause" follows a road that leads not to an earthly paradise, but rather to an earthly hell in all of its manifestations. The political faith rejects the basic reality of the human condition—that human beings are flawed and driven by self-interest—and rests on the erroneous assumption that humanity is malleable and can be reshaped into a more perfect form. This premise spawned the nightmarish repressions and genocidal campaigns of Stalin, Mao, Pol Pot, and other communist dictators in the twentieth century. Under their rule, more than one hundred million human beings were sacrificed on the altar where a *new man* would ostensibly be created.[8]

The believer, of course, is completely uninterested in the terrifying ramifications of his pernicious ideas. Preoccupied only with alleviating his own personal pain, he is indifferent to what effect the totalitarian experiments actually have. That is why the Left never looks back.[9]

It is crucial to emphasize, however, that the believer is indifferent to the consequences of his own ideology only in the sense that he needs to deny them *in public*. This is because he fears that their exposure will delegitimize his pursuit of his own neurotic urges. The believer therefore consistently denies what is *actually* happening within the totalisms he worships. Even if it is proven to him that his revolutionary idols perpetrate mass oppression and slaughter, he will take pains not to speak of it. But privately he approves of the carnage; indeed, that is *what attracts him in the first place*. The believer is well aware that violence is necessary to clear the way for the earthly paradise for which he longs. But he is careful never to acknowledge the actual process of destruction, and to always label it the opposite of what it actually is. Thus, in public, the believer pretends he is attracted to "peace," "social justice," and "equality."

The lust for destruction is at the root of Marxism. In Marx's apocalyptic mindset, catastrophe gives rise, ultimately, to a new, perfect world. And so it is no surprise that Marx often invoked, as he did in *The Eighteenth Brumaire of Louis Napoléon*, a dictum of Goethe's devil: "Everything that exists deserves to perish." Marxism, of course, did not disappoint in that part of its promise, earnestly wreaking the mass death and destruction its architect intended.[10] It is this same dreadful formula of thought that led to the Left's post-9/11 attraction to the ruins of Ground Zero.

While he dreams of destruction, the believer compensates for his lonely madness by telling himself that he is not estranged, but is actually a member of a vast community. The reality, however, is that all of his supposed friendships are with other estranged people, and he establishes no genuine, intimate ties outside the politics of the radical faith. Indeed, believers' friendships are seldom based on what they might actually like about each other *as human beings*; they are based only on how their political beliefs conform to one another's. As Che Guevara, Fidel's executioner, stated: "My friends are friends only so long as they think as I do politically."[11] This is why believers so readily accept the fact that their "friends" may be eliminated *for the idea* if they are deemed to stand in its way. As we will see in chapter three, for instance, the American fellow traveler Anna Louise Strong and the Stalinist German writer Bertolt Brecht, two typical believers, were completely undisturbed by the arrests and deaths of their friends in the Stalinist purges.

The political faith, therefore, is not at all a search for the truth. It is a *movement*. For the believer, consequently, changing his views becomes nearly inconceivable, since doing so means losing his entire community and, therefore, his personal identity: he is by necessity relegated to "non-person" status. Even so, many believers have gathered the courage to abandon the movement. The believers who have walked through this leftist valley of membership death include, in our time, David Horowitz, Ronald Radosh, Eugene Genovese, Phyllis Chesler, and Tammy Bruce.[12]

Horowitz has profoundly described the dark reality of how the ties between progressives include few actual human connections and are formed mostly on commitments to the same political abstractions.[13] He recollects the haunting experience of attending his father's memorial service, during which not a single "friend" of his father (a communist) named anything he knew or liked about Phil Horowitz personally:

> The memories of the people who had gathered in my mother's living room were practically the only traces of my father still left on this earth. But when they finally began to speak, what they said was this: *Your father was a man who tried his best to make the world a better place....* And that was all they said. People who had known my father since before I was born, who had been his comrades and intimate friends, could not remember a particular fact about him, could not really remember *him*. All that was memorable to them in the actual life my father had lived—all that was real—were the elements that conformed to their progressive

Idea. My father's life was invisible to the only people who had ever been close enough to see who he was.[14]

The believer attempts to fill the void left by the lack of real human connection with a supposed love for humanity as a whole. The believer loves people from a distance, though he hates individuals up close and in particular. The human beings he imagines he loves, meanwhile, become part of his fantasy community.

These people whom the believer loves from a distance are always the supposed victims of capitalism and American "imperialism." He agonizes over their suffering and revels in the moral indignation he feels about it. The megalomania and narcissism from which most believers suffer reinforce this dynamic. Convinced that the world revolves around him, the believer clings to the notion that the suffering of capitalism's supposed victims is somehow his personal business. And to legitimize his identification with them, he envisions himself to be a victim of capitalist oppression as well. Meanwhile, by condemning his own society, he provides himself not only a sense of belonging with the other supposed victims, but also a feeling of moral superiority that helps counteract the humiliation he experiences as a result of his real-life estrangement.

A self-reinforcing circle emerges: the more victimized the believer envisions himself to be, the closer he feels to the supposed victims of capitalism; the more the victims of capitalism suffer, the greater the indignation the believer can feel through his empathy for them. The more victims there are to identify with, the larger the community the believer belongs to. It becomes clear why the existence (real or imagined) of the impoverished and alienated classes under capitalism is so vital for the believer. His entire identity is wrapped up in his vision of their victimization.

Guilt is instrumental in the rotation of this circle. Usually coming from and/or occupying a position of privilege, the believer is guilt-ridden about his material comfort and high social status. Ashamed that he is not a genuine victim, he creates the myth that he is. By making himself a member, in his imagination, of the poor, the oppressed, and the downtrodden, he feels a sense of atonement. He is paying his karmic debt by being a believer.

In this way the believer keeps his delusions secure. Yet because those delusions are founded on the shakiest of ground, the leftist must be extremely rigid in denying basic, common-sense realities (e.g., communism is evil, al-Qaeda is a terrorist enemy that needs to be fought, and so on). If a leftist were to admit these things, his belief system would collapse entirely.

The desperation with which the believer clings to his belief system becomes understandable. It fuels the rage and fury that is already at the root of his psychological makeup. At this point, another dynamic element enters the circle: the rage that manifests itself in the need to hold onto the belief system meshes with the rage that gave life to the belief system in the first place.

We can now gauge why believers cheered the 9/11 hijackers and intimately identified with them. The act of the hijackers confirmed, in the believers' minds, the existence of an oppressed class—which legitimized their rage against America. They saw the hijackers as people who not only were performing a noble and necessary duty (i.e., dealing a deadly blow to America), but also were, like them, members of the poor, the oppressed, and the downtrodden classes. The believers lived vicariously through the hijackers' violent strike against the supposed oppressors.

Meanwhile, the believer is utterly indifferent to the real-life suffering of the actual human beings victimized by the regimes that he glorifies. The victims of adversarial ideologies do not fit into the believer's agenda, and so they do not matter and are not, ultimately, even human in his eyes.[15] Because they are not human for him, the believer sees them as enemies and, therefore, supports their extermination. Once again, in the mutated Judeo-Christian imagery, blood cleanses the world of its injustices and then redeems it—transforming it into a place where the believer will finally find a comfortable home.

Beneath the believer's veneration of the despotic enemy lies one of his most powerful yearnings: to submit his whole being to a totalist entity. This psychological dynamic involves *negative identification*, whereby a person who has failed to identify positively with his own environment subjugates his individuality to a powerful, authoritarian entity, through which he vicariously experiences a feeling of power and purpose. The historian David Potter dissects this phenomenon:

> [M]ost of us, if not all of us, fulfill ourselves and realize our own identities as persons through our relations with others; we are, in a sense, what our community, or as some sociologists would say, more precisely, what our reference group, recognizes us as being. If it does not recognize us, or if we do not feel that it does, or if we are confused as to what the recognition is, then we become not only lonely, but even lost, and profoundly unsure of our identity. We are driven by this uncertainty into a somewhat obsessive effort to discover our identity and to make certain of it. If this quest proves too long or too difficult, the need for identity becomes psychically very burdensome and the individual may be driven to escape this need by renouncing his own identity and surrendering himself to some seemingly greater cause outside himself.[16]

This surrender to the totality involves the believer's craving not only to relinquish his individuality to a greater whole but also, ideally, to sacrifice his life for it. Lusting for his own self-extinction, the believer craves martyrdom for *the idea*. As Hoffer points out, the opportunity to die for the cause gives meaning to the believer's desire to shed his inner self: "a substitute embraced in moderation cannot supplant and efface the self we want to forget. We cannot be sure that we have something worth living for unless we are ready to die for it."[17]

Believers' desire to give up their lives for the cause therefore unsurprisingly pervades the Left's history. The sixties radicals are typical of this phenomenon. Jerry Rubin's *Do It*, for instance, is rife with the veneration of death. At one point, he and a mob of fellow radicals blocked the path of a police car carrying a Berkeley activist who had violated the university's rules. Describing what became a thirty-two-hour ordeal, Rubin wrote:

> As we surrounded the car, we became conscious that we were a new community with the power and love to confront the old institutions. Our strength was our

willingness to die together, our unity.... Thirty-two hours later, we heard the grim roar of approaching Oakland motorcycle cops behind us. I took a deep breath. "Well, this is as good a place to die as any."[18]

In another scene described by Rubin, an activist lay face down on a train track in Berkeley to stop a train from taking American GIs to the Oakland Army Terminal. With great awe, Rubin recounted how this person would have died if not for four fellow activists who hauled him off the tracks a second before the train roared through.[19]

The phenomenon of believers supporting death cults and idealizing their own martyrdom has carried into the era of the terror war. The murder by Iraqi terrorists of American hostage Tom Fox in March 2006 is a perfect example of this phenomenon. Fox was among four members of the leftist group Christian Peacemaker Teams who were kidnapped in Iraq in November 2005. The group consistently speaks of its longing for death in its supposed quest for peace, and it is no coincidence that Fox died at the hands of the terrorists he was supporting.[20] Similarly, the leftists who set out to serve as human shields for Saddam, or the International Solidarity Movement activists who stood in front of Israeli soldiers, were not engaged in anything new, but just continuing a long leftist tradition.

Another element of the believer's diagnosis is the desperate search for the feeling of power to help him counteract the powerlessness he feels in his own life. This is connected, in part, to the lessening of authority in Western society, which leads believers to scapegoat their own society and forge alliances with the authority represented by adversarial despotic regimes. This explains, as Potter notes, the progressives' cult around Mao Tse-tung and "the compulsive expressions of adoration for a Hitler or a Stalin." He writes:

> Negative identification is itself a highly motivated, compensation-seeking form of societal estrangement. Sometimes when identification with a person fails, a great psychological void remains, and to fill this void people incapable of genuine interpersonal relationships will identify

with an abstraction. An important historical instance of identification with abstract power has been the zealous support of totalitarian regimes by faceless multitudes of people. The totalitarian display of power for its own sake satisfies the impulse to identify with strength.[21]

In our contemporary terror war, the believer has filled the void left by communism's disappearance with radical Islam. Instead of living vicariously through the oppression imposed by the KGB or the Red Guards, the believer now satisfies his yearnings through the violence perpetrated by suicide bombers. We can see a balance in this scale. The less brutal an ideology is, the less interest the average believer has in it and the less praise he is inclined to give it. By contrast, when the death cult is in full gear, the believer supports it most strongly. As will be demonstrated in Part II, the fellow travelers always flocked to communist regimes in largest numbers when the mass murder had reached a peak—Stalin's terror, Mao's Cultural Revolution, Pol Pot's killing fields. And as Part IV will reveal, the Left's rallying cry for militant Islam is loudest when the terrorists are waging their most ferocious campaigns against innocent civilians.

Rejecting the personal freedom that comes with modernity in a democratic society, the believer yearns for uniformity, stability, and purpose. Indeed, as will be shown in Part II, the fellow travelers who visited communist countries consistently referred to the "sense of purpose" they imagined they saw on people's faces—which they somehow never witnessed on faces in their own society. American sociologist Paul Hollander explains how these hallucinations are rooted in a "crisis of meaning":

> [T]he restlessness of estranged intellectuals and the hostility of the adversary culture are in all probability generalized responses to the discontents of life in a thoroughly modernized, wealthy, secular, and individualistic society where making life meaningful requires great ongoing effort and remains a nagging problem—at any rate for those whose attention does not have to be riveted on the necessities of survival.[22]

A simple dynamic feeds the believer's attraction to vicious adversarial cultures: he admires whomever his own society disapproves of and fears. As the enemy of his own society, the adversarial society is also the enemy of all the things the believer claims he hates therein (materialism, racism, sexism, homophobia, poverty, etc.).[23] The historical evidence, however, proves that the believer is not truly concerned with these social ills at all, seeing that these are always far worse in the adversarial societies—and this is especially true of militant Islam.

The believer's idolization of an alien culture goes back farther, of course, than the twentieth century. Alienated Western intellectuals have always dreamt of a foreign place they imagined as being better and purer than their own society. The idea of the "noble savage" was formulated in the late seventeenth century, but it is most closely associated with Jean-Jacques Rousseau, who saw man in the "state of nature" as essentially pure and good— before society corrupted him with greed and private property. The noble savage, in this paradigm, is born free and has not been shackled by the chains of civilization.

Following Rousseau, left-wing Western intellectuals have habitually looked to the Third World for personifications of primeval innocence. To alienated intellectuals of the nineteenth and early twentieth centuries, the noble savage represented everything that Western man was not. And since these intellectuals felt displaced in their own societies, they envisioned the noble savage as a guide who could help them navigate the stormy seas of life toward beachheads of meaning, satisfaction, and happiness. The classic case was Margaret Mead's 1928 bestseller *Coming of Age in Samoa*, which became the Left's bible.[24] Mead's fantasies about a guilt-free sexual utopia were typical of the Western intellectuals' dreams about the noble savage.

To be sure, there wasn't anything actually noble about the savage. And the believers knew that. But *that is precisely why they admired him.* They desired to harness his savagery in order to destroy all of their own society's modernity and freedom—as did the 9/11 terrorists who transformed the World Trade Center into Ground Zero.

The savage represented an idealized and mythical purity, but also the potential for destruction, which, as we have seen, the believer imagines to be the only path to renewed purity on earth. This is why communism and the Third World blurred into each other as objects of affection for believers. As Hollander notes:

> Certainly, the appeal China, Cuba, and North Vietnam had to the eyes of many Western intellectuals was part of the more general appeal of the Third World. Underdevelopment in the eyes of such beholders is somewhat like innocence. The underdeveloped is uncorrupted, untouched by the evils of industrialization and urbanization, by the complexities of modern life, the taint of trade, commerce, and industry. Thus, underdevelopment and Third World status are, like childhood, easily associated or confused with freshness, limitless possibilities, and wholesale simplicity.[25]

Therefore, the manner in which Western intellectuals idealized the noble savage serves as a crucial lens through which to observe how the longing for purity and innocence leads the believer to a lust for death. Unable to cope with the confusion, risks, and challenges inherent in individual freedom, the believer dreams of a world where, as a child again, he will be taken care of by a father-god who has everything under control and can make the decisions. The road to this fairy-tale world, in turn, can only be paved with human corpses.

The writings of believers are filled with allusions to the necessity of this violent destruction before the secular utopia can be built. In his introduction to Rubin's *Do It*, Black Panther Eldridge Cleaver affirmed: "If everybody did exactly what Jerry suggests in this book—if everybody carried out Jerry's program—there would be immediate peace in the world." Suffice it to say that Rubin's "program" consists of chaotic and scattered expressions of rage that have no unifying theme other than the desire to annihilate civil society. This is why Cleaver emphasizes that he can "unite" with Rubin "around hatred of pig judges, around hatred of capitalism, around the total desire to smash what is now the social order in the United States of Amerika, around the dream of building something new and fresh upon its ruins."[26] In other words, the "peace" that Cleaver and Rubin long for is the kind of peace that can be built only on Ground Zero.

In their yearning for a new earth, many Western intellectuals were also attracted to fascism,[27] the ideological cousin of communism and Islamism. Communism, of course, had a more popular appeal, since it possessed the reputation (albeit totally undeserved) of being on the side of humanity. But many believers could have gone either way. Indeed, many of the modern Left's ideas are rooted in fascism, especially in the ideology and practices of Benito Mussolini.[28] And the cult of sadism embodied in Hitler tempted their ideological appetites. Author Paul Berman reflects on Nazism's glorification of death:

> On the topic of death, the Nazis were the purest of the pure, the most aesthetic, the boldest, the greatest of executioners, and yet the greatest and most sublime of death's victims, too—people who, in Baudelaire's phrase, knew how to *feel* the revolution in both ways. Suicide was, after all, the final gesture of the Nazi elite in Berlin. Death, in their eyes, was not just for others, and at the final catastrophe in 1945 the Nazi leaders dutifully converted their safehouses into mini-Auschwitzes of their own.[29]

Because the believer possesses so many of these dysfunctions and adopts so many embarrassing political dispositions to safeguard them, remaining in denial takes on a life-and-death importance. *Everything* is at stake when a political or social reality is confronted. More than anything, the believer must constantly rationalize the annoying presence of human happiness around him. Common people who are happy with their circumstances, and who do not see themselves as victims, pose a serious threat to the believer's imagined community membership and thus to his personal identity. In response, the believer must tell himself that these individuals are content with their own society only because they have been brainwashed. In other words, they think they are happy, but in fact they are not. A "false consciousness" that capitalist forces have instilled in them rules them, and they can only be liberated from this mental enslavement by the revolution that the believers have appointed themselves to lead.

For the radical, experiencing joy means succumbing to this false consciousness and becoming distracted from the constant vigilance necessary to launch a revolutionary battle. This is why Lenin refused to listen to music, since, as he explained: "It makes you want to say stupid, nice things and stroke the heads of people who could create such beauty while living in this vile hell."[30] For Lenin violent revolution was the priority—a priority endangered by the emotions music could induce.

Needing to remain angry and full of gloom no matter how comfortable and joyful life in a free society might truly be, the believer invariably holds his own society to full moral accountability, but never does the same for enemy societies. The clear implication is that his society is actually superior, since it must be held to a higher standard. But the leftist must assiduously deny this implication, lest he be forced to confront the bigotry on which his own belief system is based.

To keep this toxic mindset in place, the believer must convince himself that *he knows something that ordinary human beings do not.* He is above ordinary human desires and affairs. As Hollander shows, left-wing intellectuals have perfected the procedure of appointing themselves the moral antennae of the human race.[31] Once again, we come full circle to the dark forces that make the progressive gravitate toward genocide: because believers consider themselves higher life forms, their inferiors become not only expendable, but necessary waste. They are nothing more than obstacles to the creation of Ground Zero and the subsequent rebuilding.

This is where the Western Left and militant Islam (like the Western Left and communism) intersect: human life must be sacrificed for the sake of *the idea.* Like Islamists, leftists have a Manichean vision that rigidly distinguishes good from evil. They see themselves as personifications of the former and their opponents as personifications of the latter, who must be slated for ruthless elimination.

As Parts III and IV will demonstrate, both Islamists and Western leftists thus see America as the Great Satan. In the American tradition, the sanctity of the individual, his freedom, and his life come before any political institution. Henry David Thoreau wrote at the close of his famous essay "On the Duty of Civil Disobedience": "There will never be a really free and enlightened State until the State comes to recognize the individual as a higher and independent power, from which all its own power and authority are derived."[32] In this formula, the sacredness of the individual *is* the political faith. For the believer and the Islamist, such a formula is anathema. The individual's right to pursue happiness, enshrined in America's foundations, interferes with the building of the perfect, unified social order; human joy and cheer are tacit endorsements of the present order that both leftist and Islamist utopians want to destroy.

The puritanical nature of totalist systems (whether fascist, communist, or Islamist) is another manifestation of this phenomenon. In Stalinist Russia, sexual pleasure was portrayed as unsocialist and counter-revolutionary.[33] More recent communist societies have also waged war on sexuality—a war that Islamism wages with similar ferocity. These totalist structures cannot survive in environments filled with self-interested, pleasure-seeking individuals who prioritize devotion to other individual human beings *over the collective and the state*. Because the believer viscerally hates the notion and reality of personal love and "the couple," he champions the enforcement of totalitarian puritanism by the regimes he worships.

The famous twentieth century novels of dystopia, Yevgeny Zamyatin's *We*, George Orwell's *1984*, and Aldous Huxley's *Brave New World*, all powerfully depict totalitarian society's assault on the realm of personal love in its violent attempt to dehumanize human beings and completely subject them to its rule. Yet as these novels demonstrate, no tyranny's attempt to turn human beings into obedient robots can fully succeed. Someone always exists who has doubts, who is uncomfortable, and who questions the secular deity—even though it would be safer for him to conform like everyone else. The desire that thus overcomes the instinct for self-preservation is erotic passion. And that is why love presents such a threat to the totalitarian order: it dares to serve itself. It is a force more powerful than the all-pervading fear that a totalitarian order needs to impose in order to survive.[34] By forbidding private love and affection, social engineers make the road toward earthly redemption much less serpentine.

As Part II will demonstrate, believers have been inspired by this form of tyranny in the Soviet Union, Communist China, and Communist North Vietnam, just as they have turned a blind eye to Castro's persecution of homosexuals. The desexualized dress that the Maoist regime imposed on its citizens especially enthralled believers. This at once satisfied the believer's desire for enforced sameness and the imperative of erasing attractions between private citizens.

The Maoists' unisex clothing finds its parallel in fundamentalist Islam's mandate for shapeless coverings to be worn by both males and females. The collective "uniform" symbolizes submission to a higher entity and frustrates individual expression, mutual physical attraction, and private connection and affection. Once again, the believer remains not only uncritical, but completely supportive, of this totalitarian puritanism.

This is exactly why, forty years ago, the Weather Underground not only waged war against American society through violence and mayhem, but also waged war on private love within its own ranks. Bill Ayers, one of the leading terrorists in the group, argued in a speech defending the campaign: "Any notion that people can have responsibility for one person, that they can have that 'out' — we have to destroy that notion in order to build a collective; we have to destroy all 'outs,' to destroy the notion that people can lean on one person and not be responsible to the entire collective."[35] In this way, the Weather Underground destroyed any signs of monogamy within its ranks and forced couples, some of whom had been together for years, to admit their "political error" and split apart. Like their icon Margaret Mead, they fought the notions of romantic love, jealousy, and other "oppressive" manifestations of one-on-one intimacy and commitment. This was followed by forced group sex and "national orgies," whose main objective was to crush the spirit of individualism.[36] This constituted an eerie replay of the sexual promiscuity that was encouraged (while private love was forbidden) in *We, 1984,* and *Brave New World.*[37]

Valentine's Day — a day devoted to the love between a man and a woman — is a natural target for both the Left and Islamism.

As we shall see in chapter ten, imams around the world thunder against Valentine's Day every year, and its celebration is outlawed in Islamist states. In the West, feminist leftists especially hate Valentine's Day. Jane Fonda has led the campaign to transform it into "V-Day" ("Violence against Women Day")—a day of hate, featuring a mass indictment of men.[38] The objective is clear: to shatter any celebration of the intimacy that a man can hold with a woman, for that bond is inaccessible to *the order*. This impulse is also manifest when Western believers dedicate themselves to the cause of "transgenderism"—the effort to erase "gender," which they believe is an oppressive social construct imposed by capitalism.

It becomes clear why totalitarian puritanism has taken on crucial significance in the terror war. As we shall see in more detail in Parts III and IV, Islamism, like its communist cousin, wages a ferocious war on any kind of private and unregulated love. In the case of Islamism, the reality is epitomized in its monstrous structures of gender apartheid and the terror that keeps it in place (from mandatory veiling and forced marriage to female genital mutilation and honor killings). Militant Islam's ruthless persecution of homosexuality, a mirror image of Castro's, is part and parcel of this phenomenon. While posing as the champions of gay rights and women's rights, believers also ally themselves with the barbaric deniers of these rights.

All these ingredients in the believer's psyche contribute to the contemporary Left's romance with militant Islam, just as they engendered the believers' love affair with communist regimes throughout the twentieth century. The pilgrimages that fellow travelers embarked on, wandering from one brutal despotism to the next, best exemplifies that love affair. In order to give the context for the story of the Left's dalliance with Islamism, we must first tell that haunting tale.

PART II

ROMANCE WITH TYRANNY

CHAPTER THREE

Worshipping the First Communist Death Cult

"We'll ask the man, where do you stand on the question of the revolution? Are you for it or against it? If he's against it, we'll stand him up against a wall."

—Vladimir Lenin

F rom the moment the Bolsheviks seized power in Russia in 1917, the Western Left reveled in the new society that they set out to create, which quickly degenerated into a prison camp ruled by terror. As new communist despotisms followed the Soviet example, believers extended their veneration from one experiment in earthly redemption to another, and they expressed their adulation through the myriad pilgrimages they made to their most beloved tyrannies. These individuals became known as "fellow travelers" and "political pilgrims."[1]

The political pilgrims began their voyages in the 1920s. They flocked to the new Soviet experiment in the hope of finding an entity before which they could prostrate themselves. The pilgrimages reached their peak in the 1930s, when Joseph Stalin was liquidating millions of his subjects. Later odysseys focused on Castro's Cuba in the early 1960s, North Vietnam in the mid- and late 1960s, Mao's China in the late 1960s and early 1970s, and Sandinista Nicaragua from 1979 to 1989. In general, any totalist regime that had adversarial relations with the United States was a potential destination.

The political pilgrims bowed before the most ruthless dictators and praised their societies in the most glowing terms. Their adulation always reached its highest level at exactly the time when the regimes reached their apex of genocide and terror. This was no coincidence, since, as indicated in the believer's diagnosis, the more brutal the regime, the greater the admiration the believer feels for it.

Though the places the political pilgrims visited were earthly hell, their hosts always worked hard to reinforce their belief that they were in heaven. And although the believers were attracted primarily by the barbarity that was now being intentionally hidden from them, they in turn would expend every effort to deny its existence and speak of the regime in terms opposite to those that would accurately describe it.[2]

The communist hosts engaged in the "techniques of hospitality," as Paul Hollander dubbed them, whereby a mythical world was carefully arranged for the visitors.[3] The techniques included latter-day Potemkin villages: officials would literally fabricate entire villages to create the illusion that communism was achieving social perfection and unbridled economic efficiency. In truth, nothing in these villages was real; even the "villagers" were actors who had been told exactly what to say.[4]

The actors didn't have to work all that hard. The pilgrims' willingness to let themselves be deceived was so strong that they were predisposed to see greatness everywhere, even in the most trivial details. If a child smiled, it meant that utopia had already arrived. (If a child smiled in the believer's own society, however, it only indicated that capitalism had succeeded in imposing a false consciousness on children.) The English historian Bernard Pares, meanwhile, found himself entranced by the "more purposeful look" that he found on the faces of ordinary Soviet citizens.[5] To be sure, Pares deemed it axiomatic that no such "purposeful" look could have existed on any face in his home society — an important aspect of the believer's diagnosis.

At first glance, there may appear to be a paradox in the believer's relationship with the Potemkin villages: if the believer yearns for death and destruction, as the necessary precursor to building the new world, then why would he need to experience the Potemkin village? The key here is that the Potemkin village symbolizes the impossible dream for the believer. He is well aware of the massive deaths that are required to realize the dream—and he supports the process. But he wants to hold in his mental vision the earthly paradise that serves as his final objective, not the carnage that brings it into being. Further, the mass slaughter that makes the earthly paradise possible is a measure of how wonderful it is. If it were easy to create—if it did not require seas of blood— then it would not be the momentous and world-transforming undertaking that inspires the imagination of the believer.

When the Bolsheviks seized power, therefore, their revolutionary acts whetted the believers' appetites and aroused their psychic lust. To be sure, Bolshevism proved itself fanatically faithful in carrying out Marx's favorite poetic dictum: "Everything that exists deserves to perish." Paul Berman profoundly captures the essence of Bolshevism's death cult:

> And, very quickly, Lenin's movement, having seized power in St. Petersburg in 1917, spread all over Europe and around the world. Everywhere the new movement displayed a weirdly frenetic dynamism, beyond anything that could have been seen in the nineteenth century. It was an emotional forcefulness that derived, ultimately, from the movement's cheerful willingness to put Bolshevism's enemies to death, and an equally cheerful willingness to put to death random crowds whose views on Bolshevism were utterly unknown, and a further willingness to put to death the Bolsheviks themselves (no one has ever murdered more communists than the Communist Party of the Soviet Union), and a willingness to accept one's own death, too— all for the best of reason. The idea was, in Baudelaire's phrase, to whip and kill the people for the good of the people. And the whipping and killing got underway.[6]

Vladimir Ilyich Lenin, the first Soviet dictator, served as the perfect engineer of the world's new killing machine. He meticulously laid the foundations for what would become one of the most despotic regimes in world history. He created the *Cheka*, the Soviet secret police, and involved himself daily in its monstrous evils. He launched the Red Terror, the mass persecution of religious believers, the systematic extermination of the so-called *kulaks*, and the concentration-camp and slave-labor system. The foundations of Stalinism were firmly constructed by Lenin.[7]

Lenin entranced leftists worldwide, as exemplified by the fellow travelers who journeyed to the Soviet Union in the 1930s and visited the dictator's tomb. The adulatory comments were unending. The American writers Corliss and Margaret Lamont were inspired by Lenin's "beautiful and resolute face."[8] American critic Edmund Wilson found a "beautiful face, of exquisite fineness...profoundly aristocratic.... Yet it is an aristocrat who is not specialized as an aristocrat, a poet who is not specialized as a poet, a scientist who is not specialized as a scientist."[9] The mausoleum also inspired Irish playwright and critic George Bernard Shaw. For Shaw, Lenin was "a pure intellectual type, that is the true aristocracy... Henceforth Napoleon's tomb ranks second instead of first."[10]

The believers worshipped Lenin not despite but *because of* the terror he inflicted. This dynamic clearly involved the process of negative identification described in the believer's diagnosis: the believer fulfills his craving for power by associating himself with the brutal display of authoritarian might. And, with his aristocratic features, Lenin served as the symbol of the earthly paradise that serves as the main inspiration to the believer.

Joseph Stalin refined and perfected the art of mass murder, annihilating his victims by the tens of millions.[11] For this achievement, believers flocked to the Soviet Union to pay homage to their genocidal secular god.

Several components formed the progressive faith's attitude toward the Soviet Union during this period. The Stalinist terror coincided with an economic crisis in the West. Believers viewed the Great Depression as a confirmation of the failure of capitalism and took it as an extra incentive to reject their own society and look admiringly to the Soviet Union. The threat of fascism also played a role. Viewing Hitler as bad because Stalin said he was, many believers were outraged that the West was not standing up to the Nazi dictator in the way that Stalin portrayed himself as doing.

Of course, as we have seen, actually opposing Hitler was the last thing on many leftists' minds. Their indignation merely served as an excuse to side with the Soviet Union. The Nazi-Soviet Non-Aggression Pact of August 1939 revealed this charade. Literally overnight, Hitler went from being bad to good in the eyes of many believers—simply because Stalin now said that the Führer was someone who could be bargained with and trusted. And while a number of believers did abandon the cause as a result of the pact, many others held on, remaining faithful to Stalin and retaining the complete indifference to Hitler that they had had in the first place—even though they had pretended that anti-fascism was fundamental to their cause.

Meanwhile, the number of political pilgrims to the Soviet Union skyrocketed during the 1930s, precisely when the terror reached its highest levels. As Paul Hollander puts it, "The Soviet Union enjoyed the greatest prestige among Western intellectuals at the times when it was most savagely repressive, most severely plagued by material shortages, and subject to Stalin's personal dictatorship—that is, during the early and mid-1930s."[12]

Leftists would make many excuses later over this inexcusable phenomenon. The most common one was that the believers "didn't know" the full extent of the horrors being perpetrated by the regime at the time they gave it their adoration. But the reality is that the evidence of the mass crimes was always available to them if they had actually wanted to know the truth. Moreover, even upon "discovering" the truth of the vicious nature of a particular regime, the believers always went on to admire the next genocidal regime. As David Caute writes, the fellow travelers "heartily welcomed the torments and upheavals inflicted on the Russian peasantry during collectivization.... The primitive aspects of Russia, and later China, captivated the imaginations of such intellectuals."[13]

There were, certainly, periods—such as the early Stalinist era—when many of the horrors were not yet completely known. Still, many published testimonies were available, along with other evidence.[14] Furthermore, the secrecy itself—especially the total restrictions on freedom of the press—provided clues about the horror that was transpiring.

Nonetheless, droves of leftists stepped forward to sing the praises of Stalinist rule. In addition to Shaw, Wilson, and the Lamonts, cited above, some of the most infamous figures included Walter Duranty, Upton Sinclair, Anna Louise Strong, Johannes Becher, André Maurois, Theodore Dreiser, and H. G. Wells. A brief examination of three individuals—Duranty, Shaw, and Strong—will help crystallize the psychology of the Left in this context.

Walter Duranty was the quintessential political pilgrim of the twentieth century. The *New York Times*'s man in Moscow during the twenties and early thirties, he deliberately spiked news of the Ukrainian famine.[15]

While Stalin starved millions of Ukrainians to death, Duranty praised the Soviet dictator and reported that Soviet granaries were overflowing. When he visited Ukraine at the peak of the slaughter in 1933, he reported that the Ukrainians appeared "healthier and more cheerful" than he had anticipated, and that village markets overflowed with "eggs, fruit, poultry, vegetables, milk, and butter." "A child," he wrote, "can see this is not famine but abundance."[16]

Duranty had already won a Pulitzer Prize for his reporting on Stalin's first five-year plan, and his lies were so far-reaching in their influence that when Malcolm Muggeridge, who was in the Soviet Union as the *Manchester Guardian*'s correspondent, managed to visit Ukraine and subsequently wrote about the holocaust there, he was not believed. Muggeridge's reports, which included descriptions of peasants kneeling in the snow and begging for crusts of bread, were ridiculed and dismissed. His reputation was so badly damaged that the *Guardian* fired him. Duranty led the chorus vilifying Muggeridge, while simultaneously admitting in private that Muggeridge was telling the truth. Duranty told a British Foreign Office acquaintance, for instance, that he was aware that at least ten million people had been killed. Duranty later handled the show trials in the same way, regurgitating the official Soviet line and demonizing the victims.[17]

Duranty fits the profile of the believer not only in terms of his blind service to the totalitarian regime, but also in terms of what led him on his political journey. He was an outcast in his own society—a drug abuser with a wooden leg who engaged in satanic sexual orgies.[18] In his alienation, he dreamt of finding a home in an adversarial society. In Stalin's Soviet Union, he found one to which he could submit.

Duranty's story is but one tragic example of the immense damage the Left's veneration of America's totalitarian enemies has caused. In 1933, Duranty was present in the Oval Office as President Franklin D. Roosevelt announced the diplomatic recognition of the USSR. The U.S. recognition of the Soviet government proved devastating in its effects. It brought legitimacy to the Stalinist regime, facilitating the workings of the Gulag Archipelago and laying the groundwork for the Cold War. Yet it is very likely that the president would have never granted this recognition if the American people had been well informed of the Stalinist terror.[19]

George Bernard Shaw matched Duranty in his adoration of the Soviet regime. Like Duranty, he revered Joseph Stalin and bought into a fantasy of abundance and richness, where in fact only famine and terror prevailed. One of the most pathetic political pilgrims of all times, he traveled to the USSR to meet the Soviet dictator in 1931. While awaiting their useful idiot, the Soviets manufactured all the seductive deceptions the playwright craved. It was love even before first sight: on his train trip to the Soviet Union, Shaw:

> strolled about the platform and then decided to look into the restaurant. Here the guide formally introduced him to two waitresses who were longing to meet the great Bernard Shaw. By an extraordinary coincidence they were intimately acquainted with his works. GBS was sufficiently moved by this remarkable evidence of Russian literacy to express the opinion that waitresses in England were not so well-read as their Soviet sisters.[20]

Delighted with such flattery, Shaw decided that he was, without doubt, about to visit paradise. Before the train crossed the Soviet border, he threw a supply of food out of the train in order to demonstrate his conviction that the reports of food shortages in the Soviet Union were capitalist propaganda. Upon arriving in the Soviet utopia, Shaw was so overwhelmed with ecstasy that *everything* he saw impressed him—especially Soviet prisons. Arranged just for him in Potemkin fashion, the prisons Shaw visited led him to the conclusion that the Soviet prison system was remarkably superior to that of Britain. In his mind, Soviet prisons were so wonderful that the inmates resisted leaving when their sentences had expired. Shaw exulted:

> When we came to the old hands in the workshops we discovered that the cardinal difference between an English and a Russian prison is that in England a delinquent enters as an ordinary man and comes out as a "criminal type," whereas in Russia he enters, like those boys, as a criminal type and would come out an ordinary man but for the difficulty of inducing him to come out at all. As far as I could make out they could stay as long as they liked.[21]

American radical activist Anna Louise Strong also found the prisons to be one of the most inspiring ingredients of the new Soviet experiment. Indeed, Strong topped Shaw in her favorable view of the prisons: while the Irish playwright perceived that Russian prisoners didn't want to leave, Strong believed that citizens "now apply to be admitted."[22] During her first visit to the Soviet Union in 1921, the slave-labor camps especially moved her. "The labor camps have won high reputation throughout the Soviet Union," she commented, "as places where tens of thousands of men have been reclaimed."[23]

Strong spent most of her years in the Soviet Union and in Communist China—devoting her whole life to these nations during what David Caute calls "the most punishing phases of socialist construction."[24] No amount of communist genocide could shake her dedication to the political faith. The more she knew about the purges, the famine, and the mass murder, the more intoxicating her Soviet romance became. When the Stalinist regime began arresting and killing her friends and co-workers, her lust for the regime increased.

Like Duranty, Strong admitted privately at the time that she knew that the victims of the Soviet (and, later, the Eastern European) purge trials were innocent, but she remained silent in public. After Nikita Khrushchev's Twentieth Party Congress in 1956, in which the new Soviet leader exposed and denounced

Stalin's crimes, Strong admitted, again privately, that she had always known about them. Still, she continued her public silence—except to blame the excesses on the secret police.[25] She never criticized Stalin himself.

Like any other believer, Strong was motivated by negative identification. For her, the Soviet monolith served as a replacement for the void in her own private life. She even spoke of it herself, referring to the Soviet Communist Party as her lifelong "boss" and "husband." The American Communist Party was far too small for her: it couldn't come close to perpetrating the violence of which the Soviet Communist Party was capable. As she explained:

> The Russian Party one could adore for its tremendous achievements: but the American Party—no! If I must have a lifelong boss, let it be a big one. Like ancient Jewish tribes wanting their Jehovah to be all-powerful, like a woman wanting an important husband.[26]

Strong was ready and willing to be devoured by the big boss-husband to whom she devoted her life. When the Soviet regime turned on her and arrested her in February 1949, she was jailed for a few days in the infamous Lubyanka Prison, branded an American spy, and expelled from the Soviet Union.[27] She wrote about her arrest, but made sure to blame everyone and everything but Stalin. The West's anti-communism, she insisted, had induced paranoia in the minds of Soviet bureaucrats. When the Soviets admitted in 1955 that they were wrong to have accused her of being a spy, she rushed back to renew her worship of her secular god.

Things weren't quite the same, however, in this second phase of Strong's Soviet odyssey. With Stalin gone and the ruthless purges coming to an end, she yearned for a new totalism to worship—a dictatorship that was, as Stalin's had been in the 1930s, at its peak of bloodshed and horror. Strong moved on to a new boss-husband, a new love: Communist China, where the wheels of the blood-drenched Cultural Revolution were just about to start turning. Until her death in 1970, she lived in China and sang Mao's praises as his regime liquidated seventy million people.

Stalin's purge trials had provided believers the special exhilaration they needed to keep their romance with the bloody Soviet experiment alive. Progressives everywhere salivated at the obvious frame-ups. Some of the loudest cheers came from the likes of the American novelist and social crusader Upton Sinclair, the French writer Henri Barbusse, and the German playwright Bertolt Brecht.[28]

Brecht rivals Duranty as the quintessential believer. A hardcore Stalinist, he excused and promoted Stalin's crimes at every turn—including the purge trials, whose victims included many of his own friends. Brecht stated:

> With total clarity the trials have proved the existence of active conspiracies against the regime.... All the scum at home and abroad, all the parasites, professional criminals, informers joined them. All this rabble had the same objectives as [the conspirators]. I am convinced this is the truth.[29]

Brecht's indifference extended to his ex-lover, Carola Neher. When she was arrested in Moscow, Brecht said there must have been evidence to warrant it.[30] Carola was never seen again, and Brecht never inquired about her again.

Brecht exemplified the believer's support for genocidal regimes not despite but because of their crimes. He revealed this in a 1935 conversation with the American philosopher Sidney Hook about the trials of Lev Kamenev and Grigory Zinoviev. When Hook commented that the Communist Party was persecuting innocent former *comrades*, Brecht rejoined, "As for them, the more innocent they are, the more they deserve to be shot."[31] When Hook asked Brecht for his reasoning, the German writer refused to explain himself. Hook had collided with the monstrous nihilism inherent in the Left's vision.

Professor Henry Pachter of City University recalled conversations in which Brecht justified the need to support the Soviet Communist Party notwithstanding its crimes. Brecht's identification with the totality also took on an expected and typical self-serving turn. One of his comments to Pachter: "Fifty years hence the communists will have forgotten Stalin but I want to be sure that they will still read Brecht. Therefore I cannot separate myself from the Party."[32]

Although Brecht relished his own role as artistic visionary, he was not a supporter of free expression. In 1938-39, for instance, he enthusiastically supported Stalin's attack on "formalism" in the arts, stating:

> The very salutary campaign against formalism has helped the productive development of artistic forms, by proving that social content is an absolutely decisive condition for such development. Any formal innovation which does not serve and derive its justification from its social content will remain utterly frivolous.[33]

In other words, Brecht could not accept any form of art that did not expressly serve as propaganda for communist ideology. Stalin himself had attacked formalism because artists—writers, painters, composers, and so on—were attempting to free their work from didactic political slavery by choosing abstract, existential subjects. Many of these Russian artists did, in fact, see their stance as a rebellion against communist tyranny, but Brecht could not accept even implicit yearnings for artistic—and thus personal—liberty.

Brecht's own work preached communist values and demonstrated the appropriate social content. In his view, all other artists were obligated to submit to a similar vision. Art's purpose was not to serve beauty or any other aesthetic value; it was to destroy the old order and thereby enable the birth of the communist utopia. Brecht and other Western intellectuals used this position to attack persecuted intellectuals under communism. As Caute writes:

> Both the Western communists and the fellow-travelling intellectuals deepened the despair of the non-official Soviet intelligentsia during the years of persecution and terror. In their darkest hours they heard themselves condemned by their own kind, by foreigners who shared their own idealistic traditions and whose immunity from imprisonment or death was due solely to accident of nationality…. The victim found himself totally isolated in a wilderness of arbitrary violence and pervasive fears. Meanwhile the "engineers of souls" in

the West lauded his tormentors and spat on his grave—then denied his death.[34]

The believers' love affair with the Soviet regime entailed, by necessity, a veneration of the dictator in charge, since Stalin was the embodiment of the Soviet system. Leftists enjoyed a wide consensus during the 1930s—the period of the greatest Soviet terror—on Stalin's virtues. They saw him as an egalitarian and a populist. Walter Duranty, naturally, led the way. Granted a personal interview with Stalin, he called the mass murderer the "greatest living statesman...a quiet, unobtrusive man." And American ambassador Joseph H. Davies, as we have seen, depicted Stalin as a type of gentle St. Francis: "His brown eye is exceedingly wise and gentle. A child would like to sit on his lap and a dog would sidle up to him."[35]

American sociologist Jerome Davis was another fellow traveler who venerated the Soviet dictator. Having visited the Soviet Union and interviewed Stalin personally on several occasions, he praised the despot and his regime at every turn in his book *Behind Soviet Power*. He insisted that Stalin was not a dictator, that the show trials were justified, and that forced collectivization was necessary. He rhapsodized about Stalin's yearning to follow the will of the people:

> It would be an error to consider the Soviet leader a willful man who believes in forcing his ideas upon others. Everything he does reflects the desires and hopes of the masses to a large degree. He always has his ear to the ground, making it his business to find out what people are really thinking. Peasants and workers are encouraged to write their frank opinions.... He both leads and follows public opinion.[36]

Davis was especially enthralled by Stalin's puritanism:

> The Soviet leader's recreational likes and dislikes are quite in keeping with his character. All Stalin's associates say that he is quite puritanical in his personal habits. He never permits smutty stories to be told in his presence. He rarely drinks *vodka*, preferring the mild Caucasian red wine. He smokes a pipe, never gambles, and never drinks in excess.[37]

Stalin's reluctance to have attention focused on him also moved Davis:

> Paradoxically enough, in view of his very real modesty and unassuming nature, Stalin permits his statue and his picture to be plastered from one end of the country to the other.[38]

Davis explained that even though Stalin found this cult around him "distasteful," he allowed it because it was the people's decision: they wanted to make for themselves a symbol of the Soviet state.[39]

Davis was insistent that "the opposition to Stalin in the Soviet Union today [1945-46] is far less than against any other ruler in any major country in the world."[40] It was simply inconceivable to Davis that there could be a serious opposition—Stalin embodied the utopian dream itself. Moreover, as Bernard Shaw put it, Stalin was "simply secretary of the supreme controlling organ of the hierarchy, subject to dismissal at ten minutes' notice if he does not give satisfaction."[41]

For many political pilgrims, their negative identification extended to a longing for their own deaths. One of the darkest impulses of the believer is the urge either to associate oneself with the power that murders, or to be murdered by that power for the sake of the idea. We need only look at the fate of so many of the Western communists who went to the Soviet Union after the revolution to help build communism—only to be killed, along with many Russian Bolsheviks, by Stalin.[42]

This was the beginning of a long tradition of communist revolutions that ate not only their own children but also those who came to pay homage to them. In more recent times, political pilgrims have ardently desired to die defending the society they idolized against an American invasion, as in Nicaragua under the Sandinistas (see chapter eight). The same is true of the leftists who set out to serve as human shields for Saddam Hussein, or the members of the International Solidarity Movement who put themselves in harm's way by obstructing the efforts of Israeli soldiers to fight Palestinian terrorists (see chapter sixteen). In the end, all these radicals desired the ultimate sacrifice: martyrdom for the idea.

The Left's idolization of Stalin would continue even after the dictator's death in 1953. Then in 1956, at the Twentieth Party Congress, Nikita Khrushchev gave his "secret speech" revealing Stalin's crimes and denouncing the "cult of personality" surrounding him. The impossible problem this presented to believers was that a Soviet leader had actually spotlighted the consequences of socialist ideas for the whole world to see.

Of course, if the Left had actually been disillusioned by the revelations of Stalin's crimes, it would have engaged in profound soul-searching and would have meticulously analyzed the possibility that the very ideological foundations of socialism had necessitated the Gulag. But because they wanted to bring about more gulags, progressives needed to create the fiction that Stalin was an aberration and that his crimes had occurred in spite of, not because of, the socialist impulse.

Another implication of Khrushchev's revelations was that Soviet mass crimes had ended and would not be renewed—at least not with the same intensity. So while the believers still were devoted to the Soviet Union, the communist paradise was no longer as exhilarating to them as it had once been. The peak of the terror-cleansing was past; no more eggs needed to be broken to make that particular omelette. For the Left, this meant a new search would have to begin for a fresh utopian paradise where revolutionaries would once again, in the tradition of Lenin and Stalin, engage in mass death and suicide—while the progressive world called it a quest for human equality and social justice.

As the historical record clearly shows, the Left would do this over and over again. Every time the elements of Stalinism were uncovered in the current favorite communist paradise, the Left would simply redirect its emotional and intellectual devotion to a new, identical experiment, where the same ingredients would lead inevitably to yet another bloodbath. This would go on until today, when al-Qaeda and Hezbollah fill the void left by the collapse of communism.

CHAPTER FOUR

The "New Left"—Renewed Instinct for Destruction

"You fucking male supremacists, arrest me, too!"

—Karen Wald, a radical at an antiwar "sit-in"

In reaction to Khrushchev's revelations,[1] some believers split off from the Communist Party and formed the "New Left." This was purportedly a path to true socialism without the Stalinist component, even though *exactly* the same ideas and goals that had engendered the Soviet terror were to be used again for the supposed betterment of humankind.

To add to the dislocation, believers confronted many new social changes that forced them to reshape the rationalizations for their destructive agendas. With the advent of the 1960s, a new generation—one that was untouched by the crises of the 1930s— came of age. This new breed of believers had no experience with any real economic hardship; material comfort, educational opportunity, and social advancement shaped their lives. Back in the 1930s, even if a particular believer was in comfortable circumstances himself, he could point to real grievances like unemployment and poverty all around him and exploit them to wage war against his society. Not so with the sixties believers: they were the most privileged generation in human history, wanting for nothing.

Whereas capitalism had momentarily appeared to be a failure in the early 1930s, by the 1960s it had clearly established itself as a tremendous success, generating massive wealth and distributing it better than any other economic system. The New Left, therefore, faced a serious crisis: since its entire *raison d'être* depended on hating capitalism and rejecting the society on which it was based, it had to come up with a new rationale. And it found it: capitalism was evil not because it failed, but *because it worked.*

The ingredients of the Left's rejection of capitalism now directly contradicted the ones exploited by the earlier generation of believers. While the older believers had rejected capitalism because it had not provided enough jobs, the new generation rejected the system for providing the *wrong kind* of jobs. A job now allegedly had to help a person find purpose in life and cure his feelings of alienation. As the Port Huron Statement—the founding document of the quintessential New Left organization, Students for a Democratic Society (SDS)—put it, "…work should involve incentives worthier than money or survival. It should be educative, not stultifying; creative, not mechanical; self-direct[ed], not manipulated, encouraging independence, a respect for others, a sense of dignity and a willingness to accept social responsibility…"[2] Held up to this ideal, almost every job could be seen as being oppressive. Capitalist society could be seen as evil because it forced people to work; in the future earthly paradise, believers envisioned no one having to work—there would just be wealth and equal redistribution of it, plain and simple.[3]

This philosophy was in perfect line with Marxism, which sees all work as an evil. Marx himself hated manual labor; he never worked a day in his life and never actually knew a single worker—except the unpaid servant in his own house. As historian Paul Johnson has made clear, Marx lived his whole life sponging off others, especially Friedrich Engels, and he developed his hatred of capitalism precisely because of his own laziness and inability to manage his finances or pay back any of his debts.[4]

Ungrateful for being the luckiest generation in world history, sixties New Leftists agonized about how affluence and security created "empty human values" and, worse still, competitive individualism. To be materially comfortable meant to be empty and selfish. And because believers themselves were among those who were materially comfortable, they became plagued by guilt, which they attempted to assuage by working toward a solution that would rid the world—and themselves—of the system that gave them all the luxurious time to think up everything they hated about it.[5] All in all, as analyzed in the believer's diagnosis, the believers found a way to fantasize that they too were victims, and to absolve themselves of their guilt by joining an imaginary community of victims.

This was nothing new. As Paul Hollander observes, "It certainly was not the first occasion in modern history that a combination of the unproblematic satisfaction of material needs and a related sense of security made a major contribution to restlessness, unease, diffuse rebelliousness, and finally political activism or (non-political) thrill-seeking."[6] This dynamic was very much a part of the development of the Romantic movement in late eighteenth century Western Europe. Bored by comfort and security, young Europeans yearned for drama and passion. And if this meant creating a problem to agonize over, then that is what they would do.

It was this same spiritual hunger that influenced the sixties believers. Craving crisis and disorder, they grasped onto whatever torments might make them righteously indignant. And these conveniently presented themselves: the Vietnam War, the race riots, government corruption, and so on. These were all realities, of course, but they were not the causes of the Left's fury—they were the occasions and pretexts for it. If problems like the Vietnam War or racial injustice had not existed, the sixties leftists would have found something else. Their rejection of their own society stemmed from their personal need to reject it. The war simply provided them with a perceived justification for doing so. As Ronald Radosh has admitted about his days as a believer:

> In truth, the end of the war produced a great void. Demonstrating, writing articles against the war, marching scores of times to the nation's capital had become the focus of our lives...the war had been the center of everything, and now it was gone. None of us admitted it,

but we almost all looked inside ourselves with a rising
sense of panic and wondered, "What now?"[7]

Similarly, when the ceasefire agreement was signed in January 1973, Weather Underground terrorist Mark Rudd wept, "thinking at first that it was for joy but realizing afterward that it was for the large part of himself that was now dead."[8] Fellow terrorist Bill Ayers agonized: "Is there life after the war?"[9]

Herbert Marcuse, often termed the "father of the New Left," outlined the rationale for the leftist hatred of the abundance of freedom in American society. Marcuse coined the term "repressive tolerance" to describe the way capitalism enslaves people by making them happy and free. Because capitalism satisfied its citizens' material needs, it distracted them from what they should be enraged about: their captivity. Human beings under capitalism lived in a false consciousness, which made them unaware of the oppression quietly destroying their lives.[10]

Leftist guru Noam Chomsky altruistically developed this theme, teaching his faithful flock that they were actually in agony even when they felt happy, since their joy was a false consciousness manufactured by capitalist elites. The capitalist oppressors used all forms of entertainment, therefore, including televised sports and movies, to distract the masses from their victimization and make them unwilling or unable to revolt.[11]

Hollander has demonstrated the significant problems that this thought-control theme posed for believers. For instance, it remained a mystery how and why, if the society had such complete control over its people's thought, the believers themselves were immune to it. A glaring contradiction existed in that at the same time that the believers argued that American society engaged in authoritarianism and thought control, they censured it for fostering too much individualism and self-indulgence. Moreover, if capitalist affluence and "repressive tolerance" were such oppressive features, why were many of the believers themselves among the greatest exploiters of their benefits? Indeed, while they furiously denounced the self-indulgence that capitalist materialism engendered, believers prided themselves on refusing to exercise even a modicum of restraint on the pursuit of their own immediate self-gratification—especially in the areas of sex and drugs.[12]

Overall, the freedom of American society allowed believers the bizarre luxury of publicly articulating how *not free* it was—with the hypocritical certainty that nothing serious would happen to them in retribution. In other words, they considered free expression their inalienable right, but hated the society whose institutions gave it to them.

The key for believers was to create an atmosphere of oppression. They quickly figured out that the best way to do this was to get themselves arrested (though they were almost always immediately released). Indeed, as the antiwar protests heated up, believers were infuriated when they *failed* to be arrested. Jerry Rubin described what occurred at one sit-in he attended:

> Finally, the cops arrived and surrounded the one thousand people sitting in.... The cops had arrest warrants for the six: Mario Savio, Stew Albert, Steve Hamilton, Mike Smith, Bill Miller, and myself. Karen Wald, another non-student sitting right in the middle of the group, was ignored. Furious, she shouted, "You fucking male supremacists, arrest me, too!"[13]

Getting arrested killed two birds with one stone: it proved that the believers lived in an oppressive society; it also proved that they were victims and that *they mattered*. They could view themselves as members of a community that was fighting injustice, which alleviated the guilt they felt for reaping the benefits of their wealthy society. As radical activist and author bell hooks put it: "My rage intensifies because I am not a victim."[14]

Inside this toxic dynamic of the New Left, myriad pathologies arose. Though they demonized competition, they competed with one another to be the greatest victim. Whites felt guilty for being white, so they wished—and sometimes pretended—they were black. Wealthy believers felt guilty about being wealthy, so they wished—and pretended—they were poor. The list goes on and on. In each case, the believer was required to identify with *anyone* who was perceived as a victim. The main tactic for achieving this end was to support the violent revolutionary vanguards in one's own society, which included, among others, the Weather Underground and the murderers, rapists, and gangsters in the Black Panthers.[15] No matter what heinous crimes such groups committed, the believers justified them—since the Left's ends legitimized every means.

Deep down, of course, the believers' rejection of their society had nothing to do with anything that was actually wrong with that society, or with anything that any society could actually mend. And that is why their desires could not ultimately be fulfilled. Jerry Rubin crystallized it best:

> Satisfy our demands and we got twelve more. The more demands you satisfy, the more we got.... All we want from these meetings are demands that the Establishment can never satisfy. What a defeat if they satisfy our demands! Demonstrators are never "reasonable." We always put our demands forward in such an obnoxious manner that the power structure can never satisfy us and remain the power structure. Then, we scream, righteously angry, when our demands are not met. Satisfy our demands and we lose. Deny our demands and through struggle we achieve the love and brotherhood of a community.[16]

Craving to be taken seriously but unable to be persecuted in their own society, the New Leftists of the sixties and seventies renewed—with vigor—the Left's tradition of venerating and visiting death cult tyrannies. That way, at least they could achieve a feeling of importance and power through negative identification. And so, they made their own political pilgrimages. Paul Hollander has described the new ingredients that inspired this new generation of fellow travelers:

> Wishing to be severe social critics of the societies they lived in and half expecting some measure of retribution or mild martyrdom for their criticism, instead they often found themselves either ignored by the holders of power or, worse, in positions of influence and high social status despite their relentless castigation of the social system which continued, almost absent-mindedly, to feed generously the mouths that so regularly bit it. Having

been so benignly treated, many social critics in the West felt ineffectual: not being denied material rewards and social status (let alone political freedom) was proof that they failed to become a threat to the system. Dark suspicions would arise: did they unwittingly sell out? By contrast in Cuba (as in the Soviet Union and China) it was possible to enjoy the blessings of the good life, that is, to consume without guilt and without twinges of doubt because this was taking place in a rational, benevolent, and egalitarian system.[17]

As the Western Left's affection for the Soviet Union waned, three new tyrannies conveniently appeared on the horizon. Fidel Castro, a brutal despot who grabbed power in Cuba, ninety miles off the U.S. coast, in 1959, ruled one. Another was the vicious dictatorship in Hanoi, which became the United States' adversary in war in the 1960s. Still another was Communist China. Mao Tse-tung had taken power there in 1949, but his mass killing machine really got underway in 1958, first with the Great Leap Forward, then with the Cultural Revolution. In all, tens of millions of Chinese were liquidated. American leftists of the sixties and seventies—Noam Chomsky, Norman Mailer, Simone de Beauvoir, Shirley MacLaine, and countless others—fawned over these despots as their role models, George Bernard Shaw, Anna Louise Strong, Bertolt Brecht, and Walter Duranty, had fawned over Joseph Stalin.

CHAPTER FIVE

Castro's Slave Camp: Affection for New Killing Fields

"Crazy with fury I will stain my rifle red while slaughtering any enemy that falls in my hands! My nostrils dilate while savoring the acrid odor of gunpowder and blood. With the deaths of my enemies I prepare my being for the sacred fight and join the triumphant proletariat with a bestial howl."

—Che Guevara, *Motorcycle Diaries*

Until July 26, 2008, Fidel Castro ruled Cuba with an iron grip for nearly five decades. On that July date in 2008, he stood to the side because of health problems and made his brother, Raul, *de facto* ruler. Raul officially replaced his brother as dictator on February 24, 2008; the regime remains just as totalitarian as before and can, for obvious reasons, continue to be regarded and labelled as "Fidel Castro's" regime.[1]

Having seized power on January 1, 1959, Fidel Castro followed the tradition of Vladimir Lenin and immediately turned his country into a slave camp. Ever since, Cuba has distinguished itself as one of the most monstrous human-rights abusers in the world.

Half a million human beings have passed through Cuba's gulag. Since Cuba's total population is only around eleven million, that gives Castro's despotism the highest political incarceration rate per capita on earth. Firing squads have carried out more than fifteen thousand executions. Torture has been institutionalized; myriad human rights organizations have documented the regime's use of electric shock, dark coffin-sized isolation cells, and beatings to punish "anti-socialist elements."[2] The Castro regime's barbarity is best epitomized by the Camilo Cienfuegos Plan, the program of horrors followed in the forced-labor camp on the Isle of Pines. Forced to work almost naked, prisoners were made to cut grass with their teeth and to sit in latrine trenches for long periods of time.[3] Torture is routine.

The horrifying experience of Armando Valladares, a Cuban poet who endured twenty-two years of torture and imprisonment for merely raising the issue of freedom, is a testament to the regime's barbarity. Valladares's memoir, *Against All Hope*, serves as Cuba's version of Solzhenitsyn's *Gulag Archipelago*. Valladares recounts how prisoners were beaten with bayonets, electric cables, and truncheons. He tells how he and other prisoners were forced to take "baths" in human feces and urine.[4] Typical of the horror in Castro's Gulag was the experience of Roberto López Chávez, one of Valladares's prison friends. When López Chávez went on a hunger strike to protest the abuses in the prison, the guards withheld water from him until he became delirious, twisting on the floor and begging for something to drink. The guards then urinated in his mouth. He died the next day.[5]

Since Castro's death cult, like other leftist ideologies, believes that human blood purifies the earth—and since manifestations of grief affirm the reality of *the individual*, and thus are anathema to the totality—mourning for the departed became taboo. Just like Mao's China and Pol Pot's Cambodia,[6] Castro's Cuba warned family members of murdered dissidents not to cry at their funerals.[7]

The Castro regime also has a long, grotesque record of torturing and murdering Americans. During the Vietnam War, Castro sent some of his henchmen to run the "Cuban Program" at the Cu Loc POW camp in Hanoi, which became known as "the Zoo." Its primary objective was to determine how much physical and psychological agony a human being could withstand. The Cubans selected American POWs as their guinea pigs. A Cuban nicknamed "Fidel," the main torturer at the Zoo, initiated his own personal reign of terror.[8] The ordeal of Lieutenant Colonel

Earl Cobeil, an F-105 pilot, illustrates the Nazi-like nature of the experiment. Among Fidel's torture techniques were beatings and whippings over every part of his victim's body, without remission.[9] Former POW John Hubbell described the scene as Fidel forced Cobeil into the cell of fellow POW Col. Jack Bomar:

> The man [Cobeil] could barely walk; he shuffled slowly, painfully. His clothes were torn to shreds. He was bleeding everywhere, terribly swollen, and a dirty, yellowish black and purple from head to toe. The man's head was down; he made no attempt to look at anyone.... He stood unmoving, his head down. Fidel smashed a fist into the man's face, driving him against the wall. Then he was brought to the center of the room and made to get down onto his knees. Screaming in rage, Fidel took a length of black rubber hose from a guard and lashed it as hard as he could into the man's face. The prisoner did not react; he did not cry out or even blink an eye. His failure to react seemed to fuel Fidel's rage and again he whipped the rubber hose across the man's face.... Again and again and again, a dozen times, Fidel smashed the man's face with the hose. Not once did the fearsome abuse elicit the slightest response from the prisoner.... His body was ripped and torn everywhere; hell cuffs appeared almost to have severed the wrists, strap marks still wound around the arms all the way to the shoulders, slivers of bamboo were embedded in the bloodied shins and there were what appeared to be tread marks from the hose across the chest, back, and legs.[10]

Earl Cobeil died as a result of Fidel's torture.

Major James Kasler was another of Fidel's victims, although he survived the treatment:

> He [Fidel] deprived Kasler of water, wired his thumbs together, and flogged him until his "buttocks, lower back, and legs hung in shreds." During one barbaric stretch he turned Cedric [another torturer] loose for three days with a rubber whip.... the PW [POW] was in a semi-coma and bleeding profusely with a ruptured eardrum, fractured rib, his face swollen and teeth broken so that he could not

open his mouth, and his leg re-injured from attackers repeatedly kicking it.[11]

The reign of terror against American POWs in Vietnam was just a reflection of Castro's treatment of his own people. In addition to physical hardships even for those who don't wind up in prison or labor camp, his police state has denied Cubans any freedom at all. Cubans do not have the right to travel out of their country. They do not have the right of free association or the right to form political parties, independent unions, or religious or cultural organizations. The regime has outlawed free expression; it has consistently censored publications, radio, television, and film. A Committee for the Defense of the Cuban Revolution (CDR) governs every single city block and every agricultural production unit. The CDR's purpose is to monitor the affairs of every family and to report anything suspicious. A Cuban's entire life is spent under the surveillance of his CDR, which controls everything from his food rations to his employment to his use of free time. A vicious racism against blacks accompanies this repression. In pre-Castro Cuba, blacks enjoyed upward social mobility and served in many government positions. In Castro's Cuba, the jail population is 80 percent black, while the government hierarchy is 100 percent white.[12]

Cuban communism follows Lenin's and Stalin's idea of "equality," wherein members of the *nomenklatura* live like millionaires while ordinary Cubans live in utter poverty. The shelves in the stores are empty, and food is tightly rationed for the average citizen. Teachers and doctors drive taxis or work as waiters to support their families. Under the system of tourist apartheid, ordinary Cubans are not allowed inside the hotels designated for tourists and party functionaries. Police wait inside every such hotel to arrest any unauthorized Cuban citizen who dares to enter.

The $5-billion-a-year Soviet subsidy that just barely kept the Cuban economy afloat during the Cold War is long gone. And notwithstanding the $110 billion that the Soviets pumped in over the decades, Cuba has become one of the poorest nations in the world. Its sugar, tobacco, and cattle industries were all major sources of exports in the pre-Castro era. Castro destroyed them all.[13] Because of his belief in "socialism or death," Cuba is now a beggar nation. Even Haitian refugees avoid Cuba.

Denied the right to vote under Castro, Cubans have voted with their feet. Pre-Castro Cuba had the highest *per capita* immigration rate in the Western hemisphere. Under Castro, approximately two million Cuban citizens (out of eleven million) have escaped their country. Many have done so by floating on rafts or inner tubes in shark-infested waters. An estimated fifty thousand to eighty-seven thousand have lost their lives.[14] Not content to trust the sharks, Castro has sent helicopters to drop sandbags onto the rafts of would-be escapees, or just to gun them all down. Epitomizing this barbarity was the Tugboat Massacre of July 13, 1994, in which Castro ordered Cuban patrol boats to kill forty-one unarmed Cuban civilians—ten of them children—who were using an old wooden tugboat in their attempt to flee Cuba.[15]

Naturally, the Left initiated a romance with Castro and his slave camp, just as it did with Lenin's and Stalin's Gulag. American leftists in 1969 formed the Venceremos Brigade, a coalition whose members traveled to work in Cuba to show their solidarity with the communist revolution. These fellow travelers participated mostly in sugar harvests in the first pilgrimages, while later brigade members engaged in various types of agricultural and construction work. High-profile Western leftists, meanwhile, including Susan Sontag, Jean-Paul Sartre, Norman Mailer, and Abbie Hoffman, also made pilgrimages to Cuba.[16]

As earlier believers had done with Stalin, Castro's devotees heaped grossly disproportionate praise upon him. Leo Huberman and Paul Sweezy made their pilgrimage to Cuba in the fall of 1960. The two believers ended up receiving all the attention they craved from their father-god, marveling at how "lucky" they were to spend "two long evenings with Fidel, in relaxed surroundings and with only a few present." After their visit, they reported that:

> Fidel is a passionate humanitarian, not in the fraudulent sense that he loves all humanity but in the meaningful sense that he feels compassion for human suffering, hates injustice because it causes unnecessary suffering, and is totally committed to building in Cuba a society in which

the poor and the underprivileged shall be able to hold up their heads and enjoy a fair share of the good things of life. He treats people within this framework—kindly, sternly, implacably, according to their actual or potential role in creating or hindering the creation of the good society.[17]

Castro personally drove his guests around to certain locations he wanted them to see. The two believers recalled this tour with great awe and emotion:

> On the way out of Havana he made a long detour through the wealthiest residential streets of the Miramar district. As he drove around, he kept saying, as much to himself as to the rest of us, "Look at how they live;" and in that brief phrase there was expressed not so much a feeling toward "them" as a sense of outrage at a system that could enable a few to live like kings while the great majority stagnated in ignorance, squalor, and often outright hunger.[18]

While trying to digest the notion that this secular messiah was driving them around, Huberman and Sweezy witnessed that they were not alone in their reverence:

> Accompanying him as he goes among his people, one not only sees it; all of one's senses are overwhelmed by it. To watch the faces light up as their owners suddenly recognized the driver of our car; to hear the delighted cries of "Fidel, Fidel;" to experience the rush of people, young and old alike, whenever the car stopped, even if only for a red light, people drawn like iron filings to a magnet, wanting to shake his hand, touch his sleeve, wish him well; to smell the sweaty bodies of hundreds of construction workers who swarmed around the car when it was halted by an obstruction in the road, pouring out to him their problems and urging that he take action to clear away obstacles to the more rapid completion of their project—those were indeed unforgettable experiences.[19]

One assumes that Huberman and Sweezy, had they been in Moscow in March 1953 and witnessed Soviet citizens sobbing hysterically upon learning of Stalin's death, would also have considered that an "unforgettable experience."

It is eerily apparent from their tone and choice of wording that Huberman and Sweezy were completely immersed in one of the key dynamics of the believer's diagnosis: the surrendering of self to a stern and all-knowing secular god. Castro was driving them, leading them, explaining all to them. They had no minds of their own, disagreed with absolutely nothing, and, like the rest of "the people" in their imagination, were completely in his hands. They were all worshipping Castro, trying to touch his sleeve, surrendering their wills to his supremacy. In this desperate attempt at a religious epiphany, Huberman and Sweezy shed their own individuality and submerged their entire beings into the collective veneration of the tyrant before them.

Huberman and Sweezy did not even consider the vital questions they ought to have asked themselves while observing the cult of personality in action: *What if one of these individuals had stood apart from the crowd and voiced his dissent? What if he had announced that he did not think like the others and that he did not approve of Castro or support his policies? What would happen to such an individual?* These are the questions that we would expect someone concerned with human dignity, freedom, and "social justice" to ask. But Huberman and Sweezy seemed completely unaware that expressions of support for a regime, and expressions of love for a leader, are utterly meaningless in a country where any contrary expression will be punished by imprisonment, torture, and execution.

Jerry Rubin joined the chorus of devotees during his trip to Cuba in 1964, when he engaged in negative identification vis-à-vis Castro's chief executioner, Che Guevara. Rubin proudly recalls:

> We were eighty-four Amerikan students visiting Cuba illegally in 1964. We had to travel fourteen thousand miles, via Czechoslovakia, to reach Cuba.... As Che rapped on for four hours, we fantasized taking up rifles. Growing beards. Going into the hills as *guerrillas*. Joining Che to create revolutions throughout Latin America. None of us looked forward to returning home to the political bullshit in the United States.[20]

Berkeley activist Todd Gitlin traveled to Cuba with an SDS delegation to a Cultural Congress in 1967. In the belly of the totalitarian beast, where he was well aware that dissidents were rotting in jail and being tortured beyond imagination, Gitlin too experienced the intoxication of negative identification. Leaving Cuba proved quite painful for him. He recalls:

> What was palpable was the pain of re-entry to my homeland.... At the Mexico City airport, having a drink with Dave Dellinger and Robert Scheer, I looked out the window and saw a billboard advertising Cutty Sark. I had to change seats: after twenty-three days where public space was turned to revolutionary use, capitalist propaganda disgusted me.[21]

What disgusted him, of course, were the withdrawal symptoms he was experiencing—analogous to a drug addict coming off his fix. For twenty-three days he had experienced his euphoria of shedding his inner self and submerging himself within the totalitarian whole. In Cuba he had found a home where even the slightest dissent would be crushed instantly and the concept of the individual was nonexistent. The advertisement he saw, therefore, was a horror to him, since it symbolized a free society where individuals could use their free will to pursue their own tastes and desires. This reality is anathema to the believer.

As Gitlin so well revealed, the persecution of intellectuals in Cuba greatly inspired Western leftist intellectuals, just as the persecution of intellectuals in Stalin's Soviet Union had inspired the earlier generation. Charmed by the notion of a society in which their own talent—as well as their entire being—would be extinguished, they continued the practice of labeling the totalitarian monstrosity the opposite of what it was.

Acclaimed American cultural critic Susan Sontag was one of many true believers who similarly engaged in this practice. After a trip to Cuba in 1968, she claimed that "No Cuban writer has been or is in jail, or is failing to get his work published."[22] She stated this falsehood with full awareness that dissident Cuban writers languished in Castro's gulag, and that not one work that was critical of the regime had been published in Cuba. Instead, she boasted that "the Cuban revolution is astonishingly free of repression.... Not only has the Cuban revolution not begun eating its children...it has no intention of doing so."[23]

Sontag believed she had found utopia in Castro's Cuba. Here human beings had been able to shed many elements of capitalist oppression, which included, as Sontag noted with satisfaction, the socially manufactured need to sleep. Sontag observed how it was completely "common," ten years into the revolution, "for people to go without sleep—talking and working several nights a week."[24] She also noted with approval how, "even deprived of the right to go into private business or to see pornographic films, the great majority of Cubans feel vastly freer today than they ever did before the revolution."[25] These insights raise several crucial questions: Why did Sontag believe she could speak for the "great majority" of Cubans? How exactly did she know that they felt "freer"? How about the ones who didn't feel freer? And what exactly would happen to an individual who *did* try to go into private business or watch pornography? Did Sontag believe that Armando Valladares, and the thousands of other political prisoners who languished in isolation cells while covered in feces, felt "freer" as well?

As leftist intellectuals like Sontag followed the tradition of venerating regimes that imprisoned, tortured, and executed intellectuals, so counterculture leftists who supported gay rights worshipped a tyranny that persecuted homosexuals, dishing out prison sentences of up to twenty years for homosexual behavior.[26]

Castro's persecution of homosexuality is part of the phenomenon of totalitarian puritanism. As discussed in the chapter on the believer's diagnosis, human beings must submit every aspect of their lives to the greater whole of the totalitarian order. Homosexuality is especially reviled in totalitarian structures: because it cannot lead to procreation, it is seen as being solely the pursuit of individual pleasure for its own sake. As Paul Hollander notes in the case of Cuba:

> Evidently the persecution of homosexuals can be explained not only by cultural traditions or *machismo*—plausible as it might seem to be—but also by the totalitarian puritanism of the new regime and its zealous

pursuit of conformity in all walks of life. Apparently prior
to the revolution no comparably massive and systematic
repressive measures were taken against them.[27]

While adamant about the right to "free love" and sexual self-
determination in their own society, believers sacrificed—and
continue to sacrifice—these principles in regard to Cuba, the
Taliban regime, the Palestinian Authority, Iran, Saudi Arabia, and
any other society that has won their affection. This is because they
see sexual freedom, like intellectual freedom, only as a weapon to
be used to destroy their own society. They don't care about these
rights and freedoms in and of themselves. Once Ground Zero has
been accomplished and the utopia they dream of is under
construction, they see them as no longer important—and even
dangerous to hold onto, since they threaten to destroy the road to
earthly redemption. Ernesto Cardenal, the Sandinista minister of
culture and one of the nine *comandantes* who ruled Nicaragua after
the 1979 revolution, represented the Left best in this regard. After
returning from a trip to Cuba, he reported that Cuba's
homosexuals "were actually happier in the concentration camps
[that Castro had built for them], a place like that where they were
all together must have been almost like paradise for them."[28]

In true leftist tradition, Western believers continue to shower
adulation on Castro to this day. Humberto Fontova has written a
succinct account of the Left's continuing dalliance with Castro in
Fidel: Hollywood's Favorite Tyrant. Here is just a portion of his
compilation of leftist praise for the death cult leader:

> "Cuba's own Elvis!"—that's how Dan Rather once
> described his friend Fidel Castro. Oliver Stone, another
> friend, describes Fidel as "very selfless and moral" and
> "one of the world's wisest men." "A genius!" agreed Jack
> Nicholson. Naomi Campbell said meeting Castro was "a
> dream come true!" According to Norman Mailer, Castro is
> "the first and greatest hero to appear in the world since the
> Second World War." Jean-Paul Sartre said, "Castro is at the
> same time the island, the men, the cattle, and the earth. He
> is the whole island...". Actress Gina Lollobrigida cooed,
> "Castro is an extraordinary man. He is warm and
> understanding and seems extremely humane." Francis

Coppola simply noted, "Fidel, I love you. We both have the same initials. We both have beards. We both have power and want to use it for good purposes." Harry Belafonte added: "If you believe in freedom, if you believe in justice, if you believe in democracy, you have no choice but to support Fidel Castro!"[29]

Steven Spielberg visited the father-god in Havana in the fall of 2002. He called the meeting with Castro "the most important eight hours of my life."[30]

Castro's Cuba has been an exhilarating gift to the American Left, presenting it with a totalitarian death cult to worship with a wonderful geographical bonus: it is close to home, just ninety miles from the Florida coast.

CHAPTER SIX

In Love with Hanoi's Butchers

"My heart jumped with pleased surprise.
This, then, was the universal pardon. I was set free."

—Mary McCarthy, after learning that North Vietnamese Prime Minister Pham Van Dong had given her a blessing to either write or not write a book about her political pilgrimage to Hanoi

In the mid-1960s, while the Stalin-like experiment in Castro's Cuba was filling believers' hearts with warmth, hope, and inspiration, the Vietnam War began significantly escalating. This gave believers a new object of worship: a ruthless dictatorship that was at war with the United States and killing American soldiers. For the Left, this was simply a godsend, just as Islamist terrorism against America would be a generation later.

Just like Stalin's Soviet Union and Castro's Cuba, Communist North Vietnam perpetrated a Red Terror on a mass scale. Purges eliminated all opposition. Trotskyites, for example, were decimated and their leader was put to death. Some fifty thousand executions occurred in the countryside alone. As Jean-Louis Margolin, the authority on the North Vietnamese gulag, has noted: "Between fifty thousand and one hundred thousand people were imprisoned, 86 percent of the members of Party cells in the countryside were purged, as were 95 percent of the *cadres* in the anti-French resistance." The regime focused its terror especially on intellectuals. Margolin notes that in 1958 alone, "476 'ideological saboteurs' were forced to make public acts of self-criticism and were sent either to work camps or to the Vietnamese equivalent of the Chinese *laogai* [camps for 're-education through labor'].["1](#)

The regime also followed its Stalinist and Maoist role models in initiating a program of forced collectivization of agriculture, with horrifying results. With instruction and supervision from their Chinese mentors, the North Vietnamese enforced a "land reform" campaign in which tens of thousands of innocent Vietnamese peasants were exterminated. Noting that this "land reform" was "a deliberate and brutal act of mass murder," American scholar Stephen Morris comments on the overall nature of North Vietnamese terror:

> It was a nation run by a Marxist-Leninist vanguard party, monolithic in its internal organization, its secret police, and its insistence on either co-opting or murdering all of its political rivals. It was Stalinist in its ambition to control every aspect of society, its intent to destroy all autonomous social forces, and its primitive ideology of a unified communist world.[2]

As occurred in every socialist testing ground that shared a border with a free society, a mass exodus ensued. More than a million northerners fled to South Vietnam to escape the monstrous communist regime.

Faced with these horrors, believers celebrated the new killing machine all the more eagerly. Content with venerating the regime from afar at first, believers could no longer contain themselves once the tyranny found itself at war with the United States. In the mid-1960s, they began making pilgrimages to North Vietnam to express their devotion in person.

This development made perfect sense. As the believer's diagnosis explains, believers' veneration for an adversarial society always increases along with that society's antagonism toward the United States. Being at war with the United States wins a totalitarian regime the most points. This reality has resurfaced in the terror war some forty years after the first pilgrimages to Hanoi.

Without doubt, the Vietnam War provided a priceless gift to the Left. Believers were now able to claim that the Vietnam conflict itself was the cause of their rage, when in fact it was, as described in chapter four, just a symptom. Jerry Rubin boasted: "If there had been no Vietnam War, we would have invented one. If the Vietnam War ends, we'll find another war."[3]

As Paul Hollander explains, leftist fury about Vietnam:

> had sources other than the aggrieved concern with the consequences of war *per se*. Vietnam mobilized the rejection, criticism, or hatred, as the case may be, of American society that had been dormant or partially articulated earlier. The war gave new vehemence and assurance to the social critics who languished during the placid fifties without major issues or causes that could have "offered the key to a systematic criticism of America." Vietnam was more a catalyst than a root cause of the rejection of American society in the 1960s. It confirmed all lurking apprehensions about the United States among the critically disposed and the estranged.[4]

The phrase Hollander quotes in this passage comes from Susan Sontag: "Vietnam offered the key to a systematic criticism of America."[5]

When the war escalated in the mid-1960s and believers began to experience the bloodshed vicariously through the Vietcong, the protests at home exploded. As Rubin put it, speaking on behalf of the antiwar activists: "And in Amerika we are all learning how to become Viet Kong."[6] Believers were able to reject their own society as never before, while identifying with a new brutal tyranny. And as they jabbed their angry fists in the air, the political pilgrimages began.

Sontag and novelist Mary McCarthy both visited Hanoi in the spring of 1968 (a few months before Sontag visited Cuba). It was a most fitting time to pay homage. In the Tet offensive of January–February, the Vietcong had done what attracted believers most: they perpetrated a massacre. Margolin notes that during the few weeks that the communists controlled the city of Hué, the ancient imperial capital:

[a]t least three thousand people were massacred, including Vietnamese priests, French religious workers, German doctors, and a number of officials and government workers. The number of deaths was far higher than in the massacres carried out by Americans. Some of the victims were buried alive; others were taken away to "study sessions;" from which they never returned.[7]

As the bloodshed peaked, believers flocked to the scene.

Sontag's memoir of her odyssey to North Vietnam, *Trip to Hanoi*, contains almost every symptom noted in the believer's diagnosis. Every page of her account gives voice to her self-flagellating sense of guilt for being a wealthy citizen of the imperialist power that was—in her mind—victimizing the Vietnamese for some vague and sinister reason. Her message is clear: she loathes herself for having been poisoned by her capitalist society and its sinful pleasures:

> Of course, I *could* live in Vietnam, or an ethical society like this one—but not without the loss of a big part of myself. Though I believe incorporation into such a society will greatly improve the lives of most people in the world (and therefore support the advent of such societies), I imagine it will in many ways impoverish mine. I live in an unethical society that coarsens the sensibilities and thwarts the capacities for goodness of most people but makes available for minority consumption an astonishing array of intellectual and aesthetic pleasures. Those who don't enjoy (in both senses) my pleasures have every right, from their side, to regard my consciousness as spoiled, corrupt, decadent. I, from my side, can't deny the immense richness of these pleasures, or my addiction to them.[8]

And so poor Susan Sontag cannot afford the luxury of living in the paradise she venerates. She does not consider herself good enough; that entitlement she leaves for the enslaved Vietnamese. A schizophrenic outlook emerges, as Sontag believes she has found paradise in Hanoi, yet considers herself luckier than the North Vietnamese because of the wealthier society from which she hails. She feels guilty for reaping the benefits of a society that she admits gives her more—but which she nonetheless hates. She forgives herself for this grievous sin by identifying herself with the victims of the society she worships.

The believer's yearning to return to childhood permeates Sontag's account. She continually refers to the Vietnamese as being like children: they are, in her view, "opaque, simple-minded, naïve."[9] She self-consciously chastises herself for making paternalistic remarks, but she cannot help herself. Longing for the fairy-tale world of innocent childhood, as all believers do, she projects it onto the adversarial society she idolizes.

Sontag exhibits self-deception, an important component of the believer's diagnosis, in her speculations about what might have motivated her North Vietnamese hosts to insist on driving her and her American comrades wherever they wished to go, no matter how short a distance, when they often would have preferred to walk. "Do they have a rule: only the best for the guests?" Sontag wonders.[10] All the experiences the pilgrims to Stalin's Soviet Union had with the techniques of deceptive hospitality—which had been exposed and widely publicized by this time—apparently had made no impression on America's cultural critic.

Sontag pretends not to notice that her totalitarian hosts are exploiting her for propaganda reasons so as to strengthen the regime and increase its chances of taking over South Vietnam. She never asks herself: *What are they getting out of my being here?* Instead she reprimands herself: "I sometimes have the miserable feeling that my being here…is a big waste of our Vietnamese hosts' time"[11]—which presumably could have been better spent building the revolution and fighting the imperialist United States.

Like Sontag, Mary McCarthy presented almost every element of the believer's diagnosis on her own trip to Hanoi. Like Sontag, McCarthy notes how her hosts don't want her going out alone, but she simply can't fathom why. She finally decides just to accept the situation, noting, "This of course limited one's bodily freedom, but I accepted it, being a law-abiding citizen."[12] This came from an individual who, like her fellow believers, promoted *every* form of lawlessness in demonstrating against the war or anything else to do with capitalism and American institutions. Yet when it came to obeying the secular deity of her imagination, she gained enormous emotional gratification from being a "law-abiding" citizen.

McCarthy was also much impressed that "in the hotel, to my stupefaction, there was hot water." She had never received such a luxury in hotels in South Vietnam. She also marveled at the other bounties of the communist paradise:

> Other luxuries I found at the Thong Nhat Hotel were sheets of toilet paper laid out on a box in a fan pattern (keys at the desk were laid out in a fan pattern, too), a thermos of hot water for making tea, a package of tea, a teapot, cups and saucers, candies, cigarettes, and a mosquito net draped over the bed and tucked in; in Saigon, I had been tortured by mosquitoes.[13]

The reality eluded McCarthy that since South Vietnam did not have totalitarian despots controlling every facet of the society, various aspects of her stay would be left to private individuals and businesses. Of course, the North Vietnamese had a much lower standard of living than the South Vietnamese. But McCarthy happily received the luxuries that Hanoi's despots made sure she was given, and concluded that all North Vietnamese people lived as she was living in the Thong Nhat Hotel. Yet she simultaneously knew very well that this could not possibly be true. This is why, like Sontag, she engaged in the schizophrenic behavior of praising the despotism for bestowing utopia upon its citizens, while condemning herself for her "knowledge of living better than others." After a while, she admitted, her uneasiness "wore off." Still, her guilty feelings resurfaced again during the trip: she was "embarrassed" to be caught with an umbrella, which others didn't seem to have.[14] She, like Sontag, absolved herself by identifying with the victims.

McCarthy's dysfunctional confessions reflect the believer's universe of contradiction and self-hatred. In the United States, believers opposed conformity, but when they were in North Vietnam they were suddenly embarrassed to have any individual habits or belongings not shared by the collective. Believers discovered paradise in the most basic items (hot water, toilet paper), which were supposedly nonexistent in South Vietnam, and yet they hated America, where these items all existed in much greater quantity and higher quality.

More than anything else, McCarthy's emotional reaction to her treatment at the Thong Nhat Hotel reveals believers' longing for a father figure who will take care of them. McCarthy knows who gave her the hot water and the toilet paper to which the others are not entitled. She feels a sense of great satisfaction that the secular deity takes her seriously and looks after her.

For McCarthy, heaven was everywhere in North Vietnam, no matter where she looked. She exclaimed, "You could have dropped from the moon into Hung Yen or Hoa Binh Province and known at once that something marvelous, in the old sense, was astir."[15] North Vietnamese society, she found, had even solved the problem of alienation: "The phenomena of existential agony, of alienation, just don't appear among the Vietnamese— probably in part because they lack our kind of 'ego,' and our endowment of free-floating guilt."

Susan Sontag, meanwhile, observed that even babies were filled with socialist joy. Even though Vietnamese babies were suffering under American imperialism, they did not feel the need to cry like babies in capitalist countries. Sontag wrote: "Though I see many small but not too well nourished children and babies [obviously America's fault], I've yet to hear one cry."[16] North Vietnamese adults had also been freed from the emotions of anger and hate. Sontag observed that her North Vietnamese hosts:

> seem astonishingly calm, and though they talk of little else but the war, their discourse is singularly unmarked by hate. Even when they use the melodramatic communist language of denunciation, it comes out sounding dutiful and a little flat. They talk of atrocities, the marrow of their history, with an almost gentle sorrow, and still with amazement. Can these things really have happened, their manner says.[17]

While the North Vietnamese were torturing American POWs in the cruelest and most sadistic ways imaginable, Sontag reflected on how the regime's love surpassed anything America could possibly equal:

> And as the quality of Vietnamese love differs from ours, so does the nature of their hate. Of course, the Vietnamese hate the Americans in some sense—but not as Americans would, if we had been subjected to equivalent punishment at the hands of a superior power. The North Vietnamese genuinely care about the welfare of the hundreds of captured American pilots and give them bigger rations than the Vietnamese population gets, "because they're bigger than we are," as a Vietnamese army officer told me, "and they're used to more meat than we are."...and in the perennial possibility of rehabilitating the morally fallen, among whom they include implacable enemies, even the Americans.... it's impossible not to be convinced by the genuineness of these concerns.[18]

Sontag concluded that human beings under capitalism are not yet complete because they lack these traits exhibited by those living under socialism. She concluded: "The Vietnamese, are 'whole' human beings, not 'split' as we are." After her odyssey, she wrote, "I found, through direct experience, North Vietnam to be a place which, in many respects, *deserves* to be idealized."[19]

Mary McCarthy, meanwhile, perfectly fit the mold of intellectual believers championing the persecution of intellectuals in their idealized adversary society. For believers, the idea of their own intellectual trade and life-purpose being annihilated was inspiring: it meant they would be submerged within the totalitarian whole of which they would become part.

At one point, McCarthy commented, "Obviously, in a short official stay in North Vietnam, I was not in a position to meet dissenters, if they existed." But that was okay with her: "The license to criticize was just another capitalist luxury, a waste product of the system." For McCarthy, the earthly paradise had already been constructed and there was no need for dissenters. While as a writer she took it as a given that her work should be published in her own society, she concluded that freedom to publish was not essential in a place like North Vietnam. "A free press is livelier than a government-controlled one," she wrote, "but access to information that does not lead to action may be unhealthy, like any persistent frustration, for a body politic."[20] In other words, information that does not lead to Ground Zero and the building of earthly paradise should not be published.

Along with praising a tyranny that persecuted intellectuals, believers like McCarthy and Sontag also worshipped at the altar of totalitarian puritanism. McCarthy, for instance, was charmed to find that Hanoi was "clean" and that there were "no prostitutes on the streets."[21] To her, this represented the return to the innocent purity of childhood for which every believer longs. It also meant the annihilation of any private agreement between individuals without the blessing of Big Brother. One wonders, of course, if McCarthy would have been equally impressed by a similarly "clean" U.S. city. If presented with an American city that had no prostitutes on the streets, she surely would have lamented that moral tyrants were forbidding women from expressing themselves sexually and from making a living in any way they deemed fit.

Sontag noticed totalitarian puritanism as well. But while a great promoter of "free love" back home, she didn't whisper one word of criticism about the lack of public sexuality in Hanoi. She noted that there was "no kissing in Vietnamese plays and films; obviously there's none in the streets or parks. I haven't seen people touching each other in a casual way."[22] It is noteworthy that she didn't wonder why this was the case. She didn't ask: *What would happen to two people who decided of their own free will to engage in the public display of affection?* It is clear that for her, as for all believers, the nonexistence of private love was a positive and revolutionary development, since human beings had now found purpose and no longer needed bourgeois and selfish capitalist distractions.

Dreaming of the day that America would be defeated by North Vietnam, Sontag admited that in her rejection of her own society, "Vietnam becomes an ideal Other." She noted that the North Vietnamese had become "stationed inside my consciousness as a quintessential image of the suffering and heroism of 'the weak.'"

The "ideal" human beings that Sontag found in Hanoi gave her hope that one of the central tenets of leftist ideologies—that human nature can actually be remolded—would soon be brought to fruition. If the North Vietnamese leaders had their way, she gleefully opined, "the process of recasting the particular historical form of our human nature prevalent in Europe and America can be hurried a little..."[23]

McCarthy and Sontag were also typical believers in faithfully perpetuating the cult of personality around the tyrants they worshipped. For Sontag, Prime Minister Pham Van Dong represented the peak of humanism. He transformed her understanding of authority:

> What I actually saw when I was there—that the North Vietnamese genuinely love and admire their leaders; and, even more inconceivable to us, that the government loves the people. I remember the poignant intimate tones in Pham Van Dong's voice as he described the sufferings the Vietnamese have endured in the last quarter of a century and their heroism, decency, and essential innocence. Seeing for the first time in my life a prime minister praising the moral character of his country's people with tears in his eyes has modified my ideas about the conceivable relations between rulers and ruled.[24]

McCarthy, meanwhile, found Pham Van Dong to be:

> a man of magnetic allure, thin, with deep-set brilliant eyes, crisp short electric grey hair, full rueful lips drawn tight over the teeth. The passion and directness of his delivery matched something fiery, but also melancholy, in those coaly eyes. An emotional, impressionable man, I thought, and at the same time highly intellectual.[25]

Before the end of her stay, she rejoiced upon learning that Pham Van Dong had given her his blessing to either write or not write a book about her trip:

> My heart jumped with pleased surprise. This, then, was the universal pardon. I was set free. He had kissed us, each, with emotion when we said good-bye, and now I did not have to feel like a Judas, whatever I would write. The North

> Vietnamese did not expect more of me than what I was.
> From each according to his abilities, which is the same as
> saying, in my Father's house, there are many mansions.[26]

Once again, we see the believer's final submission to the totalist authority.

Noam Chomsky followed the path of McCarthy and Sontag. He journeyed with other fellow travelers to Hanoi in 1970 to pay homage to the tyrants. While there, he discovered that their revolutionary activities reflected "the capabilities of the human spirit and human will." He regarded Hanoi as "a radical version of the Eternal City."[27] When the communist hosts applied their techniques of hospitality and took Chomsky on rigidly controlled guided tours, the guru of the believers soaked it all up. As Stephen Morris notes, "Chomsky repeated the accounts of his official guides uncritically, as if their information carried some certainty of truthfulness, rather than simply being official government propaganda."[28]

When Jane Fonda went to Hanoi in July 1972 with her future husband Tom Hayden and other fellow travelers, it was evident she was pursuing the believer's sacred quest. She left no ambiguity about her mission when she posed on a North Vietnamese anti-aircraft gun used to shoot down U.S. planes and announced to the world that American POWs were living in the lap of luxury.[29]

In 1975, as Sontag, McCarthy, Fonda, Hayden, Chomsky, and all other believers hoped would happen, the North Vietnamese conquered South Vietnam. With their antiwar protests, the believers had helped bring about the communist victory and paved the road for the bloodbath that followed. David Horowitz was one of the organizers of the first campus demonstration against the war at the University of California at Berkeley in 1962. He later reflected on the tragedy of how the Left facilitated the communist victory:

> Every testimony by North Vietnamese generals in the
> postwar years has affirmed that they knew they could not
> defeat the United States on the battlefield, and that they

counted on the division of our people at home to win the war for them. The Vietcong forces we were fighting in South Vietnam were destroyed in 1968. In other words, most of the war and most of the casualties in the war occurred because the dictatorship of North Vietnam counted on the fact Americans would give up the battle rather than pay the price necessary to win it. This is what happened. The blood of hundreds of thousands of Vietnamese, and tens of thousands of Americans, is on the hands of the anti-war activists who prolonged the struggle and gave victory to the communists.[30]

After Saigon fell to North Vietnam in 1975, the summary executions of tens of thousands of innocent South Vietnamese followed. The new government threw two million refugees and more than a million people into "re-education camps." Tens of thousands of South Vietnamese "boat people" perished in the Gulf of Thailand and in the South China Sea in their attempt to escape what the likes of Sontag, McCarthy, and Chomsky had helped create.

The victory also led to the communist takeovers of Laos and Cambodia. The Khmer Rouge victory in Cambodia led to the killing fields in which some three million Cambodians were exterminated. In just a few years after the communist takeovers in South Vietnam, Laos, and Cambodia, the communists killed more Indochinese citizens than had died on both sides in the whole Vietnam War. And the Left could take full credit for this new era of death. Not only had American leftists abetted the communist victory, but the intellectual leaders of the Khmer Rouge—they called themselves *Angka Loeu*, "the Higher Organization"—had been radicalized in French universities.[31]

In the face of these mass crimes committed by their heroes, believers again manifested their typical behavior: they blamed the genocide on the United States. In 1977, after the boat people had begun fleeing and the re-education camps had been set up, a group of leftists took out an ad in the *New York Times* in which they blamed the suffering of the Vietnamese people entirely on the war, "for which the United States bears the continuing responsibility."[32] In reaction to the Khmer Rouge's genocide, Chomsky denied the extent of the massacres, dismissed eyewitness reports, and compared Pol Pot's Cambodia with Revolutionary America. Regarding any atrocities that may have occurred, Chomsky followed the believers' paradigm of *the devil made them do it* and argued that it was the fault of the United States.[33] As we shall see in Part IV, Chomsky would later represent the Left with this very same strategy in his reaction to 9/11 in particular and the terror war in general, blaming the victims of militant Islam for having provoked the wrath of the Muslim world.

Once again, the believers did not care about the victims of their idols. In the eyes of the Left, those victims had merely gotten what they deserved—because their existence was an obstacle in the path to the earthly utopia.

Mary McCarthy's reaction was typical. In a November 1967 letter to the *New York Review of Books*, Diana Trilling criticized an article by McCarthy in which McCarthy had promoted an immediate American withdrawal from Vietnam. Trilling suggested that it would trouble America's conscience if a military withdrawal were to leave millions of South Vietnamese vulnerable to the wrath of the vengeful North Vietnamese. In response, McCarthy stated: "Mrs. Trilling has the gift of prophecy. I have not. I do not know what will happen to millions of human beings in Southeast Asia if the Americans pull out." [34] She did, of course, know. The issue is *whether she cared*. The answer to that question is obvious.

After 1975, the Left's interest in Vietnam unsurprisingly began to wane. The crisis and the war were over. It was time for believers to move on to new killing fields.

The opportunity arrived with the Marxist revolution in Nicaragua in 1979, where a new set of social redeemers—the Sandinistas—attempted a new round of Stalinist experiments on mankind. But before we examine the Left's romance with the Sandinistas, we must first tell the tale of a leftist love affair next door to Vietnam—in Maoist China.

CHAPTER SEVEN

Flirting with Mao's Executioners

"Mere anarchy is loosed upon the world,
The blood-dimmed tide is loosed, and everywhere
The ceremony of innocence is drowned;
The best lack all conviction,while the worst
Are full of passionate intensity.

—W. B. Yeats

The *People's Republic of China* came into being on October 1, 1949. The newly empowered social redeemers were headed by Mao Tse-tung, who would become one of the greatest mass murderers of the twentieth century. Mao launched his own personal version of Stalinist terror immediately upon seizing power, initiating the mass killing of "social enemies" and "counterrevolutionaries." In the immediate post-revolutionary period alone, as many as fifteen million Chinese were murdered.[1]

In 1958, Mao launched the Great Leap Forward, an industrial and agricultural program intended to make China the world's largest steel and grain exporter. Involving demented economic schemes and brutal forced collectivization, the Great Leap was an unparalleled human disaster, exterminating approximately thirty-eight million people through government-engineered famine.[2] Mao's starving victims were reduced to eating grass, dirt, leaves, and tree bark in the attempt to survive. They picked through horse manure for undigested grains of wheat, or cow manure for worms. They also resorted to cannibalism, digging up freshly buried corpses. Mad from hunger, parents ate their own children—or swapped children with other parents in an attempt to ease the horror of the act. Children were also killed, boiled, and used as fertilizer. Machine gun fire mowed down desperate villagers who abandoned their homes and traveled to other towns in search of food.[3]

Mao intentionally created this horrifying tragedy—the greatest famine in all human history. While millions starved, plenty of food existed in state granaries. The army, however, guarded these granaries under strict order: "Absolutely no opening the granary door even if people are dying of starvation."[4] Mao biographers Jung Chang and Jon Halliday concluded that if food had not been exported and instead had been distributed among the Chinese people, "very probably not a single person in China would have had to die of hunger."[5]

In 1966, Mao launched the Cultural Revolution, designed to purge the country of all dissent and bring it completely under the dictator's vicious rule. Millions of schoolchildren became the infamous Red Guards, whose task was to destroy anything connected to traditional culture and philosophy. As Paul Johnson put it, the Cultural Revolution became "a revolution of illiterates and semi-literates against intellectuals, the 'spectacle-wearers' as they were called.... It was the greatest witch-hunt in history, which made the Zhdanov purges in post-war Russia seem almost trivial."[6]

In the Cultural Revolution, almost every expression of human emotion—and every cultural ritual whose purpose was to honor the sanctity of human life and relationships—became illegal, including weddings, funerals, and even the simple act of holding hands. The Red Guards humiliated, beat, and murdered teachers, school administrators, bureaucrats, foreign diplomats, technicians, artists, intellectuals, and, eventually, anyone and everyone. "Class enemies" experienced every humiliation the Red Guards could think up; the Guards smeared their faces with ink, forced them to get down on all fours and bark like dogs, and made them eat grass. The Red Guards also literally feasted on those they had murdered. In Guangxi, where at least 137 "animals" ("class enemies"), mostly teachers and college principals, were killed, the Red Guards cooked and ate them.[7]

An immense concentration camp system, the *laogai,* spread through China like a cancerous growth. It operated under the pretense of "reform" or "re-education" through labor and self-denunciation. The horrors of the *laogai* almost defy description. Harry Wu, who spent nineteen years in the *laogai,* has given an account of its vicious dynamics in *Laogai: The Chinese Gulag.*[8] Bao Ruo-Wang has done the same regarding his seven years in the *laogai* in *Prisoner of Mao.*[9] Wu and Bao did for China what Armando Valladares did for Cuba in *Against All Hope,* and Aleksandr Solzhenitsyn did for the Soviet Union in *Gulag Archipelago.*

Between 1949 and 1980, some fifty million Chinese people passed through this system of terror.[10] Like Stalin's Gulag, Mao's *laogai* took on a life of its own, continuing its bloody work unabated until Mao's death from Parkinson's disease in 1976. In all, Chinese communism would extinguish the lives of over seventy million people in the twentieth century.[11]

This horror represented the natural order of things for Mao. Indeed, while millions of his people were starving to death, the dictator habitually informed his inner circle that it did not matter if people died and that, in fact, death was to be deemed a cause for celebration and rejoicing.[12] This was because, naturally, destruction was necessary in order for the earthly heaven to be built. Mao wished destruction not only for his own country, but for the entire universe. As he explained: "This applies to the country, to the nation, and to mankind.... The destruction of the universe is the same.... People like me long for its destruction, because when the old universe is destroyed, a new universe will be formed. Isn't that better!"[13] Mao stated that it would be ideal to sacrifice about three hundred million Chinese lives for the world revolution, since "It's best if half the population is left, next best one-third..."[14]

As in Cuba, mourning for the dead was forbidden. Mourning implied something wrong with death—a notion that a death cult obviously couldn't allow. Moreover, grieving for a dead person singularized the individual and his private reality. Mao therefore outlawed the shedding of tears at funerals and even ordered peasants to plant crops over burial grounds—since he believed that deaths "can fertilise the ground."[15]

Mao's horrifying reign of terror, and the philosophy it was based on, predictably exhilarated believers. As they had done with all the other communist tyrannies, they lavished praise on the Chinese killing machine and flocked to visit its terrain—especially during the period, once again, when the genocide was at its peak: the 1950s and 1960s.[16] As Paul Hollander observes about these particular fellow travelers: "The sharply defined and binding values of Chinese society appeared as refreshingly firm guideposts to life which freed people of the burden of agonizing choices, of living with ambiguity and uncertainty."[17]

Fellow traveler Carol Tavris, an American psychologist, clearly reflected this disposition. She wrote:

> When you enter China you walk through the looking glass into a world that reflects a reality antithetical to ours. You leave Watergate, the energy crisis, crime, privacy, dirty movies, cynicism, and sex at the border, and step across into safety, stability, enthusiasm, clean streets, clean talk, and positive thinking. Most of all, you leave diversity and controversy, the hallmarks of America, to be wrapped in a uniformity of belief and singlemindedness of purpose.[18]

Here we see once again the devotion to totalitarian puritanism, the craving for "cleanliness," and, of course, the overall longing for a collective order in which humanity is purged of the expressive possibility of individualism and freedom of thought.

Anna Louise Strong, as we have seen, played a starring role among the political pilgrims to China. After she had finished her Stalinist odyssey, she moved on to China, settling there around 1960. Worried that her own writing might cross some unknown political line, she herself requested a Chinese "adviser" to censor her articles. In letters to friends in America, she alluded to some problems in Chinese society, but warned them never to mention them. An enthusiastic supporter of the Cultural Revolution, she received the honor of admission into the Red Guards. Not once did she utter a single syllable of criticism against their monstrous excesses—even after they had arrested a number of her friends.

When Strong became ill, she was hospitalized in Peking. She died in 1970, shortly after China's premier and foreign minister, Chou En-lai, visited her hospital room to pay his final respects.[19]

The French "feminist" intellectual Simone de Beauvoir, who pimped young girls for her lover, the Stalinist apologist Jean-Paul Sartre,[20] went on her own six-week China pilgrimage in 1955. Unsurprisingly, she found earthly paradise. Denying that there was state repression of any kind, she avowed: "Never has a popular democracy carried liberalism so far.... The Chinese intellectuals are now in a position to invent anew an ideology that will give adequate expression to the new world."[21] The techniques of hospitality were implemented to an extreme during de Beauvoir's visit; even the French-speaking Chinese woman assigned to accompany her was not allowed to speak with her without going through the interpreter.[22]

For these steadfast believers, not only was repression nonexistent, but, as for Walter Duranty in the Soviet Union, there wasn't any famine, either. For instance, during the peak of starvation in the Great Leap Forward, American journalist Edgar Snow admitted that there were some food shortages, but insisted that no one starved. He maintained that the government had done much to alleviate the problem and that the majority of the population was healthy.[23] Hewlett Johnson, the "Red Dean" of Canterbury, went further, stating that, "but for communes and communism, millions of people would have died...."[24]

Shirley MacLaine's brief journey to China in 1972—as part of a delegation of American women—became, like Sontag's and McCarthy's pilgrimages to Hanoi, a classic example of the believers' veneration of the communist killing machine. From the very beginning of her trip, MacLaine found a sense of purpose in the totalitarian society, and experienced a feeling of bonding with it:

> Here too I began to feel a sense of strength, a common bond among these people, joined together in a common task. They were not producing junk to sell for profit in some second-rate department store. They were feeding China. It was no small thing to them, and their sense of pride and purpose was infectious.[25]

Everything she saw represented utopia. Immediately upon her arrival she noticed that speaking in a loud voice was no longer necessary. There was, she wrote, "a sense of peace, and of safety, and it was immediately infectious; I found myself speaking in a quieter tone, and so did the other women."[26] Had MacLaine encountered such conditions in an American city, she would most surely have complained that a "false consciousness" was forcing women to speak "in a quieter tone."

The Chinese children who had not died of starvation or been eaten by their starving parents greatly impressed MacLaine. As Susan Sontag had noted that babies in the North Vietnamese paradise didn't have the need to cry, so MacLaine observed that Chinese children were impeccably behaved. MacLaine was not alone; another political pilgrim, British surgeon Joshua Horn, remarked that children in Communist China didn't even need to be disciplined.[27] Indeed, there was no longer a need for parents in the new communist paradise. Visiting Chinese nurseries, MacLaine became convinced that the Chinese had found a way to bring security to infants, and that it was only capitalism that made people believe that "mothers and fathers were necessary to children."[28] Along with eliminating private property, individual thought, and personal love, the earthly paradise had also eliminated the family. Children became the collective responsibility of the utopia.

British filmmaker Felix Greene discovered that capitalist-style competition could not be found anywhere in Chinese society; even among the leaders, he found no rivalry for power.[29] Greene's discoveries in China may have been somewhat colored by his longing for a dictatorial, one-party state, which he had publicly advocated for America. His overall views on China were perhaps best represented by his perspective on the Cultural Revolution, which he felt was a profound process of national self-inquiry that was necessary to wipe the slate clean from the slavery of bourgeois conditioning.[30] This view of the Cultural Revolution was not unusual for fellow travelers: the British economist Joan Robinson, for instance, concluded that the Cultural Revolution came from the bottom up—it was "spontaneous" and "unregulated."[31]

Believers discovered paradise wherever they cast their glances. As Paul Hollander put it: "The poetic qualities of the Chinese countryside were especially hard to resist. For many visitors it was inconceivable that there could be disharmony between mellow landscapes, gentle people, and the political system superimposed on them."[32]

Orville Schell, dean of the Graduate School of Journalism at UC Berkeley, made a tremendous discovery: humor in the Chinese paradise had been liberated from any bitter or angry emotion. Unlike Western humor, it "rarely seems to involve cruelty, sarcasm, or cynicism at someone else's expense. Indeed, one rarely sees anyone laugh derisively when someone else is awkward, hurt, or foolish. The first reaction seems to be to help."[33] Schell wasn't too preoccupied with one little detail that may have been lightly interlinked with his profound observations: Mao had criminalized humor. His regime had illegalized "speaking weird words"— which involved anything from asking strange questions to articulating dissatisfaction to making any kind of wisecrack. These offenses would get one classified as a spy—the consequences of which were obvious.[34]

For her part, meanwhile, MacLaine observed the tranquillity in China on an even grander scale:

> I hadn't seen any examples of hostility in China since the Cultural Revolution, not even a simple quarrel between bus driver and passenger, and it slowly dawned on me that perhaps human beings could really be taught anything, that perhaps we were simply blank pages upon which our characters are written by parents, schools, churches, and the society itself.[35]

Viewing human beings as entirely malleable, MacLaine fundamentally rejected the notion of human nature, whether spiritual or biological; the human being is simply a social creature with no inherent value or character. As such, morality itself is purely a matter of social engineering, for human beings are not in themselves good or bad; like blank pages, they bear only the impress of societal perfection or the lack thereof.

Pat Branson, another member of MacLaine's delegation, made her own earth-shattering observation: she noticed that the Chinese people wouldn't tolerate—not for one second—the kind of dirty tricks that politicians pulled on the public back home. In her lecture tour after her China odyssey, she recalled how "the Chinese take a stand for what they believe in. We could do the same thing. People here sit back and let everyone else do the work. The Chinese don't do that. They're involved. If somethin' is wrong, they fix it."[36] A couple of mysteries need solving here: if the American people sat back and didn't do anything, then who was the "everyone else" to whom Branson referred? And what was it, exactly, that the Chinese people were "fixing" in a totalitarian society that was suffering from genocide and famine?

The Chinese paradise overwhelmed one of the women in MacLaine's delegation, whom MacLaine referred to only as "Karen." She broke down and sobbed as MacLaine held her in her arms. As MacLaine recalled:

> The words poured out of her. China, she said, was the only place where she ever had felt safe. In America, she lived with the door locked, but here, the Chinese were so kind and sensitive and good that she knew no harm would ever befall her. She talked about things that had happened to her in her short life that caused her to be distrustful of people, and she said she would give anything to stay in China.[37] She sobbed harder: American school kids were cruel because America was a warlike nation; when she tried to work against the Vietnam War, she had been criticized; money and power and ruthlessness were all Americans cared for. But here in China, she "belonged." The tears were pouring, and I held her tight, trying to comfort her.[38]

The ingredients of the believer's diagnosis are written all over Karen's nervous breakdown, which had absolutely nothing to do with China and everything to do with her. She was confusing her own personal neuroses with social criticism. The whole episode leads to a few interesting questions: Did Karen shed a single tear for the millions of Chinese prisoners who passed through the *laogai*, or the millions of victims of the Red Guards? Would the victims of Maoist terror believe their persecutors to be as "kind and sensitive and good" as Karen had found her Chinese hosts? Did MacLaine spare a thought for the Chinese mothers who had seen their own babies starve to death, or who had eaten a dead child during Mao's famine?

Karen's yearning to "belong" was an emotion that MacLaine, like every other believer, shared. MacLaine wrote:

> I had spent a lot of my life feeling lonely in the individualistic West, but here, in this "collective place," where I knew neither the language nor the people, I was not lonely, I almost felt at home. And I hadn't smoked a cigarette in five weeks.[39]

While capitalism created a void in human beings that had to be filled with smoking, Communist China relieved its citizens of such harmful habits by imbuing them with hope and purpose.

As MacLaine and her delegation marveled at every sight and sound in the Chinese earthly paradise, the techniques of hospitality were clearly on display. MacLaine, like Sontag and McCarthy in Hanoi, pondered the fact that she was unable to roam about freely but could not, for the life of her, figure out why. She expressed her regret to her hosts about the "lack of contact" she had with the people, but accepted their explanation that it was the result not of the authorities' directive, but of the Chinese people's wishes: they had decided to keep their distance as a sign of "respect" for the guests, understanding how overpowering the whole experience was and not wanting to overwhelm them any further. MacLaine was filled with gratitude for such sensitivity: "It was as if they realized how difficult the adjustment to China would be for so many of us, how brimming over we were with questions that they might not be able to answer. It was easier to maintain space between us."[40] It is interesting to ponder what would have happened if MacLaine had just informed her hosts that she was *not* overwhelmed or confused and that she would prefer to go about as she pleased and speak with whomever she chose. That would have settled quite quickly whether or not her hosts' explanation was legitimate. MacLaine, of course, never chose to do this.

MacLaine also pondered, again without momentous results, the fate of Chinese intellectuals:

> How did the intellectuals who had been assigned to the countryside really feel about being "re-educated by the workers, peasants, and soldiers"? What could a plow-wielding peasant actually teach a Shanghai poet after the novelty of the first few weeks was over? Sometimes intellectuals were required to stay in the countryside for years. Was this de-emphasis of the elite a good thing? Did it help equalize the entire society, or did it abort intellectual creativity? Should *anyone* be considered special in a society where *everyone* was considered equal? The questions came in waves, but I really didn't have answers yet.[41]

The answers to these questions would not have been particularly difficult to find: by the time of MacLaine's visit, information about China's persecution of intellectuals was widely available.

While MacLaine and other fellow travelers remained completely indifferent to the fate of China's intellectuals, the nonexistence of escapees from Chinese prisons charmed them. In their eyes, this had nothing to do with the features of totalitarianism in the rest of Chinese society (i.e., there was nowhere to escape to)—it was simply that prisoners were so happy in the *laogai* that the thought of leaving would never even have entered their minds. Just like George Bernard Shaw and Anna Louise Strong in the Soviet Union, fellow travelers to China concluded that incarcerated Chinese requested to stay in prison even when they had served their sentences.[42] Why wouldn't they? After all, de Beauvoir visited Bolchevo Prison in Peking and found it located "in the depths of a kind of park...no warders, no guards, only...unarmed overseers...a theatre where a movie is shown or a play presented once a week."[43]

MacLaine was especially enthralled with the method of "self-criticism" that served as the underpinning of the Chinese revolution. Everyone, she was told, was subjected to criticism, and this helped the Chinese people see their faults and become perfect people, fit to live in utopia. MacLaine could have inquired into the way self-criticism was conducted as a form of torture in the *laogai*, but she didn't.

MacLaine recorded that in the self-criticism sessions, the most ordinary people confronted the most important leaders. "The honesty demanded by the people was excruciating," she affirmed. "I wondered how our politicians would stand up in sessions like that."[44] To be sure, one could imagine how nervous Chairman Mao was on the nights before his self-criticism sessions in front of common Chinese people ready to confront him on the excesses of the Great Leap Forward and the Cultural Revolution.

More than anything else, MacLaine adored "self-criticism" because it had eliminated the need for individual expression:

> Perhaps honest group communication reduced the need for individualistic artistic expression in the New Society. Since so many human creative forces are based on a desperate need to communicate one's feelings, perhaps the need is displaced in a society that practices intercommunicative therapy. In that case, perhaps I wasn't seeing a censored artistic community, but rather a community that simply had no need to express itself in art.[45]

MacLaine didn't fabricate these thoughts out of whole cloth. Her Chinese hosts graciously put her in contact with many Chinese artists who told her this was the case. MacLaine tells us:

> I had talked to many artistic people—writers, filmmakers, dancers, and directors...all seemed to feel they were currently living through a transition period—a creative and artistic pause which would help facilitate a more important goal if they applied their creative abilities to the revolution rather than pursuing individualistic artistic needs and desires. The purpose of art and literature was to serve the people and the revolution *now*. Later on—who knew? Would there even be art and literature later on? And would anybody miss it?[46]

For MacLaine, who was herself an artist, the prospect that art, literature, and all other forms of creative expression would eventually be annihilated in the earthly paradise to which she would submit presented the ultimate fantasy.

Like all other communist tyrannies, China enforced a ruthless attack on personal love and sexual pleasure. Sin was criminalized: sodomy earned its practitioners a death sentence, and sex outside of marriage was punishable by a prison sentence. China also imposed a unisex form of dress on its citizens, intended to minimize individuality and the chances of private attractions, affections, and desires.

Orville Schell fell in love with China's enforced mode of dress the moment he was exposed to it. Foreshadowing believers' ecstatic support of radical Islam's covering of women, he praised the "baggy uniformlike tunics" and wrote admiringly, "The question of the shape of a person's body is a moot one in China."[47] Schell also approved of the fact that physical attributes were subordinated in intimate relationships. He wrote that the Chinese had "succeeded in fundamentally altering the notion of attractiveness by simply substituting some of these revolutionary attributes for the physical ones which play such an important role in Western courtship."[48] Schell also noted approvingly that "The notion of 'playing hard to get' or exacerbating jealousies in order to win someone's love does not appear to assume such a prominent role."[49]

Hewlett Johnson was glad to find that:

> China's cinemas start with a clean sheet. Hollywood productions neither enter China now nor are sought there. The huge market which once was open to U.S. films is now closed and likely to remain so until Hollywood is purged from its crudity, its brutality, and its low sexual morality…. The life of Chinese men and women is too full of creative activity to seek "escape" in fatuous or horrific films; the youth, full of adventure and enabled, if they wish it, to embark on early and satisfying married life, do not seek the stimulation of coarse sexual films.[50]

MacLaine joined Schell and Johnson in championing China's totalitarian puritanism. Like all believers, she would have viewed any restriction on attire or sexual impulses in her own society as "capitalist oppression." Yet for the Chinese people, the suffocation of unregulated love and sex was beautiful:

> I could see for myself that in China you were able to forget about sex. There was no commercial exploitation of sex in order to sell soap, perfume, soft drinks, soda pop, or cars. The unisex uniforms also de-emphasized sexuality, and in an interesting way made you concentrate more on the individual character of the Chinese, regardless of his or her physical assets, or lack of them.... women had little need or even desire for such superficial things as frilly clothes and makeup, children loved work and were self-reliant. Relationships seemed free of jealousy and infidelity because monogamy was the law of the land and hardly anyone strayed.... It was a quantum leap into the future.[51]

For Claudie Broyelle, a French believer, one of the key accomplishments of the revolution was the cancellation of the "privatization of love."[52] Love in China, she pointed out, was now to be expressed not through personal and selfish capitalist avenues, but only through "revolutionary commitment."[53] Broyelle noted approvingly that good looks were no longer important for Chinese women. Unlike the sexualized image of women in Western advertising, she boasted, in China there was a different image, "on wall posters, in newspapers, on the stage, everywhere. It is the picture of a worker or a peasant, with a determined expression and dressed very simply.... You can see her working, studying, taking part in a demonstration."[54]

Once again, Schell, Johnson, MacLaine, and Broyelle never reflected on the brutal truths staring them right in the face. Indeed, how could jealousy be nurtured and infidelity be practiced in a society where privacy did not exist and infidelity would land you in a concentration camp at best, and get you executed at worst? MacLaine never asked: What if a Chinese citizen chose *not* to forget about sex and made his lack of forgetfulness evident? What if a man or a woman wore clothes that did *not* de-emphasize his or her sexuality? Hewlett Johnson never asked: What about Chinese men and women whose married life was *not* satisfying? What choices did they have? And what if certain Chinese citizens *did* seek "the stimulation of coarse sexual films" and got their hands on such films? What would happen to them?

Besides championing China's totalitarian puritanism, believers also continued the Left's tradition of forming a personality cult around the tyrants themselves. Chairman Mao and Premier Chou En-lai became the recipients of the believers' unbridled worship.

MacLaine saw that Mao "was a leader who seemed genuinely loved, people had great hopes for the future."[55] MacLaine's fellow delegate Pat Branson was convinced that "Mao Tse-tung and Jesus Christ were brothers under the skin."[56] Hewlett Johnson detected in Mao something no picture has ever caught, an inexpressible look of kindness and sympathy, an obvious preoccupation with the needs of others: other people's difficulties, other people's troubles, other people's struggles. These formed the deep content of his thoughts and needed but a touch or a word to bring this unique look of sympathy to his face.[57]

Johnson also noted:

> It was not hard as you talked with Chairman Mao to understand the deep affection men feel for this man who has organized life on a human basis for hundreds of millions of Chinese men and women. All men—intellectuals, peasants, merchants—regard Mao as the symbol of their deliverance, the man who shared their troubles and has raised their burdens. The peasant looks at the land he tills: Mao's gift. The factory worker thinks of a wage of 100 lb. rice instead of 10: Mao's gift. The intellectuals rejoicing in freedom from the menace of armed censorship regard that too as Mao's gift.[58]

The greatness of Chou En-lai also captivated Johnson:

> Handsome, courteous and gently spoken, [he] hides under a modest urbane presence a courage of steel with reasoning power swift and trenchant as a *rapier*.... Mr. Chou's face once seen is never forgotten. An alert and kindly face, youthful, almost boyish, set in a frame of dark hair, with dark eyes, shining beneath dark brows.... A very warmly kind face too, and with eyes that look

straight at you. I cannot imagine a less aggressive face, or a gentler one. But under the charm and the calm was a complete assurance and a sense of command....

Chou is an intellectual. He is cultivated.... He himself has all the elements of literary genius.[59]

American author and photojournalist Audrey Topping also saw remarkable traits in Chou En-lai:

Dinner with the Premier of China is not only a gourmet's delight, it is mixed with words of wisdom and wit. Every visitor leaves with his own impressions of Chou, but everyone seems to agree that he radiates intelligence and worldly charm. I found him to be a virtual prism, shooting off flashes of light in all directions, yet he possesses a calm dignity and projects an inner strength that to me reflects the face of New China itself.... he also has a remarkably keen wit, a warm humor and an appealing sense of the ridiculous.[60]

With all these heavenly qualities that believers discovered in China's despots, it is no wonder that it was painful for them to leave this paradise. MacLaine, who stoically held back her tears until she had left China, began to sob the moment she arrived in Hong Kong. During her first capitalist meal at the Hilton, when she had cut into a piece of meat, tears began to splash on her butter, and she excused herself to go to the ladies' room. She wrote:

As soon as I closed the door of the cubicle, I knew it would take a while. And then I started to cry. I didn't really know why, but it had something to do with all those people in a place called America, all those faces I had seen in crowds and in the living rooms, all the betrayed and insulted people I had seen.... It had something to do with them, and the women on my delegation and their confusing hang-ups, and it had something to do with George McGovern coming across those two hard years, to see it all go wrong at the end. It was about him, and about the cookie jar in my mother's kitchen, and the white pigeons in the yard, and the people who were going to jail because they were forced to be criminals, and the families

who couldn't make the payments that month on their cars
and their mortgages....[61]

After these precious moments of self-discovery, MacLaine
returned to the United States, where she concluded that the
Chinese communists had "caused the better side of human nature
to dominate." And while she celebrated the fact that artistic self-
expression was no longer necessary in China's earthly paradise,
she decided to continue her own career on stage, explaining to a
reporter that it was Mao Tse-tung who inspired her to do so. That's
because, as her friend Margaret Williams explained to the reporter,
"China makes you believe that everything is possible." MacLaine
made sure to emphasize that when Williams said this, she was
"jovial and ever cheerful" and "standing amidst the flowers and
telegrams."[62]

As with the Soviet Union, when the genocide slowed down,
the pilgrimages and adulation waned as well. Once President
Nixon made the opening to China in 1972, the Left's veneration of
the tyranny started to dissipate. After Mao's death in 1976, when
a Khrushchev-like thaw set in, most believers became bored with
China. Though Americans found it much easier to get into China
after 1972, their interest had become more a matter of curiosity
than of veneration.

And so, once again, believers began to look for new horizons,
and they soon found them in Nicaragua.

CHAPTER EIGHT

Nicaragua:
The Last Communist Hope

"In this tiny, sparsely populated land, where Christ's words are taken literally, the Sandinista revolution provides a different example."

—Günter Grass, on his political pilgrimage to Marxist Nicaragua

L ike all their communist role models, when the Sandinistas captured power in Nicaragua in July 1979, they immediately imposed a ruthless dictatorship to maintain rigid control.[1] Following in Castro's footsteps, they set up local spy networks. Each neighborhood had a *Comité de Defensa Sandinista* (CDS—Sandinista Defense Committee), which served the same totalitarian purpose as the Cuban CDR and the Nazi regime's block overseers—although the power of the CDS extended far beyond the Nazis' model.[2]

Emulating Stalin, Mao, and Castro, the Sandinistas took control of everything in the country. They censored all publications, suspended the right of association, and ruthlessly crushed the trade unions. They seized the means of production, and incentives for foreign investment disappeared. To put it plainly, another twentieth century experiment with socialism annihilated a nation's economy.[3]

The new despots imprisoned or executed Nicaraguans who attempted to protect their property. Moreover, unlike the authoritarian but not totalist regime of Anastasio Somoza, whom the Sandinistas overthrew, they did not leave the native populations on the Atlantic coast of Nicaragua in peace. In Khmer Rouge style, the Sandinistas forcibly relocated tens of thousands of Miskito Indians from their land. Like Stalin and Mao, the new regime used famine as a weapon against these "enemies of the people." The Sandinista army killed or imprisoned approximately fifteen thousand innocent Miskitos.[4] The Sandinista crimes included a calculated liquidation of the Miskitos' entire leadership—as the Soviets had done to the Poles in the spring of 1940, when, at Katyn Forest and other locations, the NKVD executed approximately fifteen thousand Polish officers.[5]

The Sandinistas quickly distinguished themselves as among the worst human rights abusers in Latin America, carrying out approximately eight thousand political executions within three years of the revolution. By 1983, the number of political prisoners in the new Marxist regime's jails was estimated at twenty thousand.[6] This was the highest number of political prisoners in any nation in the hemisphere—except, of course, Castro's Cuba. By 1986, a vicious and violent "resettlement program" forced some two hundred thousand Nicaraguans into 145 "settlements" throughout the country. This monstrous social-engineering program included the designation of "free-fire" zones, in which government troops had carte blanche to shoot and kill any peasant they spotted.[7]

The Sandinistas also institutionalized torture. Political prisoners in jails such as Las Tejas were consistently beaten, deprived of sleep, and given electric shocks. They were routinely denied food and water and kept in dark cubicles known as *chiquitas* (little ones), that had a surface area of less than one square meter. These cubicles were too small to sit up in, were completely dark, and had no sanitation and almost no ventilation. Prisoners were also forced to stand for long periods without bending their arms or legs; they were locked into steel boxes exposed to the full force of the tropical sun; their wives and daughters were sexually assaulted in front of them; and some prisoners were mutilated and skinned alive before being executed. One Sandinista practice was known as *corte de cruz*: this was a drawing-and-quartering technique in which the prisoner's limbs were severed from the body, leaving him to bleed to death.[8] The result of all of these horrifying cruelties was yet another mass exodus from a country enslaved by communism, with tens of thousands of Nicaraguans escaping and settling in Honduras, Costa Rica, or the United States.

With Soviet and Cuban aid, Nicaragua developed the biggest and best armed force in Central America. In attempting to export its Marxist revolution, it posed a serious threat to stability and democracy in the whole region, and thus to the United States.[9] In response, the Reagan administration backed a group of rebels, the "Contras," who sought to bring democracy to their homeland. The Contras were mostly peasants led by former Sandinistas who felt betrayed by the totalitarian turn of the revolution.[10]

As with North Vietnam twenty years earlier, the Contras' rebellion gave Sandinista Nicaragua an extra titillating attraction for believers: a military conflict in which America became involved. Paul Hollander notes the psychology of the leftists who hailed the Sandinistas:

> Quite possibly the single major reason for the surge of affection for the communist government of Nicaragua was the hostility shown toward it by the Reagan administration. Given the unpopularity of Reagan in the adversary culture it was axiomatic that whatever or whoever he opposed was deserving of support. Nicaragua came to benefit from the irresistible emotional logic of the impulse to treat the enemies of one's enemies as friends.[11]

This time around, believers' pilgrimages were labeled "political tourism"; thousands of Americans came to Nicaragua for prolonged stays designed to help build the revolution. Perhaps the most infamous group to embark on this totalitarian odyssey was the *"internacionalistas"*—foreign volunteer workers, similar to the Venceremos Brigade in Cuba. Coming for "humanitarian" reasons, they were especially involved in propaganda, attempting to convince the media worldwide of Sandinista Nicaragua's greatness, and giving instructions on how to oppose U.S. policy.

Overall, throughout the 1980s, a quarter of a million Americans visited Nicaragua. Hollywood led the way: the likes of Ed Asner, Michael Douglas, and Susan Anspach flocked to pay homage to the revolution.[12] Many familiar faces from previous political pilgrimages arrived in Nicaragua; indeed, Vietnam-era believers played starring roles. Hollander lists a few leading members of the cast:

> [t]he Berrigan brothers, Julian Bond, Noam Chomsky, Ramsey Clark, William Sloane Coffin, Harvey Cox, David Dellinger, Richard Falk, Allen Ginsberg, Bianca Jagger, Staughton Lynd, Jessica Mitford, Linus Pauling, Adrienne Rich (the radical feminist poet), Bernard Sanders (the socialist former mayor of Burlington, Vt., elected to the House of Representatives in 1990), Dr. Spock, George Wald, and the entire Institute for Policy Studies, among others."[13]

Once again, the techniques of hospitality were clearly in evidence. Just as the Soviet train carrying George Bernard Shaw employed waitresses who coincidentally had read the playwright's works, Nicaraguan actors were positioned to play certain roles.

One of the Sandinistas' favorite techniques for impressing their visitors was to allow them the honor of meeting one of the nine *comandantes* who made up the Sandinista National Directorate. As Shaw, Sontag, and MacLaine had experienced in other totalitarian settings, this strategy gave the believers a feeling of tremendous importance and *power*. The Sandinistas went further in this regard than any previous regime, allowing as many meetings as possible between the worshipping visitors and their earthly deities. Comandante Ernesto Cardenal, the minister of culture, played a central role in this realm of hospitality. He consistently played up his distinguished life: he was not only a Sandinista, but also a priest and a poet.

Tomás Borge, the interior minister, also played a prominent role in greeting the travelers. He actually had two different offices, one for work and one for the Potemkin-village charade. According to Alvaro José Baldizon, a former assistant of Borge's who defected in 1985, Borge's first office, where he met with fellow travelers, contained photographs of children, gilded carved crucifixes, and a Bible or two. If the group of travelers in question was a religious delegation, Borge would refresh his memory on Bible passages which he could quote to impress his guests. Borge's real office, which was used for his duties as interior minister, contained no crucifixes or Bibles but, as Baldizon recalled, "only Marxist literature and posters of Marx, Engels and Lenin."[14]

Like earlier political pilgrims, believers were especially enchanted with the prison system. The view of German writer Günter Grass was typical.[15] Borge didn't take him, naturally, to Las Tejas to show him prisoners who were starved, beaten, deprived of sleep, and tortured with electric shocks. He didn't introduce him to the prisoners lying in the dark *chiquitas*. Instead, he took Grass to the Tipitapa prison, which had been well prepared for its leftist admirers.

Tititapa exhilarated Grass. "The humane way in which sentences are carried out" and how "Saturdays and Sundays are kept free for visitors who come each week and are allowed to stay for three or four hours" amazed him. He was especially impressed that there was absolutely no room for any kind of "revenge" for wrongs committed by the previous regime, either at Tipitapa or in the society at large—because Tomás Borge told him so. Borge explained to Grass how even Sandinistas who didn't behave humanely were punished by the regime. These wonders led Grass to conclude that the cause of the Sandinistas vis-à-vis the United States was analogous to the Polish Solidarity movement's cause vis-à-vis the Soviet regime. Grass concluded that "in this tiny, sparsely populated land, where Christ's words are taken literally, the Sandinista revolution provides a different example."[16]

Benedict Alper, a criminology professor at Boston College, also received the honor of touring a Sandinista prison. Like Grass, he was pleasantly surprised at the excellent treatment prisoners received, especially the "compassion" that officials and guards showed them. He later advocated that America should adopt Nicaraguan methods of rehabilitating prisoners.[17] No one asked him if he was referring to the main ingredients of the "rehabilitation" process in the Nicaraguan gulag: sleep deprivation, beatings, torture, electric shock, denial of food and water, and confinement in *chiquitas*.

Overall, the Sandinistas' techniques of hospitality were especially successful in the prison tours. Humberto Belli, a former Sandinista, commented on these techniques:

Many visitors to Nicaragua are misled in regard to human rights by a model prison, the "Open Farm" fourteen miles from Managua, where the inmates can be seen working the one hundred and twenty-five acres of farmland and enjoying a most benign penal regimen, which requires no security of any kind. Although this prison, a prison "without walls," only houses a fraction of the total inmate population (chosen on the basis of good behavior), many visitors mistake it for a representative sample of the entire correctional system. They are seldom taken to the "Zona Franca," the huge master prison where thousands of inmates are crammed into filthy cells.[18]

It is no great surprise that the likes of Grass believed that Christ's words were taken literally in Sandinistaland. Joan Patajon, an American *internacionalista*, echoed Grass's sentiment in her observation that "Jesus would be very happy with Nicaragua today."[19]

As always, fellow travelers saw heaven everywhere they looked. And when they didn't see hell, that meant it did not exist. James Harrington, legal director of the Texas Civil Liberties Union, believed there was no malnutrition or begging in Nicaragua because he did not see any.[20]

Believers also fantasized about the Sandinista paradise spreading throughout Central America. Michael Harrington, the American representative to the Socialist International's Committee to Defend the Nicaraguan Revolution, referred to Nicaragua as the "good domino," a play on the "domino theory" which U.S. officials had used in their argument (tragically prophetic) that if Vietnam fell to the communists so would the rest of Southeast Asia. For Harrington, it would be a *good* thing if the remaining Central American nations fell like dominoes and became carbon copies of Communist Nicaragua. Harrington was certain of the truth of his vision because, like myriad other fellow travelers, he had learned it directly from the Sandinistas in Managua. After this encounter, he wrote that he was "deeply moved by the sincerity and passion" of those with whom he met. He also insisted that the Sandinista revolution was "democratic and pluralist," and that if the regime had committed any excesses, they were the fault of the United States.[21]

In the end, just as believers' lies about the Soviet Union had helped to legitimize a genocidal regime, and just as antiwar protesters had helped pave the way for a bloodbath and the enslavement of millions of people in Southeast Asia, so too pro-Sandinista groupies bolstered the strength of this new tyranny by consistently promoting it in the American media. Fellow travelers openly strategized with the Sandinistas. A typical scene occurred in the bar at the Intercontinental Hotel in Managua in 1983, where American University professor William LeoGrande and Robert Borosage, director of the Institute for Policy Studies, sat with Alejandro Bendana, secretary general of the Foreign Ministry, and other Sandinistas, candidly exchanging thoughts as to which U.S. publications, laid out on the table before them, could be "played" for maximum advantage. They also discussed which American radicals, such as Michael Harrington, could be counted on to help the regime. LeoGrande and Borosage assured Bendana that the Sandinistas just had to outlast the Reagan administration in order to survive.[22]

The greatest damage the believers inflicted, of course, was interfering with the Reagan administration's aid to the Contra freedom fighters. Left-wing activists succeeded in limiting Contra funding to meager amounts, stopping it for long periods of time and then having it completely terminated in 1988. Pro-Sandinista Democratic senators like John Kerry and Christopher Dodd spearheaded this effort.

While helping to keep their beloved tyranny in power, some of the fellow travelers continued their predecessors' tradition of longing for their own deaths for the sake of the idea. The *internacionalistas*, for instance, consistently voiced their craving for an American invasion. Paul Rice was a typical *internacionalista*: a venerator of Mao, he openly discussed his fantasy of not only sacrificing his own life for the revolution against an American attack, but also killing his former high-school buddies in the Marines if they invaded Nicaragua.[23]

The Nicaraguan people themselves despised the believers who came to Nicaragua, since they understood that the visitors worshipped their persecutors. Martin Kriele, a German visitor to Nicaragua, recalled:

> From the very evening I tried to make contact with ordinary people and hear their views. At first, people were mistrustful, reticent. But I was not long in discovering a method of gaining their confidence and getting them to talk. They always asked whether I came from East or West Germany. When answering all I had to do was to add that I was not one of the *"internacionalistas,"* if possible throwing in a sarcastic remark. This provoked relieved laughter and was almost always followed by the whispered comment: *our situation is very, very grave*. The moment had come to ask them to elaborate, and they would begin to talk (emphasis added).

Kriele quickly learned that for Nicaraguans, *"internacionalistas"* had connotations of social leprosy. Indeed, Nicaraguans referred to the *internacionalistas* with the disgusting term *pacusos*—which indicates people with stinking feet, arses, and armpits.[24]

In the end, the Nicaraguans were able to oust their oppressors. On February 25, 1990, under massive international pressure, and intoxicated by their own propaganda with regard to their popularity, the Sandinistas held an election. But the dictators had fundamentally failed to gauge what the people were really feeling. The Coalition of Nicaraguan Opposition Parties, headed by Violeta Chamorro, ousted the Sandinistas, led by Daniel Ortega, from power.[25]

While Nicaragua obviously did not heal overnight, the Sandinistas could no longer torture their own people in a position of total power. They made sure, of course, to fulfill their Marxist legacy by swiftly "privatizing" the huge property holdings they had confiscated during the revolution. But the reign of terror was cut short.[26]

The Left, consequently, fell into a profound despair. Once again, believers began to yearn for new tyrannical adversaries of the United States, which would sacrifice human blood on the altar of utopian ideals. David Horowitz observed this as he watched the leftist fellow travelers during his trip to Managua in 1987:

> We recognized the journey they were on; it was one that had only beginnings, and certainly no middles. When only beginnings failed, these radical travelers would always find another. For them, history was a giant station at which there was always another train about to leave.[27]

The circumstances of the post-1991 era, however, made it more difficult to find a new death cult, since communism had disintegrated throughout Eastern Europe in 1989-90, and the Soviet Union had finally collapsed in 1991. The North Korean regime founded by Kim Il Sung still exists, of course, and Robert Scheer, for instance, believed it represented humanity's greatest hope and led many leftists in idealizing it.[28] But basically, with communism gone, believers had to seek out new objects of adoration.

The underdeveloped Third World served part of believers' purposes: it represented for them the fantasy of purity, simplicity, and innocence, within which they could indulge their craving to return to childhood and safety. But no entity in the Third World appeared strong enough to satisfy believers' most powerful motivating urge: to destroy Western civilization and freedom and replace them with despotism and backwardness.

The Left did not have to despair for long. A new and glorious gift was soon delivered to believers: Islamism, a totalist ideology that, in believers' eyes, was a rebellion against American imperialism and capitalist oppression. The Islamist threat had first surfaced significantly back in 1979, with the revolution in Iran. In January of that year, Islamist fanatics overthrew the American-allied government of the Shah, who had ruled Iran for thirty-eight years and had brought the country into the modern world, instituting many changes, including new rights for women. Now, a brutal and totalist regime took power, headed by a Shi'ite cleric, Ayatollah Khomeini. Rivers of blood began to flow as the Islamists initiated the ugly process of purifying humankind. Iran's pro-Western disposition was reversed. The new civil rights, especially those for women, were ruthlessly terminated.

The blood-soaked Iranian revolution gave exhilarating inspiration to Islamic fanatics worldwide. They conspired more fervently and confidently to destroy modernity in their own societies and to wage terror against America and the West. Islamism would fill the void left by communism's collapse. But before we tell the horror story of the believers' romance with Islamism, we must first define the new enemy.

PART III

THE DEATH CULT COUSIN: ISLAMISM

CHAPTER NINE

Yearnings for Death and Suicide

"If faith, a belief, is not watered and irrigated by blood, it does not grow."

—Ali Benhadj, a leading Algerian Islamist

T*he horrifying image of the Twin Towers* burning and then collapsing on September 11, 2001, forced Americans to focus on the monstrous death cult that poses the greatest threat to freedom in the early twenty-first century. The enemy was yet another vicious totalist ideology: Islamism, which seeks to force *sharia* (Islamic law) on all the inhabitants of the earth.

A by-product of Islamic fundamentalism, Islamism is also, as Paul Berman has profoundly demonstrated, partly a manifestation of the post-1914 revolt against liberalism in Europe that spawned fascism and communism. As Berman notes, Islamism is "the Muslim variation on the European idea."[1]

It is therefore no surprise to find that fascism and communism were centrally involved in the birth and development of Islamism. The Nazis, for instance, helped create Egypt's Muslim Brotherhood, a pioneering Islamic extremist group founded in 1928.[2] The Nazis hoped to use the organization as a weapon against the British in the Middle East.[3] Hassan al-Banna, the founder of the Muslim Brotherhood, was a devout admirer of Adolf Hitler.[4] These Nazi roots helped facilitate the seamless incorporation of a virulent anti-Jewish strain into Muslim totalitarianism.

Islamism also has roots in Marxist-Leninist philosophy. As Muslim author Mustafa Akyol has pointed out, Marxism had a profound influence on the godfathers of Islamism, notably Sayyid Qutb, an Egyptian Muslim radical and Muslim Brotherhood theorist; the Pakistani Sayyid Abul A'la Maududi, a chief architect of the present-day Islamic resurgence; and Ali Shariati, a philosopher who helped lay the groundwork for the Iranian revolution. It is not surprising, then, that many ex-Marxists joined Islamist circles (e.g., Carlos the Jackal, now imprisoned in France),[5] and that a writer such as Sayyid Maududi consistently appropriated Marxist language in his writings.[6] The Soviet regime, meanwhile, had a long record of using its influence to set militant Islam onto an anti-American path.[7]

The Iranian revolution provides a particularly good example. Although the "ayatollahs' revolution" was widely viewed as a matter of imposing religious purity, it also had strong Marxist underpinnings. Iranian-born leftist intellectuals such as Jalal Al-Ahmad and Ali Shariati made significant contributions to the discourse of militant Islam, incorporating major Marxist themes into its dogma of hate.[8] These thinkers strongly influenced Khomeini, as did texts such as *The Wretched of the Earth*, by the Martinique-born Marxist author Frantz Fanon. Khomeini introduced into radical Islamic thought the central Marxist paradigm of a world divided into oppressors and oppressed; he did this by utilizing the moral terms of Islam—*mostakbirine* ("the arrogant") and *mostadafine* ("the weakened").[9] The despot completed his revolution's alignment with the Left by introducing the terms "Great Satan" and "Little Satan" to describe the United States and Israel.[10] In this light, it is not surprising that Khomeini gained the support of the Western Left as well as that of the Moscow-aligned Iranian Communist Party.[11]

While militant Islam has its own unique religious component, it shares with the secular totalitarianisms the impulse to create an earthly paradise by washing the slate clean with human blood. No sacred/secular distinction exists in Islam, and Islamists envision enforcing the kingdom of heaven on earth. The greatest obligation of the Islamist, like that of the believer in the other two totalisms, is to submit his will to the deity and, if the opportunity arises, to give his life for it. Martyrdom and suicide become the favored expressions of this submission and of the radical desire for perfection. It is precisely this ingredient that has so attracted the Western Left to Islamism.

The Islamist craving for death is clearly outlined in the works of one of Islamism's godfathers, Sayyid Qutb (1906-1966). His massive thirty-volume commentary, *In the Shade of the Quran*, has had enormous influence on today's Muslim warriors worldwide. For Qutb, a non-Islamic state has no right to exist. In his view, violent jihad is necessary to achieve worldwide Islamic law, and the death of the Islamic warrior is a crucial element of this process. Qutb consistently stressed that it was necessary to submit oneself to the totality (Allah), that truth could not be reached by spiritual vehicles alone, and that violence was critical for the cause.[12] In his profound study of Qutb's writings, Paul Berman outlines how Qutb linked truth and martyrdom and how, in so doing, he illuminated the Islamist synthesis of the totalitarian idea and the death cult. Berman writes:

> Qutb's doctrine was wonderfully original and deeply Muslim, looked at from one angle; and, from another angle, merely one more version of the European totalitarian idea. And if his doctrine was recognizable, its consequences were certainly going to be predictable. Qutb's vanguard, if such a vanguard ever mobilized itself, was going to inaugurate a rebellion—this time, a rebellion in the name of Islam, against the liberal values of the West. (Totalitarian movements always, but always, rise up in rebellion against the liberal values of the West. That is their purpose.) And rebellion was bound to end in a cult of death. For how were any of Qutb's goals to be achieved? What could it possibly mean to treat the entire Muslim population of the world, apart from the followers of his own movement, as *jahili* barbarians who were bringing about the extermination of Islam?.... The successes of the Islamist revolution were going to take place on the plane of the dead, or nowhere. Lived experience pronounced that sentence on the Islamist revolution—the lived experience of Europe, where each of the totalitarian movements proposed a total renovation of life, and each was driven to create the total renovation in death.[13]

Overall, militant Islam needs to kill in order to survive. Peter Raddatz, a German scholar of Islamic studies, notes that this culture is based on the "enemy principle": the culture can exist only as long as enemies exist, and it can live only as long as it can kill.[14]

The French-born strategist Laurent Murawiec summarizes the ideology's overriding theme as "I kill, therefore I am."[15] In his study of the Islamist terrorist's mindset, he writes, "...the means has become the end. The blood of the enemy renews the identity of the lynch mob.... Death is not an instrumentality—like the death of the enemy on the battlefield—it has become an end in itself..."[16] Murawiec points out that the suicide-killing manual left behind by Mohammed Atta, the leader of the 9/11 attacks, included a provision commanding that before going on his mission, the Islamic warrior must make sure his knife is sharp: "you...must not discomfort your animal during the slaughter."[17] The animal being referred to is the non-Muslim whom the Muslim is instructed to kill. As Murawiec correctly observes, we see here the element of human sacrifice for the sake of pleasing God.[18]

A stunning example of the importance of spilling human blood in this sacrifice was the assassination in 1971 of Jordan's prime minister, Wasfi al-Tell, by PLO terrorists. As al-Tell lay dying on the marble floor of the Sheraton Hotel in Cairo, one of the terrorists knelt down and began lapping up his blood.[19] Murawiec cites a long sequence of such incidents of blood worship in what Saudi lawyer Sheikh Mohsin al-Awaji has referred to as the Islamic jihad's "industry of death."[20]

In the process of killing its enemies, this culture kills its own children. For the Islamist, as for his totalitarian cousins, the goal of life is not to treasure it—and definitely not to utilize it to pursue individual happiness or fulfillment. The goal of life is to lose it, in the very act of eradicating the enemy. This is why the idea of America, and its sacred principle of "the pursuit of happiness" embedded in the Declaration of Independence, is anathema to Islamism, just as it was anathema to fascism and communism (and to the Western Left).

The pursuit of happiness implies that the individual and his will matter. An individual's pursuit of happiness, moreover, implies that the world can be accepted for what it is—and human beings can be accepted for what they are. This is a deadly violation of the totalist code, since it contradicts the necessity of destroying the world and rebuilding it. Happiness is betrayal. Rage is a glorious commitment to the cause.

This psychotic mindset explains why Jew hatred is such an important component of Islamism, as of most other death cults. Two of the most outstanding Jewish characteristics are the love of life and the enduring struggle to survive. For Islamists, as for Nazis and communists, this is an egregious transgression against their faith. To Qutb, a truly "contemptible characteristic of the Jews"—as identified by the Koran—was their "craven desire to live, no matter at what price, regardless of quality, honor and dignity."[21]

The Algerian militant Ali Benhadj crystallizes Islamism's central tenet that death serves to purify the earth:

> If faith, a belief, is not watered and irrigated by blood, it does not grow. It does not live. Principles are reinforced by sacrifices, suicide operations, and martyrdom for Allah. Faith is propagated by counting up deaths every day, by adding up massacres and charnel-houses. It hardly matters if the person who has been sacrificed is no longer there. He has won.[22]

This Islamist thirst for human blood was tragically conspicuous on September 11, 2001, when nineteen radical Muslims "won" by crashing commercial airliners into heavily populated buildings. The horror of that day testified to the mind-numbing fact that when Maulana Inyadullah, a member of al-Qaeda, bragged that "the Americans love Pepsi Cola, we love death," he meant it.[23]

One of the most frightening manifestations of this death cult is the way it has infected contemporary Palestinian culture. The outcome of the Camp David talks in July 2000 demonstrates this haunting reality. Israeli prime minister Ehud Barak offered the Palestinians 95 percent of their negotiating demands. He offered them their own sovereign state in Judea, Samaria, and the Gaza Strip, more than 90 percent of the West Bank, and a capital in Jerusalem. He also offered them sovereignty over all Arab-populated parts of East Jerusalem, over all of the Old City except the Jewish Quarter, and over the Temple Mount, with Jewish sovereignty only over the Western Wall below the Mount.

This was more than Israel had ever offered before and, most likely, ever would again. The Palestinians had a chance to enter a new era of peace, with their own state, on incredibly generous terms. Instead, they chose death.

Yasser Arafat rewarded the Israelis for their offer by initiating an onslaught of terror that became known as the al-Aqsa Intifada.[24] On the principle that murdering Jews was a Muslim obligation, the Palestinians strapped bombs onto themselves, boarded Israeli buses and went into Israeli cafés and discotheques, and blew themselves up alongside innocent Jews. The deadly suicide massacres began with the bombing of a Tel Aviv disco catering to teenagers in June 2001. The suicide bombings quickly escalated. Mass murder became an everyday affair in Israel. Palestinian children blew themselves into smithereens while their parents celebrated, proud that their offspring had become *shahid* (martyrs).[25]

These horrifying developments raise the question: what would the Palestinian culture do without the existence of Israel next to it? How then would it pursue its yearning for death? The Palestinian dynamic is in perfect continuity, after all, with the way communist revolutions devoured their own children. After overthrowing the targeted enemy, the killing machine always continued, requiring the bloody sacrifice of countless innocents.

The Palestinian Intifada is just one more outbreak of the Islamist death cult in the years since the Islamist virus surfaced in the Iranian revolution. Upon coming to power in 1979 with the help of Democratic President Jimmy Carter,[26] the Iranian Islamists immediately indulged the overriding impulse of their ideology. Ayatollah Khomeini killed more human beings (approximately twenty thousand) in two weeks than the Shah (who had been widely denounced in the West for human rights violations) had killed during his entire reign of thirty-eight years. Khomeini followed this immediate burst of terror by sending hundreds of thousands of his people to die in a pointless war with Iraq. Many young Iranians eagerly rushed to their deaths. Berman describes the horrifying pathology:

> Khomeini's revolution, by contrast, worshipped piety, the flip side of which was martyrdom—the martyrdom that was needed to bring about the resurrection of the Islamic Empire. And so, in a pious and revolutionary spirit, Khomeini organized his "human wave" attacks—mass frontal assaults by thousands of young men, advancing to certain death...Khomeini whipped up a religious fervor for that kind of mass death—a belief that to die on Khomeini's orders in a human wave attack was to achieve the highest and most beautiful of destinies. All over Iran, young men, encouraged by their mothers and their families, yearned to participate in those human wave attacks—actively yearned for martyrdom. It was a mass movement for suicide. The war was one of the most macabre events that has ever occurred—a war between love and piety, which was, from another angle, a war between cruelty and suicide.[27]

The Iranian revolution was clearly about irrigating the earth with human blood. This is precisely why, as Amir Taheri notes, when pilgrims visit Iran, they:

> start their guided tour of the Islamic Republic with a visit to the *Behest Zahra* (Paradise of Flowers) graveyard south of Tehran. They are invited to stand for a minute's silence in front of the Fountain of Blood, a 4.5-meter-high fountain out of which surges a blood-red liquid, symbolizing, in the words of the guide, the essence of Islam's message.[28]

That is also why, when the mullahs discovered that Iraq planned to start killing Iranians in a manner that would not cause blood to flow, they immediately sought a truce. As Peter Raddatz explains:

> In the Iranian death cult, there is a Shiite "Fatwa" ruling the exorbitantly important question of "martyrs" dying of poison gas. At the end of the Iran-Iraq war, Saddam's troops had started sending rockets onto Tehran with rumours going that they would soon be equipped with Tabun and Sarin nerve gas. The truce was accelerated as

the jurists ruled that a Muslim dying from a gas rocket
would not enter paradise since there would be no blood
involved, which must flow generously in order to
constitute martyrdom.[29]

Khomeini's Islamic state gave powerful inspiration to militant
Islam worldwide. Islamic fundamentalists were now confident that
a domino effect would start in their favor. The Soviet invasion of
Afghanistan, which rallied Muslims all over the world to the
special cause of defending a Muslim nation, reinforced this
inspiration. When the Soviets were finally defeated in Afghanistan,
militant Muslims worldwide celebrated their victory over a
superpower. When the Soviet Union collapsed a few years later,
this impression was reinforced. Islamists believed that their future
war on America would be simple in comparison.

In 1996, Islamists, in the form of the Taliban, achieved their
next victory: they established another death cult in Afghanistan.
This regime annihilated all civil rights. Public executions of
homosexuals and of women accused of adultery or premarital sex
became common.[30]

The Taliban also hosted al-Qaeda—providing the terrorists a
safe haven in which to build terror-training camps. The means
were now in place with which to attack directly the last
remaining superpower, the most powerful symbol of everything
militant Islam reviled. Within this dynamic of totalitarian terror,
9/11 materialized. It served the perpetrators in delightful ways,
for the terrorists who carried it out achieved every Islamist's top
two objectives: (1) to spawn Ground Zero and (2) to die a bloody
death in the process.

While Islamism's death cult is, as Berman has noted, partly
an importation of the European totalitarian virus, it is also
obviously the natural outgrowth of its own unique religious
roots. One of these roots is religious hatred—analogous to the
racial and class hatred that drove Nazism and communism. In the
Islamist paradigm, those who are not part of the faith are seen as
enemies; thus, violent jihad ("struggle") must be waged against
them. In other words, Islamist terror is in one sense simply the
continuation of Islamic holy war against non-Muslims, which, as

will be shown below, is considered a central duty of every Muslim and is, therefore, a constant in Islamic history.

Before we proceed further, it is crucial to stress that there is a struggle taking place for the soul of Islam at this very moment, and many Muslims who oppose extremism and fanaticism are courageously fighting to bring their religion into the modern world. Individuals such as Canada's Irshad Manji and Italy's Sheikh Abdul Hadi Palazzi, and groups such as Muslims Against Sharia and the Center for the Study of Islam & Democracy, are all part of this effort.

It will be no easy thing for Muslim reformers to buck nearly fourteen hundred years of tradition. But they do have the power to bring out the tolerant and civilized components of their religion. For instance, they can take a Koranic verse such as Sura 2:256, which states, "There is no compulsion in religion," and make it the most important and influential verse for their brand of Islam. As historian Daniel Pipes has shown, the "no compulsion" verse is very complex; it has had numerous interpretations throughout history and has often been read as not implying tolerance of any kind.[31] But this is part of the larger point Pipes himself is making: on their own playing field, Muslims have some scope for making a verse mean *what they want it to mean.* This is not an easy process, but, as Pipes puts it in his analysis of this verse's historical interpretations:

> First, it shows that Islam—like all religions—is whatever believers make of it. The choices for Muslims range from Taliban-style repression to Balkan-style liberality. There are few limits; and there is no "right" or "wrong" interpretation. Muslims have a nearly clean slate to resolve what "no compulsion" means in the twenty-first century.[32]

In other words, a new generation of Muslims can renew Islam and reinterpret its teachings and commandments. They can allow verses that teach tolerance and peace to supersede and negate those verses that advocate intolerance and violence.

The efforts of the Turkish Muslim writer Mustafa Akyol serve as a perfect example of the possibility of an Islamic reformation.

Fighting for a modern, tolerant, and pro-Western Islam, Akyol stresses that Muslims must question certain traditional teachings, because they can no longer apply "a medieval political doctrine to the twenty-first century."[33]

It is one of the central premises of this work that Muslim voices such as Akyol's offer true hope in the battle for the soul of Islam. The course of the terror war and the future of freedom are very much dependent on whether or not the voices of reform-minded Muslims prevail. The West has a huge stake in the success of such teachers as Mustafa Akyol, Irshad Manji, and Abdul Hadi Palazzi, and must do everything in its power to support them.

At the opposite end of the Islamic spectrum are extremists like the Wahhabis. Wahhabism, founded by the Sunni reformer Sheikh Muhammad ibn Abdul al-Wahhab (1700-1792), is one of the most powerful strains of radical Islam.[34]

Osama bin Laden, himself a Wahhabi, has repeatedly made clear that militant Islam's war against the West is based on religious hate. In 1996, in his declaration of jihad against the United States, the terror master gave a long laundry list of his organization's grievances against America, the central one being this:

> The latest and the greatest of these aggressions...is the occupation of the land of the two Holy Places [i.e., Saudi Arabia]—the foundation of the house of Islam, the place of the revelation, the source of the message and the place of the noble Ka'ba, the Qiblah of all Muslims—by armies of the American Crusaders and their allies. (We bemoan this and can only say: "No power and power acquiring except through Allah.")[35]

The refusal to accept anyone who is religiously different would be totally unacceptable for any modern Western nation. Yet for Islamists, human beings who hold different beliefs represent a lower species and defile not only Muslim lands, but the entire earth.

Islam specifically forbids non-Muslims from entering certain areas that are considered sacred. Non-Muslims, for instance, are not allowed to stay in the "*Hijaz*"—the area around Mecca and Medina—for more than three days, and they can stay that long only to obtain something they need. They cannot enter the holy cities themselves at all. These rules are directly founded on mandates of the Prophet Muhammad, who on his deathbed said: "Let there not be two religions in Arabia."[36] The prophet also stated, "I will expel the Jews and Christians from the Arabian Peninsula and will not leave any but Muslims."[37]

As mentioned earlier, Islam also commands the faithful to engage in jihad. According to the Koran and the *hadiths* (recorded teachings of the Prophet Muhammad), jihad must be waged against unbelievers until they are defeated, subjugated, and forced to submit to Islamic law. Islam also possesses an understanding of the "spiritual" jihad, the "inner" jihad, which is the Muslim's personal struggle to reach a higher level of moral purity and conform his life to the will of Allah. Unfortunately, the Koran does not teach that the inner jihad is the most vital jihad.

Myriad Koranic verses emphasize the importance of fighting unbelievers. The famous Verse of the Sword (Sura 9:5), for instance, which is considered the Koran's final word on jihad and nullifies all contrary teachings, instructs Muslims to attack and kill non-Muslims as a means of achieving world hegemony under Islam.[38] Many *hadiths*, such as *Sahih Muslim* 4294, also enjoin war against unbelievers.[39] Muslim reformers may be able to change this reality, but the fact is that violent jihad remains a primary commandment in the Islam *that is.*

Muhammad himself was a living example in this regard, making frequent war against unbelievers. By the end of Muhammad's life, Islam dominated Arabia, and Muslim armies were set to expand outward to battle the Byzantine and Persian empires. After Muhammad's death, Muslims engaged in ferocious attacks on their non-Muslim neighbors, and the Islamic empire grew quickly, extending into Syria, Egypt, and eventually all of the Middle East and North Africa. Those who were conquered were given three choices: converting to Islam, living as a second-class citizen and paying a poll tax (the *jizya),* or being sold into slavery or killed.[40] Those who chose second-class citizenship became part of the historical phenomenon called the *dhimma*—the structure of oppression that non-Muslims suffer under Islamic rule. The conquered peoples are known as the *dhimmis,* the "protected people" (primarily Jews and Christians, although other groups, notably Hindus, have enjoyed this "protection" at various times in history), who are allowed to lie but are deprived of many rights and freedoms.[41] All of this is based on Muhammad's instruction to be "harsh" or "ruthless" to unbelievers.[42]

To say the least, the concepts of equality and multiculturalism do not exist in Islam. As British author David Pryce-Jones notes, "Set up by Muslims for Muslims, every Arab state is explicitly Islamic in confession. Religious and ethnic minorities have been persecuted everywhere. Nowhere is there participation in the political process corresponding to any conception of representative democracy."[43]

A manual of Islamic law includes, among other things, the instructions that "protected people" must:

> pay the non-Muslim poll tax (*jizya*) and [must be] distinguished from Muslims in dress, wearing a wide cloth belt (*zunnar*); are not greeted with "*as-Salamu 'alaykum*" [the traditional Muslim greeting, "Peace be with you"]; must keep to the side of the street; may not build higher than or as high as the Muslims' buildings, though if they acquire a tall house, it is not razed; are forbidden to openly display wine or pork...recite the Torah or Evangel aloud, or make public display of their funerals or feast days; and are forbidden to build new churches.[44]

Islamic law also mandates that the religious symbols of other faiths be destroyed. This is why, during Muhammad's own time, the shrines of non-Muslims were destroyed upon his personal orders.[45] When Muslim warriors attacked Rome in 846, they were only following their religion's commandments in sacking the basilicas of St. Peter and of St. Paul and in desecrating the graves of the pontiffs.[46] The same applied to Muslim conquerors who came to India starting in the tenth century: they destroyed thousands of Hindu shrines and temples and built mosques from their debris.[47]

These realities of Islamic religious despotism explain why Islam became dominant in the places it entered. The Syrians, Egyptians, Persians, and others who became Muslim under Islamic conquest did not embrace Islam on their own accord; rather, they did so because of the dire choices they faced.[48]

Jihad and *dhimmitude* have never been renounced, and their barbarities are abundantly present in the modern era. In the twentieth century, exposure to the totalitarian ideological virus only strengthened the death cult that had been part of Islam from the beginning. During and immediately after World War I, Muslim Turks massacred more than one and a half million Armenian Christians. Later in the century, in Uganda, Idi Amin slaughtered some three hundred thousand of his own people, mostly Christians. He perpetrated these massacres only *after* he embraced Islam. In the twenty-first century, Indonesian Muslims of the Laskar Jihad have killed approximately ten thousand Christians. Laskar Jihad's leader, Jaffar Umar Thalib, has issued numerous statements making clear that his struggle is a religious one.[49] The horrifying genocide in the Darfur region of Sudan is a typical example of Islamic jihad and Arab racism. The Muslim government in Khartoum has killed more than two million black Christians and displaced four million since imposing Islamic law nationwide in 1993.[50] In Algeria, Muslim radicals terrorize the populace in the name of jihad; by 1999, they had killed some hundred thousand.[51]

It quickly becomes clear that Islamism is the greatest threat to freedom in the twenty-first century. We must now delve deeper in our analysis of this totalism that thirsts for mass death and suicide. We journey next into the pathology that serves as the foundation of most suicidal cultures and ideologies: misogyny and the fear and hatred of women's sexuality. No ideology exemplifies these suicidal ingredients better than Islamism.

To Hate a Woman

"Democracy is when a woman can talk of her lover without anyone killing her."

—Sheika Dr. Souad M. Al-Sabah,
widow of the founder of modern Kuwait

L*ike every other death cult*, Islamism wages a ferocious war on the individual. As we have seen in our examination of Stalin's Russia and Mao's China, a human being's pursuit of his own desires, passions, and pleasures threatens the very foundation of a totalitarian structure. For the totalism to survive, the reality we know as love must be annihilated.

Islamism wages war on unregulated love by instituting a vicious structure of gender apartheid. This structure, like Mao's totalitarian puritanism, includes an enforced collective mode of dress. In this case, men wear long, shapeless robes, while women, before venturing outside the home, don garments that cover their entire body, head, and face (except for their eyes in Saudi Arabia; under the Taliban, the whole face was veiled). By imposing this collective body covering, Islamism frustrates individual expression and mutual physical attraction.

As in Mao's China and Castro's Cuba, the hatred of personal sexual freedom extends to a ruthless persecution of homosexuals.[1] However, Islamism's war on private love derives most of its energy from a deep-seated misogyny. Women's empowerment, independence, and self-determination—especially the sexual variety—pose a threat to Islamism's very existence. Just as Nazism dehumanizes Jews, and communism scapegoats property owners, Islamism mandates the hatred of women.

Although the Islamic system of gender apartheid clearly adopts many ingredients from European totalitarianism, it is crucial to point out that Islamism also obviously derives many of its elements from its own unique Islamic sources. It is also vital to stress that the Islamic world must not all be tarred with the same brush. A wide diversity of ideas exists in different Muslim societies; especially in the matter of women's rights, some Muslim countries are more liberal, while others are far more backward. However, the liberal elements that exist in certain Muslim societies are not necessarily outgrowths of any accepted strains of Islam, but in fact represent a *relaxation* of Islamic principles. Cultural differences, in other words, depend on just how Islamic the societies in question are.[2]

In appreciating these realities, we may still hope, as noted in chapter nine, that moderate Muslims will have the power to reform their religion and culture. In the matter of misogyny, reformers face a huge task. Fatima Mernissi, a Moroccan sociologist, has shown how successive Muslim leaders manipulated Islamic texts to enforce male privileges; she argues that Muslims can reinterpret these teachings anew, in a way that brings rights to women *within* their religion.[3] Muslim feminist activist Irshad Manji has also argued optimistically that Muslims can renew their religion and allow it to empower women and to promote pluralism and diversity.[4] And indeed, reformers in Morocco and Indonesia have recently pushed through legislation that promotes gender equality on Islamic grounds, thus demonstrating that progressive change can come from *within* Islam.[5] However, certain fundamental Islamic teachings, rooted in the Koran and the Sunnah, cannot easily be transformed—for example, the mandate for men to beat their wives (Sura 4:34).

The reality remains that, as noted in chapter nine, it will be a huge task for Muslims to reverse fourteen hundred years of tradition and completely remake their religion. Aside from Morocco and Indonesia, there is, to date, no evidence that any large-scale feminist reform movement exists—or that the existing feminist reformers have any significant influence within the *ummah* (the nation of Islam) as a whole. A large percentage of Muslims revile and have threatened Irshad Manji and other Muslim feminists. Although they may have a following in private, as Manji says she does, it is risky for any co-religionist to support them in public. But reformers such as Manji are doing crucial work and, despite the heavy odds against them, they do possess the power to make a change. The West has a huge stake in their success and must support them in every battle.

The basic point is that Islamist misogyny derives from various ingredients within Islam itself. The notion that women are, by their very nature, inferior to men is the underpinning of the entire structure and derives its legitimacy from numerous traditional teachings.[6]

The belief in women's inferiority provides theological justification for violence against females from the very moment of their birth. Indeed, baby girls are simply not wanted in large segments of the Arab Middle East. When a father is asked how many children he has, he will give only the number of male children. One has to inquire specifically about daughters to find out how many offspring he really has. As David Pryce-Jones writes about Arab culture: "Boys are regarded from birth as capital investment...while girls are the fountainhead of shame, valued only because in due course they will develop into the producers of boys or of more capital."[7] Egyptian feminist author Nawal El Saadawi recalls her grandmother repeatedly telling her that she wished she had been born a boy.[8] And Souad, the Palestinian survivor of an attempted honor killing, recalls, "Every birth of a girl was like a burial in the family."[9] Indeed, within the blurred boundaries of Arab culture and militant Islam, women are seen as less worthy than cows and sheep—a fact that Souad's father never let his daughters forget.[10]

In such an environment of hate, the mother is always blamed for bringing a non-child (a girl) into the world—even though biologically it is the father's seed that determines the child's sex. Saadawi recalls a typical occurrence in her native Egypt in the event of a baby girl's birth:

As a child, I saw one of my paternal aunts being submitted to resounding slaps on her face because she had given birth to a third daughter rather than a male child, and I overheard her husband threatening her with divorce if she ever gave birth to a female child again instead of giving him a son. The father so hated this child that he used to insult his wife if she used to care for her, or even just feed her sufficiently. The baby had died before she had completed forty days of her life, and I do not know whether she died of neglect, or whether the mother smothered her to death in order to "have peace and give peace," as we say in our country.[11]

Upon first laying eyes on a newborn girl, the paternal grandmother in an Arab society traditionally sings, "Why did you come, girl, when we wished for a boy? Take the *zala* (jar) and fill it from the sea; may you fall into it and drown." And in fact baby girls are often killed and disposed of in many parts of the Arab world. The death rate for Arab girls is significantly higher than for Arab boys. In Egypt, for instance, among families with low levels of education, baby girls are twice as likely to die as their male counterparts.[12] Souad recalls that her mother suffocated nine of her own baby daughters, twice right in front of Souad.[13]

If a baby girl manages to elude her paternal grandmother's wish for her, she will very likely confront vicious maltreatment nonetheless. As she grows, her entire being—her sexuality in particular—poses a major threat to the social order. It is no coincidence that the Arabic word *fitna* has two meanings: a beautiful woman and social chaos.[14] As Fatima Mernissi notes, the "entire Muslim social structure can be seen as an attack on, and a defense against, the disruptive power of female sexuality."[15]

The will of Mohammed Atta, the 9/11 terrorist hijacker, eerily reflects this dark phenomenon. He sternly warned against women being present at his funeral—or at his grave at any later date. He also instructed that "He who washes my body around my genitals should wear gloves so that I am not touched there." Atta, obviously, was a troubled man. But far from being the testament of an alienated madman, his will revealed the deep-rooted hatred and fear of female sexuality that permeates Islamist-Arabic culture.

Fatna Sabbah has documented that the criteria on which women are judged in many Islamic societies are silence, immobility, and obedience. Women are supposed to dehumanize themselves in order to be tolerated. Males are taught to control desire (*shahwa*). Women are considered to be the incarnation of *shahwa*, which comes from the devil. The association of *shahwa*, the devil, and woman is rife throughout Islamic religious literature.[16] Indeed, the woman is seen, as Mernissi notes, as the "symbol of unreason and disorder," an "anti-divine force of nature and disciple of the devil."[17]

In this environment, the pathological notion arises that a man and a woman cannot be alone without the ominous threat of evil in their midst—i.e., without evil sex occurring. The threat of sin, guilt, and punishment looms large. A much-quoted proverb in the Islamic-Arab world asserts: "Whenever a man and a woman meet together, their third is always Satan."[18]

Where tribal Arab culture and militant Islam meet, a man is forbidden not only to touch any woman other than his wife and close relatives, but even to look at such a woman. Sex outside of marriage is known as *zina*—illicit copulation.[19] *Zina* is considered not only a sin, but a criminal offense punishable by public flogging for males and execution for females. Muslim society's dread of *jahiliya*—the time before Islam,[20] which Muslims see as a horrifying period of barbarism and ignorance permeated with female sexual freedom—compounds the fear of female sexuality.[21]

Therefore, many Muslim men develop a disdain for women because the latter are symbols of the formers' own lust. The men denigrate the object of their lust so as to diminish their own shame. In this dynamic of sexual repression and misogyny, love is reduced to violent domination, which becomes directly intertwined with terrorism against societies that allow women freedom, especially sexual freedom—as will be explored in chapter eleven.

The totalitarian puritanism that permeates this whole system entails—as in the communist paradigm—the demonization of private love. As Mernissi notes, "the breakdown of sexual segregation permits the emergence of what the Muslim order condemns as a deadly enemy of civilization: love between men and women in general, and between husband and wife in particular."[22] Allah, like the secular god in communist totalisms, cannot permit this: he demands *all* of his people's love. Deep interpersonal love is a great threat to the Islamist order: the values within a fulfilled marriage of equal rights and the pursuit of personal happiness will extend into the society. Islam, therefore, must destroy such love in order to maintain itself in power.

Toward this end, Islam enforces myriad structures to minimize the possibility of private love even among married couples. Marriage in the Islamic-Arab world is usually not based on love and free choice between the parties. Instead, heads of families arrange marriages for their children. In analyzing Arab society, David Pryce-Jones notes:

> Love comes to be valued not for itself but for its instrumentality. Arabs of both sexes pay a terrible price for this.... Group defense is inseparable from Arab sexuality. Far from being an absolute and incontestable value, love is careerist aggrandizement and simply that part of the money-favor nexus which takes place in the domestic arena.[23]

Islam teaches that the sexual act is dirty, and consequently surrounds it with rituals. The objective is to build a wall between the lovers themselves. In many segments of Islamic culture, a male must engage in various ceremonials and incantations so that the end result of his erection, which is looked upon with dread, is not the complete merging with the female force of evil and unreason. The man must constantly keep Allah in his thoughts during intercourse. At the moment of ejaculation, when the union of the lovers reaches its full potential, the male is supposed to pronounce praise to Allah.[24]

Islam also uses two legal devices to weaken the dangers that a couple's love poses: polygamy and repudiation (whereby a husband can divorce his wife by simply pronouncing certain words). By allowing the Muslim man to take many wives, Islam minimizes the ability of a couple to nurture a deep emotional connection. And by making it extremely simple for the husband to shatter the marital bond, Islam keeps couples in a state of fear, uncertainty, and disorder.[25]

The role of the mother-in-law in Muslim society, meanwhile, undermines any remaining possibility of personal intimacy between husband and wife. In countries such as Morocco, the bridegroom's mother often lives with the new couple in the early years of their marriage. This creates a situation in which the son lavishes attention and love upon his mother while neglecting his wife, with whom privacy is rendered almost impossible. As Mernissi writes:

> In a traditional setting the mother's involvement with her son is not limited to material things. It goes so far as to prevent his being alone with his wife. A husband and wife cannot be together during the day without being conspicuously anti-social. The social space in a family dwelling is centred on one local room, *al-bit alkbir* (the big room). It is here that everything happens and that everyone is encouraged to spend most of their time. Individual privacy is vehemently discouraged.... The anti-privacy structure of Moroccan society facilitates—almost requires—the mother-in-law's intervention in her son's physical intimacy with his wife.[26]

Because of these circumstances, there is, as Saadawi notes, "rarely any genuine feeling between the couple."[27]

Islam's revulsion toward Valentine's Day further exemplifies its hatred of personal love. Just as the hard Left's totalitarian puritanism abhors Valentine's Day, as we saw in chapter two, so too Islam hates the idea of a day marked to celebrate personal love: in both cases, such a day distracts citizens from the priority of submission to the higher authority. It is no surprise that the Left and Islamism come together on this issue; indeed, it perfectly illuminates what brings these two ideologies together and sparks their romance.

The Muslim world reacts violently on each and every Valentine's Day. On February 10, 2006, for instance, activists of the radical Kashmiri Islamic group *Dukhtaran-e-Millat* (Daughters

121

of the Community) went on a rampage in Srinagar, the main city of the Indian portion of Kashmir. Some two dozen black-veiled Muslim women stormed gift and stationery shops, burning Valentine's Day cards and posters showing couples together.[28]

Of course, they were just following Islamic tradition. As Daniel Pipes has reported, the Saudi regime takes a firm stand against celebration of the day, and the Saudi religious police monitor stores selling roses and other gifts. They have even arrested women for wearing red on that day. The Iranian despotism, meanwhile, has ordered shops to remove heart and flower decorations and images of couples embracing.[29] In Pakistan, the student wing of the fundamentalist Islamic party Jamaat-e-Islami has called for a ban on Valentine's Day celebrations. Khalid Waqas Chamkani, a leader in the party, calls it a "shameful day."[30]

Valentine's Day is a "shameful day" for these Muslims because female sexuality and the female herself are considered shameful. And this in turn explains why many men in Muslim culture prefer a female's anus over her vagina for sexual intercourse. As Peter Raddatz notes:

> Being legitimized religiously, male dominance assumes godlike qualities and condemns not only women as an animal-like existence but also their sexual organ as a despicable opening far below the biological "honor" of man. Therefore, the anus is preferred to the vagina to an extent that has raised the attention of UN institutions and secular Muslim scientists. Anal intercourse appears as an unusually common practice and corresponding hospital reports often indicate brutal extremes in which terrible injuries have been inflicted in this area. This puts more light, clearly, on the alleged rejection of homosexuality in Islam.[31]

Indeed, the hatred of female sexuality is directly connected to the widespread practice of homosexuality in this culture, which, as we shall see in chapter eleven, is simultaneously demonized and denied.

In the context of this fear and hatred of private love and female sexuality, the guardians of purity inflict numerous punishments to keep women confined in slavery. One of the most frightening manifestations of this hatred of women is also the most direct assault on their sexuality. In its effort to deny women even the possibility of personal happiness and sexual satisfaction, the law of men mandates that at the age of seven or eight—before their menstrual periods begin—their sexuality be amputated.[32] This is the so-called "female circumcision," more accurately described as female genital mutilation (FGM), based on the notion that a girl's genital area is dirty and unacceptable.[33] An uncircumcised girl is called *nigsa* (unclean); the only way she can become non-*nigsa* is to have part of her external genitals sliced off. How much is amputated varies among cultures. In Egypt only the clitoris is amputated; in countries like Sudan the woman-haters are not so kind. In a savagery called infibulation, the girl's external genital organs are completely removed: the clitoris, the two major outer lips (*labia majora*) and the two minor inner lips (*labia minora*).[34] In Sudan, the term used for this is *tahur*—which means "cleansing" or "purification."

FGM predates Islam and is not exclusively Muslim; many non-Islamic parts of Africa whose cultural traditions also dehumanize women practice FGM. The fact remains, however, that Muslims are the principal religious group that practices this sexual violence against women. In Egypt, for instance, 97 percent of girls are circumcised. Saadawi relates how, at the age of six, she was assaulted with FGM at the hands of strangers and how she saw her mother "right in the midst of these strangers, talking to them and smiling at them, as though they had not participated in slaughtering her daughter just a few moments ago."[35]

More than 130 million women living today have suffered through this horrifying practice, and more than two million girls face assault by it each year: that is more than five thousand girls every day. Many girls lose their lives during FGM, which is often done with broken glass. Most victims suffer from chronic infection and pain for the rest of their lives. The mutilation robs women of their ability to enjoy the fullness of their sexuality. Approximately 75 percent of women cannot achieve orgasm without clitoral stimulation; thus the possibility of sexual satisfaction has been obliterated for millions of women in the Muslim-Arab world.

Islamists will not easily abandon this practice. The Egyptian government, for example, banned FGM in 1996, but an Egyptian court overturned the ban in July 1997. And militants can point to traditional teachings that sanction FGM. Islamic tradition, for instance, records the Prophet Muhammad emphasizing that circumcising girls is "a preservation of honor for women."[36] A legal manual endorsed by Al-Azhar University of Cairo, which is the oldest and most prestigious university in the Islamic world, states that circumcision is obligatory for both boys and girls.[37]

Many Islamic clerics and educators do all they can to keep FGM in place. Egyptian Sheikh Mustafa Al-Azhari has led the way by arguing, among other things, that the attempt to stop female circumcision is a Western conspiracy designed to spread promiscuity among Muslims and, therefore, to cause the downfall of Islam. For him, the Egyptian media's attempt to stop female circumcision is a "crime."[38] A surgical specialist at Al-Azhar University, Dr. Muhammad Rif'at Al-Bawwab, agrees, arguing that the pleasure that women derive from the clitoris is unnatural, abnormal, and leads to moral degradation.[39] Sheikh Muhammad Sayyid Tantawi, the grand sheik of Al-Azhar—who is, according to a BBC report, "the highest spiritual authority for nearly a billion Sunni Muslims"—considers FGM "a laudable practice that [does] honor to women."[40]

Hope remains, of course, that Muslim reformers can organize and use their power to purge their societies of this horrific practice. Some sheikhs, such as Al-Azhar's Mahmoud Shaltout, argue that there is nothing religious or moral about FGM.[41] These people can cite the fact that the Prophet Muhammad did not have his own daughters circumcised. Muhammad has also been recorded as declaring that girls should be treated gently during circumcision and that it should not be done severely.[42] "Non-severe" mutilation is still mutilation, of course. But reformers can work with this material to move away from the savage pathology of practices such as infibulation. Thankfully, FGM is rare in some Muslim countries—notably Jordan, Syria, and Turkey.

Unfortunately, the sexual mutilation of women is in the interests of those who control the structure of gender apartheid in

Arab tribal culture and militant Islam. Keeping FGM legitimized and institutionalized is one of the most effective means to keep women subjugated and caged.

Many supporters of FGM in the West try to excuse this torture by arguing that it is usually carried out by women. But the women have no choice but to perpetuate this barbaric practice: if their daughters are not circumcised, they will be considered ineligible for marriage. Moreover, it appears that in many cases the victims of gender apartheid have internalized self-hate and are reenacting the horrors done to them on females over whom they have power (i.e., their own daughters). Overall, the key issue here is that those who try to excuse this practice by arguing that it is not Islamic or that it is carried out by women usually do absolutely nothing to defend the victims—and future victims.

At the foundation of FGM is an obsession with keeping girls virgins until marriage. The assumption is that amputating the clitoris will lessen the woman's sexual desire and thereby reduce the chances that she will have sexual intercourse until she has a husband who wants to have it.

Virginity is so morbidly tied to honor in this culture that, as Saadawi notes, a girl's hymen is considered much more valuable than any external body part, such as an eye, an ear, or a leg. In fact, "if a girl lost her life, it would be considered less catastrophic than if she lost her hymen."[43] In Islamic-Arab societies, a girl must bleed on her wedding night. If she does not, it is concluded that she was not a virgin and she suffers great shame and punishment—often death. Since roughly 30 percent of girls do not bleed during their first sexual act, one can only imagine the number of injustices perpetrated against girls who were indeed virgins until their wedding night.[44]

At about the same time as their sexual mutilation, young girls are also hidden from sight, covered up with veils. Many defenders of this tradition argue that Muslim women choose of their own accord to wear the veil, but in many Islamic societies women have absolutely no choice. Some who have dared to venture out without the veil have suffered horrifying consequences: gang-rape, mutilation, killing, being doused with gasoline, having acid thrown in their face, as has occurred in Iran and Saudi Arabia. The problem, once again, is that the clerics who enforce these rules can point to texts that show the Prophet commanding his wives to wear the veil.[45]

Even a woman who has not deliberately eschewed the veil can be made to pay. In Mecca in 2002, religious police, the *mutaween*, pushed fifteen fleeing female students back into their burning school because they were not properly veiled. All fifteen girls died.[46]

In Jordan, there is a law stipulating that a murderer must be punished by years in prison. But next to this law are two small articles, 97 and 98, specifying that judges will be lenient with those found guilty of "honor crimes."[47] The penalty is reduced to anywhere from six months to two years in prison, and the condemned almost never serve their whole sentences. An additional issue here is that a woman doesn't even have to engage in consensual sex outside marriage to get her death sentence. She could be punished by death for being raped or for people saying she was raped. In many cases, she need only look in the eyes of a male outside her family or be seen talking to one—or have someone say that she talked to one; women who dare to be seen unveiled in public are easy targets for such accusations.

The accused woman is considered a *charmuta*—a whore. She will have to die because her blood is deemed the only substance capable of washing away her family's and her community's shame. And there will be no hearing, no lawyer, and no defense for her. The male with whom she associated (in reality or in someone's imagination) is always exonerated. And the family member who kills or maims her may, as stated above, receive a token punishment, but he will be respected in the community for what is considered a noble and necessary deed. This tragic phenomenon is all too common. According to the Human Rights Commission of Pakistan, for instance, on average two women a day are slain in Pakistan alone so that "family honor" can be restored.[48]

Postmortems conducted on victims of honor killings often prove that the girl in question was a virgin. Many instances occur of a father killing his daughter after her wedding night because the new husband claims she was not a virgin, only to have the medical exam reveal that the husband was mistaken or lying. Not infrequently, it turns out the husband lied to protect himself from embarrassment about his own impotence.

In all of these circumstances, forced marriage looms front and center. With her genitals mutilated and her body and face veiled in public, and having been brought up illiterate, a young woman has no higher aspiration than for a brutal marriage. And this marriage might well be to a cousin, which leads to a high incidence of severely handicapped children.

Throughout this process, constant beatings keep girls and women in line. Once again, cultural and religious paradigms legitimize the abuse. The Koran, for instance, teaches that a woman must obey the male members of her family, especially her father and her husband, and that if she shows even the slightest hint of disobedience, then they have not only a right but an obligation to beat her.[49]

A telling cross-cultural incident occurred when Spanish Muslim cleric Mohamed Kamal Mustafa wrote his book *Women in Islam*, in which he gave men specific instructions on how to beat their wives. To Mustafa's great surprise, a Spanish court prosecuted him and sentenced him to fifteen months in jail. His confusion about being charged was understandable. As his defense correctly argued, he was only repeating and interpreting passages from Islam's religious texts (such as Sura 4:34). Mustafa, incidentally, was somewhat liberal, for he stressed that the beating should not inflict permanent damage. He writes: "The blows should be concentrated on the hands and feet using a rod that is thin and light so that it does not leave scars or bruises on the body."[50] In the end, Mustafa did not serve any time, since Spanish law suspends sentences of less than two years for first offenses.

Saudi instructional TV programs on wife beating are especially illuminating. Jasem Muhammad Al-Mutawah, an "expert" on Islamic family matters, hosts *Disciplining Wives and Children*, on Iqraa TV. In one show, he discussed how to discipline a wife when she is disobedient. Picking up several different-sized rods, he explained how a husband should use each one. At the end of the program, he boasted how Islam has solved a serious psychiatric problem in marriages: when the husband is a sadist and the wife is a masochist, they are able to soothe each other's neuroses and become satisfied through a beating sanctioned by the Koran.[51] It becomes understandable, therefore, that the Pakistan Institute of Medical Sciences estimated that over 90 percent of Pakistani wives had been struck, beaten, or sexually abused for offenses such as cooking an unsatisfactory meal.[52]

As noted earlier, it is not just wives and mothers, but all females who suffer this abuse. Souad tells how her father and brother routinely beat her and her sisters:

> That is what it was like in our village. It was the law of men. The girls and women were certainly beaten every day in the other houses, too. You could hear the crying. It was not unusual to be beaten, to have your hair shaved off and be tied to a stable gate. There was no other way of living.[53]

Wife beating and abuse of women is known to some degree in all cultures. The difference is that in the United States, for example, such conduct is illegal and punishable through the courts, whereas in Islamic societies the institutions and laws themselves sanction—even promote—the beating of a wife.

The institution of polygamy is also sanctioned in the religious/cultural paradigm. In many areas of the Islamic world, a man is allowed to marry four wives at a time.[54] The Prophet Muhammad established the precedent and led by example, taking more than nine wives himself. A man can also go through serial marriages, since he is allowed to dissolve a marriage unilaterally at any time by simply saying to his wife: "You are repudiated." The woman who is repudiated suffers great shame and is ostracized from her community.

Within this system, the society sees the individual woman as entirely expendable. Hence the misogyny in which many Muslim boys grow up. They have all kinds of siblings born of different women, which gives them the idea that none of these women—including their own mother—was good enough to be cherished alone. The boys internalize this misogyny, which leads in turn to self-hate, since they come from their mothers. These feelings, as will be discussed more fully in chapter eleven, lead many Muslim men to psychologically abandon their mothers. This situation, as psychoanalyst and Arabist Nancy Kobrin has demonstrated, becomes directly connected to their urge for terror and suicide.[55]

The promise of the *houris* (eternal virgins with whom the Muslim warrior is purportedly rewarded for dying in holy war against nonbelievers) compounds the expendability of women. To add to this culture of misogyny, even the individual *houri* herself is expendable and not sacred or special in any way. As Fatna Sabbah notes, she "has no spiritual dimension; she is a thing because she has neither will nor any possibility of development.... [She] has no intellect; she does not think. She is a thing that awaits consumption."[56]

The hatred of women is directly correlated with another aspect of the Islamist death cult. Women become mandatory victims in a culture whose lust for death necessitates scorn and loathing for the gender that bestows life. Western values, therefore, pose a severe danger to the death cult, since they threaten to liberate all the women in the world. In the age of globalization, mass communication, and the Internet, the West's values are spreading with lightning quickness. The death cult's response takes two forms: a war fought within the culture to eradicate the essence of what is female within its own women, and a jihad against free nations to crush the expansion of liberty and pluralism.

The war on terror, therefore, cannot be crystallized any more powerfully than with this formula: one side allows human freedom, including its sexual component, and accepts all the risks and costs that come with such freedom; the other side lusts for the incineration of every element of human desire, yearning for a sterilized utopia where human beings will be purged of what and who they are.

The hatred of women in the Islamic world has fertilized the soil in which terrorism and the new death cult have grown. In the next chapter, we show exactly how this deadly process occurs.

CHAPTER ELEVEN

The Seeds of Death

"Allah did not create man so that he could have fun."

—Ayatollah Khomeini

No *society can be truly modern,* civilized, or democratic if its women are caged and treated as second-class citizens. Because of the cruel system of gender apartheid in the (overlapping) Islamic and Arab worlds, a culture of failure has manifested itself in virtually every facet of these societies, from the political to the economic to the social. As David Pryce-Jones observes:

> In the years of independence, the Arabs have so far made no inventions or discoveries in the sciences or the arts, no contribution to medicine or philosophy. Among those millions of quick and gifted people of individualistic outlook, and heirs to one of the world's civilizations, hardly a single Arab has earned an international reputation except as the beneficiary of his country's politics or his country's oil extraction.[1]

Because of this failure, the males in this culture experience an agonizing sense of humiliation that leads, in turn, to violent rage. Since most of these men cannot imagine that their powerlessness stems from their culture's misogyny (along with other dysfunctional ingredients), they rationalize it as the result of the threat of freedom *from without and within.* The solution for

Islamists thus lies in eradicating the threat of freedom from within their own culture, and destroying the examples of success and freedom that surround it (i.e., the West in general and America and Israel in particular).

The concept of humiliation plays a key role in Islamist terror. Almost every statement issued by Islamist terrorists echoes the theme of humiliation—as well as its twin sisters, shame and disgrace. Osama bin Laden's videotape of October 7, 2001, the first that was released after 9/11, is emblematic of this: he complained about the "eighty years of humiliation and disgrace" that the Islamic world had endured.[2]

Bin Laden's statement was an obvious reference to the grave offense committed by the secular Turkish leader Kemal Atatürk, who dared in the 1920s to separate religion from state *within* the Islamic world. Atatürk did this primarily by abolishing the *caliphate*, the institution governing, at least in theory, the *ummah*. The *caliphate* represented the line of Sunni Muslim leaders dating back to the death of Muhammad in 632.[3] In ending this Islamic political reign, Atatürk brought Turkey into the modern age, establishing it as a secular state. It is no surprise that Sayyid Qutb spent an enormous amount of time and energy fulminating against Atatürk. Atatürk's act was tantamount to a declaration of war.

In much of this culture, modernization is seen not only as an enemy; worse still, it represents "inherent degradation." As Pryce-Jones explains, the "more the Arabs modernize, the less Arab they become: the more they assert themselves as Arabs, the less they truly modernize. Definitions of progress, in the circumstances, are neither continuous nor coherent."[4] In what becomes a vicious circle, Arab culture becomes all the more backward in the face of modernity with all its successes.

This dysfunctionality is further compounded by the fact that this culture rejects human reason and individual responsibility as important values. Like fascism and communism, Islamism sublimates the individual into the collective whole, making it virtually impossible for individuals to take any real action to fix a societal problem. Sayyid Abul A'la Maududi, a leading twentieth century Islamic thinker and activist, gave voice to this deep cultural neurosis in his writings:

> No one has the right to become a self-appointed ruler of men and issue orders and prohibitions on his own volition and authority. To acknowledge the personal authority of a human being as the source of commands and prohibitions is tantamount to admitting him as the sharer in the Powers and Authority of God. And this is the root of all evils in the universe.[5]

The individual who lives within an established Islamic system must always be subservient. His duty and obligation are simply to carry out its mandate. To attempt to change or reform this system is perceived as blasphemous.

In contrast, Western civilization—starting from its roots in the Hellenic tradition—possesses a strong counter to this totalitarian tendency. As literary scholar M. H. Abrams argues, the concept developed particularly in the eighteenth century that the human being is, at his best, an artist whose powers are modeled upon those of the divine creator himself.[6] This concept is the basis for humanism and for the eventual rise of liberal, democratic values all through the West. From this perspective, precisely because the individual has within him a divine power, his creative activity is not blasphemous, but is rather a proper fulfillment of his own nature.

But this developed sense of himself that the infidel displays further inflames the Islamist. Like bin Laden, Ayatollah Khomeini was preoccupied with the themes of humiliation and disgrace—and blaming the "Great Satan" for them. In this way, as Pryce-Jones notes, Khomeini could take the self-pity resulting from a bankrupt culture and convert it into "the blind but absolving rage of the helpless."[7]

The inhabitants of this culture suffer an excruciating dissonance: while convinced that their values and way of life are superior to those of the West, they must witness, in every facet of human existence, a contrary reality. The superiority of the West's medical industry is just one of myriad examples. Pryce-Jones writes:

It remains noticeable that the rulers of Saudi Arabia and the Gulf states, and their relations and tens of thousands of their citizens, prefer to place themselves in the hands of doctors in the West; that Nasser, seriously ill, chose to be treated in the Soviet Union; that even Ayatollah Khomeini has sent members of his family and his entourage to the United States to be cured by the doctors of what he likes to call "the Great Satan."[8]

Theodore Dalrymple touches on this phenomenon in his observations regarding the ambivalent lives of the terrorists who perpetrated the London suicide bombings in 2005:

[T]hey led highly Westernized lives, availing themselves of all the products of Western ingenuity to which Muslims have contributed nothing for centuries. It is, in fact, literally impossible for modern Muslims to expunge the West from their lives: it enters the fabric of their existence at every turn. Usama bin Ladin himself is utterly dependent upon the West for his weaponry, his communications, his travel, and his funds. He speaks of the West's having stolen Arabian oil, but of what use would oil have been to the Arabs if it had remained under their sands, as it would have done without the intervention of the West? Without the West, what fortune would bin Ladin's family have made from what construction in Saudi Arabia?[9]

Unable to accept that Westernization is the only way out of their failure and humiliation, Islamists convince themselves that Westernization is actually the root of the problem. They conclude that they must resurrect the world of Islam as it existed in the seventh century, during Muhammad's time—and then continue violent jihad until the whole earth is ruled by Islamic law, bringing about paradise on earth. This, again, is the common denominator between the Left and Islamism: Ground Zero must be engendered everywhere so that the earthly paradise can be built on its ashes.

As we explore the Islamist urge for destruction, the evidence emerges that generalized feelings of impotence in the face of the infidel's greater power are exacerbated by specifically sexual feelings of emasculation. Because of the prevailing totalitarian puritanism and the hatred of women and their sexuality, the Muslim Arab male is consumed with feelings of sexual frustration, confusion, and inadequacy. It is crucial to examine the dynamics of this phenomenon, since they are directly related to the spawning of the terror culture.

To begin with, in a structure in which a woman has no sexual freedom, the husband will never know whether he himself would have been the woman's real choice. He will also never truly know if he is better as a lover than other men could have been—or could be—to his wife. Moreover, if the wife is circumcised, she is unable to experience a full measure of satisfaction, further increasing the husband's insecurity. And when he is forced to confront the existence of sexually fulfilled women in the West, his feelings of self-doubt and inadequacy grow even stronger.

John Racy, a psychiatrist with much experience in Arab societies, has touched on many of these themes. He notes how the culture "promotes in men and women a rising and threatening sense of inadequacy." Impotence and related problems, he confirms, are common reasons for men seeking psychiatric help.[10] As Pryce-Jones notes, the Arab man becomes obsessed with proving his sexual superiority.[11] This obsession finds its expression by targeting the Western infidel. To put it starkly: By not veiling its own women and by giving them personal and sexual freedom, the West infuriates Islamists, leading them ultimately to unleash terror in a furious attempt to keep their own culture free of Western influences.

The trauma of the sexual abuse many Muslim men suffer in childhood reinforces their feelings of emasculation. And the hatred of females is part and parcel of this vicious circle. Indeed, in all environments where men are segregated from women, there is an increase in homosexual behavior and in the sexual abuse of boys by older males. Even though, in the Islamic world, homosexuality is strictly prohibited and punishable by imprisonment and/or death, having sex with boys or effeminate men is a social norm. Males serve as available substitutes for unavailable women. A man who does the penetrating is not considered to be homosexual or emasculated any more than if he had sex with his wife, while a man who is penetrated is emasculated. A boy who is penetrated, however, is not seen as emasculated since he is not yet considered to be a man.[12] Overall, penetration is a manifestation of male power, conferring a status of hyper-masculinity. An unmarried man who has sex with boys is simply doing what men do.[13] As the historian Bruce Dunne has demonstrated, sex in Islamic societies is not about mutuality between partners, but about the adult male's achievement of pleasure through violent domination.[14]

While secrecy and taboo surround the phenomenon of homosexual behavior, some Arabs have dared to discuss it. Walid Shoebat, a former Palestinian terrorist, has openly related the abuse of young boys in Palestinian Muslim society; he himself witnessed a line of shepherd boys waiting for their turn to sodomize a five-year-old they had caught while he was on a hiking trip.[15] Amnesty International, meanwhile, reports that Afghan warlords routinely sodomize young boys and film the orgies.[16] (The sexual abuse of young girls is also widespread in this environment, a crime for which the perpetrators are not punished.)[17]

While she was in Afghanistan in 1961, author Phyllis Chesler saw homosexuals roaming the streets, holding hands in broad daylight and gazing into each other's eyes. "One of the pair," she writes, "might sport a flower behind his ear; another might be wearing lipstick or have rouged cheeks." At the same time, Chesler observed that everyone, including her husband, was in denial about this common social reality, refusing to admit that it was homosexuality.[18]

A deafening silence surrounds this mass cultural pathology. The denial forces the victims into invisibility. Psychologically scarred by the violation of their manliness, many Arab boys spend the rest of their lives trying to recapture it. The impossible problem is that with women out of touch—indeed out of sight—until marriage, males experience premarital sex only in the context of being with other males. And this mostly means males victimizing younger males—just the way they were victimized.

In these dysfunctional and terror-ridden circumstances, the idea of love is completely absent from men's understanding of sexuality. It is reduced to a form of prison sex: hurting others with violence. As noted in chapter ten, the culture does everything it can to prevent the development of harmony, affection, or equality between men and women. And in relationships between men, affection, solidarity, and empathy are left out of the picture, as these would threaten the hyper-masculine order.[19]

It is no surprise that many men in these cultures find their only avenue for gratification in the act of humiliating the foreign "enemy" — or that, when they get the chance, Islamic terrorists engage in sexual mutilation of their victims. Psychiatrist David Gutmann notes this in the Israeli context:

> The Israelis perform in this Arab psychodrama of gender as a potent, destabilizing threat: to begin with, as a people they broke out of the deprecated but tolerated status of *dhimmi*—a kind of submissive "woman"—to the "masculine" status of pioneer, rebel, warrior and nation builder. In retaliation, in their wars and Intifadas the Arabs strive to castrate the uppity masculinizing Jew— and this project is carried out quite literally on the battlefield, where the bodies of fallen Jews have been mutilated in the most obscene ways.[20]

Terrorism is thus a direct outgrowth of the Islamist's rationalization that he is purifying himself when he engages in violence against *the other*. He believes that jihad against the enemy and violence against women disinfects him from the poison he feels has invaded him. Thus, just as the Islamist militant mutilates the foreign enemy on the battlefield after he has killed him—and just as his society routinely mutilates Muslim girls with FGM—so too Muslims who engage in rape almost always mutilate their victims, sexually disfiguring them in crude and horrifying ways. Typical is the *pogrom* that three hundred Muslim men waged against thirty-nine women in Hassi Messaoud, a town in eastern Algeria, in July 2001. The women had been imported from another province of Algeria to work as cleaning personnel and secretaries for foreign oil companies. In

137

his sermon one Friday, Imam Amar Taleb called them "immoral" and instructed his male congregants to launch a "jihad against Evil." This jihad consisted of the violent torture, gang rape, and murder of these poor women—and the violence invariably included the mutilation of their genitalia.[21]

In this pathological dynamic, the perpetrator believes his violence against the female not only will purify him, but will also save his social group from similar infection. The "impure" must be purged in order to bring purity to the environment. Thus outsiders must be attacked by sexual mutilation—especially when the female insiders have all been "purified" by FGM. Pryce-Jones recounts a revealing story:

> Peroncel-Hugoz tells of an Egyptian villager who married a French wife and then felt that her introduction into his village would create shames with which he could not cope. Eventually his wife persuaded him otherwise, and over a period of time, she succeeded in making friends with the local women. One day, these village women noticed her body hair and overpowered her in order to discover if she was "clean." They thought it was a kindness to make her "clean" by circumcising her on the spot, and she died as a result.[22]

The "shame" with which this Egyptian villager could not cope was that this woman had not been dehumanized; she still had the potential of experiencing sexual pleasure. This was a dangerous threat. The mutilated women around her had internalized their culture's message to such a degree that they needed to take steps to disinfect the foreign agent. Her death was better than her life, for her blood purified the environment. Also, as noted in chapter ten, Muslim women often re-enact the violence done to them by doing it to a female over whom they have power (whether their own daughters or a lone French woman).

Many Muslims have transported this violence into non-Muslim countries to which they have emigrated. Muslim newcomers are significantly overrepresented among convicted rapists and rape suspects in nations such as Australia, the Netherlands, Sweden, Norway, and Denmark.[23] These immigrants are doing in their new societies what they learned back home. In some rural areas of Pakistan, for example, gang rape is officially sanctioned as a way of keeping women in their place.

This is a natural outgrowth of Islamic teaching. The Koran permits Muslim men to enslave—and to have sexual relations with—the women of unbelievers captured as the spoils of war.[24] The Islamic legal manual cited earlier, *Umdat al-Salik*, which embodies Sunni orthodoxy, affirms that Muslims can enslave infidel women and make them concubines.

To compound this pathology, a notion has developed within Islam that a woman who does not veil herself is responsible for any harm done to her. In the mental gymnastics that sustain gender apartheid, the unveiled woman must be sexually punished for violating the modesty code. When the mufti in Copenhagen, Shahid Mehdi, publicly declared in 2004 that women who refuse to wear headscarves are "asking for rape,"[25] he was merely repeating a popular theme among Muslim clerics.

In the Netherlands, there are women who bear the horrible scar known as "smiley," whereby one side of the face is cut up from mouth to ear, a war mark left by Muslim rapists as a warning to other women who don't veil themselves. In France, gang rape as punishment for non-veiling even has a word to describe it: *tournante* (take your turn). In areas where Muslims form the majority (e.g., Courneuve, a suburb of Paris), even non-Muslim women feel pressured to veil themselves for fear of being raped.

Overall, the main theme is crystal clear: the Muslim woman who does not abide by the rules of the group is an enemy—and enemies must be punished. And no punishment is considered too barbaric for those outside the Muslim clan. As the French sociologist Juliette Minces has noted, "Even more than an Arab woman, a Western woman is seen as potential prey."[26] Once again, purification is achieved through violence.

As our analysis deepens in exploring how misogyny spawns terror in this culture, we come to the reality that the hatred of earthly desire leads to a rejection of all earthly joy and cheer. As we saw in chapter two in the case of communists and leftist believers, the celebration of life on this earth is furiously rejected. This is a crucial component in the Left's love affair with the death cult.

Sayyid Qutb serves as a perfect example of Islamism's rejection of the joyous celebration of *this* world and *this* life. In his work *Milestones*, this godfather of Islamism demonizes the pursuit of individual interests and sensual pleasures—above all sexual pleasure—and of personal happiness and fulfillment. The word "desire" reverberates through *Milestones* as a diabolical entity.[27]

America is the main target of Qutb's fury. He lived in Colorado from 1948 to 1950, and Americans' interest in having "a good time" and "fun" enraged him. He despised all the comforts of modern American life. A dance he witnessed after a church service particularly repulsed him. He writes with horror: "The dancing intensified.... The hall swarmed with legs.... Arms circled arms, lips met lips, chests met chests, and the atmosphere was full of love."[28] Here we see totalitarian puritanism as well as the totalitarian craving to reject the reality of personal love.

Qutb also reviled something that most totalist ideologies despise: music. Like Lenin, he deemed music a distraction from the raging hatred necessary for destruction. He was stunned when the pastor himself dimmed the lights at the church dance, creating "a romantic, dreamy effect," and played a popular record of the time: "Baby, It's Cold Outside."[29] Qutb hated this song, just as he hated all American popular music. "Jazz is the favourite music," he writes. "It is a type of music invented by Blacks to please their primitive tendencies and desire for noise."

The rejection of this form of creative expression goes back to the beginning of Islam. *Umdat al-Salik*, the Islamic legal manual, quotes Muhammad:

> Allah Mighty and Majestic sent me as a guidance and mercy to believers and commanded me to do away with musical instruments, flutes, strings, crucifixes, and the affair of the pre-Islamic period of ignorance.
>
> On the Day of Resurrection, Allah will pour molten lead into the ears of whoever sits listening to a songstress. Song makes hypocrisy grow in the heart as water does herbage.

140

> "This community will experience the swallowing up of some people by the earth, metamorphosis of some into animals, and being rained upon with stones." Someone asked, "When will this be, O Messenger of Allah?" and he said, "When songstresses and musical instruments appear and wine is held to be lawful."

> There will be peoples of my community who will hold fornication, silk, wine, and musical instruments to be lawful.[30]

Throughout Muslim history, various branches of Islam have tried to eradicate music. The reforming Mughal emperor Muhyi al Din Aurangzeb (reigned 1658-1707) attempted to purify his land (which included most of the Indian subcontinent, plus part of Afghanistan) by banning music there. In our own day, Laskar Jihad, the extremist Islamic group in Indonesia, considers music "a distraction from God." In the Malaysian state of Kelantan, the government—controlled by Islamic fundamentalists—has banned singing, dancing, and even the ringing of church bells, since these things could lead to "immoral activities."[31] The Taliban illegalized music completely in Afghanistan, and Ayatollah Khomeini banned most music from Iranian radio and television. In Khomeini's mind, music was "treason,"[32] because, as he told Italian journalist Oriana Fallaci, it involves "pleasure and ecstasy, similar to drugs."[33] Khomeini's rejection of music—like Qutb's and indeed the Prophet Muhammad's—was directly connected to his revulsion at any form of cheer or joy in human life. He explained:

> Allah did not create man so that he could have fun. The aim of creation was for mankind to be put to the test through hardship and prayer. An Islamic regime must be serious in every field. There are no jokes in Islam. There is no humor in Islam. There is no fun in Islam. There can be no fun and joy in whatever is serious.[34]

A comedy club could never exist in this environment; even laughter is discouraged—and is actually forbidden for women, and especially young girls. Nawal El Saadaw remembers that, growing up in Egypt, "If I laughed, I was expected to keep my voice so low that people could hardly hear me, or better, confine myself to smiling timidly."[35] When Souad, the Palestinian survivor of an attempted honor killing, was flown to Switzerland, she was shocked to find females dressing as they wished, smiling and laughing without being punished, and having people actually say "Thank you" to her—which had not happened once her entire life.[36]

The late American journalist Steven Vincent, a warrior for the rights of women under Islam,[37] made a careful study of these phenomena during trips he made, at great peril to himself, to Iraq. In his Iraq memoir, he noted that, at one point, he was sitting by the swimming pool at the Al-Hamra Hotel in Baghdad, where Western journalists stay. He heard two American women laughing, and a "chill" shot right through him. Their laughter made him realize that he had not heard a woman laugh in Iraq, "not in a free and unguarded manner, at any rate." That laughter, he says, was music to his ears, and at that moment, he reflects, "I became a feminist."[38]

In an interview I conducted with Vincent, I asked him for his thoughts on Islam's hatred of women's laughter. He replied:

> Remember Umberto Eco's *The Name of the Rose*? The murders of the monks in the English monastery were part of an attempt by religious despots to conceal the existence of Aristotle's lost treatise on Comedy. They knew that laughter is uncontrollable, subversive—especially to the clerical mindset. This is especially true in Islam—which demonstrates no sense of humor whatsoever. Combine the seditious nature of laughter with the equally dangerous—to the patriarchal tyrant—power of femininity and you have a force that can sweep away the kings of the earth.

> I have this fantasy that fills me with particular joy. I think of some cranky bearded cleric—say, Moqtada al-Sadr—spouting the usual anti-American, anti-Semitic bilge when suddenly the women in his mosque laugh. Imagine that moment! All that Islamofascist hatred and resentment and grandiosity washed away in a torrent of feminine amusement and ridicule. How could the cleric's hold over the imaginations, spirits, and desires of his flock withstand the charisma of feminine laughter? Add in the even more volatile force of sexual freedom and you would reduce 90 percent of Islam's *ulema* [legal scholars] to

pathetic old men in back-street mosques, preaching their
misogynistic claptrap to ever-dwindling congregations.
And no better fate could befall them.[39]

Vincent's shrewd and profound analysis crystallizes perfectly
why female laughter poses such a threat to Islamism and the
Arab tribal culture.

The hatred of joy and laughter is also connected to the dearth
of toys and games for children in the Muslim-Arab world. Pryce-
Jones notes:

> There appears never to have been any such thing as an
> Arab toy or games for children, in the sense that Western
> children have had a ball or a hoop, a shuttlecock or board
> games. To this day, toys and games and bicycles are
> Western imports or imitations. Similarly, there are old and
> often striking folktales that Arab children may enjoy, but
> no classic such as *Robinson Crusoe* or *Black Beauty*
> conceived specifically for the imaginative child.[40]

The only game permitted to many Arab children is "kill the Jew" —
and the game becomes reality when they become suicide bombers.
After the kidnappings and beheadings started in Iraq, the "take the
hostage and behead him" game became very popular among Arab
youngsters.[41] We begin to see why Islamist terrorists so often hit
places of enjoyment in their deadly strikes: dance halls, nightclubs,
beaches (e.g., Israeli discos, the Bali resort). All things connected to
earthly pleasure must be extinguished.

In the end, therefore, as we examine this culture that is rife
with feelings of humiliation, shame, impotence, emasculation,
and rage, combined with the rejection of earthly joy and pleasure,
it becomes obvious why so many Muslim men choose death.

CHAPTER TWELVE

Killing and Dying for Purity

"Thank God, my son is dead."

— A Muslim Palestinian mother celebrating
that her son has become a *shahid*

For most men living in the confines of militant Islam, there exist very few reasons to value their time on earth. For a militant Muslim, it is only through sacrificing his own life that he can cleanse himself of the sinful nature of earthly existence. And since almost every other form of individualism is closed to him, killing himself and others in Islamic jihad becomes the principal means by which he can express himself.

A special problem plagues those who have experienced the temptations of Western freedom. Islamists fault America and the West for the excruciating guilt they feel over the desires that freedom plants within their hearts; consequently, their impulse is to lash out violently at the tempter. It is in this light that Theodore Dalrymple analyzes the motivations of the young suicide bombers who struck in London in July 2005. He demonstrates that they saw no way out of their confrontation with freedom and modernity except death:

> Muslims who reject the West are therefore engaged in a losing and impossible inner jihad, or struggle, to expunge everything that is not Muslim from their breasts. It can't be done: for their technological and scientific dependence

is necessarily also a cultural one. You can't believe in a return to seventh century Arabia as being all-sufficient for human requirements, and at the same time drive around in a brand-new red Mercedes, as one of the London bombers did shortly before his murderous suicide. An awareness of the contradiction must gnaw in even the dullest fundamentalist brain.

Furthermore, fundamentalists must be sufficiently self-aware to know that they will never be willing to forgo the appurtenances of Western life: the taste for them is too deeply implanted in their souls, too deeply a part of what they are as human beings, ever to be eradicated. It is possible to reject isolated aspects of modernity but not modernity itself. Whether they like it or not, Muslim fundamentalists are modern men—modern men trying, impossibly, to be something else.

They therefore have at least a nagging intimation that their chosen utopia is not really a utopia at all: that deep within themselves there exists something that makes it unachievable and even undesirable. How to persuade themselves and others that their lack of faith, their vacillation, is really the strongest possible faith? What more convincing evidence of faith could there be than to die for its sake? How can a person be really attached or attracted to rap music and cricket and Mercedes cars if he is prepared to blow himself up as a means of destroying the society that produces them? Death will be the end of the illicit attachment that he cannot entirely eliminate from his heart.

The two forms of jihad, the inner and the outer, the greater and the lesser, thus coalesce in one apocalyptic action. By means of suicide bombing, the bombers overcome moral impurities and religious doubts within themselves and, supposedly, strike an external blow for the propagation of the faith.[1]

The promise of otherworldly rewards fuels this temptation to suicide, as noted earlier. These rewards are delineated in the Koran itself, as the Prophet Muhammad promised Muslim warriors not simply high spiritual positions in paradise, but carnal pleasures as well.[2] The Muslim warrior who dies in battle is promised that the *houris* who reside in heaven are at his disposal for eternity. Pre-pubescent boys are also referred to—they will be like "scattered pearls" of "perpetual freshness."[3] It is no coincidence that the pleasures denied on earth are *exactly* the pleasures offered in heaven. For a Muslim male who wants to engage in various sexual acts outside of marriage without offending Allah, the only avenue possible for him is to die for Islam.

Pierre Rehov, the French filmmaker who produced the documentary *Suicide Killers*, spent hours speaking with would-be martyrs in Israeli jails and with their families. He notes how, in this culture, the dream of becoming a suicide bomber starts in the mosque, where the imams continually tell their congregations that Jews are the descendants of apes and pigs and are oppressors of humanity in general and of Palestinians in particular. Sacrificing one's life to rid the earth of such an enemy becomes the highest value to which the Muslim boy can aspire.

And since one is not allowed to do almost anything pleasurable on earth, one seeks to die in order to do it in heaven. As Rehov writes:

> Imagine a world where separation between men and women is virtually absolute. Where not only sex is a taboo, but where a woman's body is considered to be so impure that it must be hidden at all times…. In this chauvinistic land, a sixteen- or eighteen-year-old boy has a 99 percent chance of having never touched the hand of a girl nor having spoken to one, except for his sister. At this age where libido is at its peak, a young male is in need of these beautiful and forbidden sensations. He needs to prove to himself that he is a man, a future man. But, in this arena, there is no hope—only frustration. Dating and flirting are forbidden. Marriage is the only tolerated path to sex in the Muslim world. But without money there is no wife. Ironically, while women are the object of the highest contempt, while the temporal existence of flesh is considered despicable ("seek for death, and eternal life will be given to you"—Prophet Mohammad), the promise of eternal life surrounded by seventy-two virgins is popularized daily through every arm of the Muslim media. The misguided kids I interviewed while shooting *Suicide Killers* spoke of the seventy-two virgins with total conviction. "No one knows how much Allah would have given me in heaven if I had succeeded," said one of them,

who described his ideal target as a mall, a school or a hospital in Netanya.[4]

Of course there are some sexual treats offered to Muslim warriors who do *not* die in battle. As mentioned in chapter eleven, while it is a sin in Islam to have sex outside of marriage, Allah makes an exception for the Muslim warrior who wants to rape the women of conquered infidels.[5] When Pakistani Muslim soldiers raped a quarter of a million Bengali women in 1971 after they had massacred three million unarmed civilians, it was not just a coincidental wave of sexual exploitation. But these sexual treats on earth are nothing compared to the eternity of sexual delights promised to the warrior who dies in battle. And this incentive is compounded by many other pleasures that are allowed only in paradise, such as "rivers of wine bestowed in heaven."[6]

Aside from sexual incentives and promises of guilt-free intoxication in wine, the prospect of pleasing his parents—a good proportion of whom want him to become a martyr—also inspires the suicide killer. Reflecting on his interviews with the suicide bombers, Rehov comments:

> It is like dealing with pure craziness, like interviewing people in an asylum, since what they say is, for them, the absolute truth. I hear a mother saying "Thank God, my son is dead." Her son had become a *shahid*, a martyr, which for her was a greater source of pride than if he had become an engineer, a doctor or a winner of the Nobel Prize.[7]

In this whole pathological paradigm, the suicide killer's road to death ultimately comes full circle in that it begins and ends with the hatred of women. Dr. Nancy Kobrin points out that because children in this culture are brought up by women who are debased and humiliated, they feel they must dissociate themselves from their mothers—and this can only be done through their own deaths. In other words, the misogynist culture leads to literal suicide as the only way young men can cure their contamination by the mother.[8]

This toxic instinct goes hand in hand, naturally, with a deep-seated Jew hatred. Kobrin has observed, for instance, that, on a deeply unconscious level, suicide bombers want to die but simultaneously yearn to merge with the source of contamination. They resolve this conflict by blowing themselves up in a way in which their blood is mingled with that of their adversaries. In Kobrin's view, the Jew functions in this context as a surrogate for the hated woman.[9]

Meanwhile, the suicide culture faces a significant dilemma in that too many males blow themselves up, while women are exempt from killing themselves. And so, in a full cyclical rendezvous with the culture's misogyny, the death cult now sees to it that women blow themselves up—whether they want to or not. It is more difficult to instill the death wish in women, who, despite their suffering in a strict Arab-Islamic society, do not experience the same hatred of earthly life as men in this culture (and who have no sexual orgy to look forward to in paradise). The woman haters solve this problem by creating nightmarish conditions in which a woman is given suicide as the only way out.

This is a growing scenario in the Palestinian territories. Fatah, for instance, runs an operation in which male terrorists seduce or rape young women and then confront them with the deadly choice: a shameful death at the hands of their own family for the sake of "honor," or the washing away of the family's shame by becoming a "martyr." Such was the case of Reem Al-Reyashi, the mother of two young children, who blew herself up in January 2004 at the Erez crossing in Israel, killing herself and four Israelis. Officials later learned that she had been seduced by a Hamas terrorist—who then offered her a choice between an honor killing or suicide by means of explosives detonated amidst as many Jews as possible. Her terrorist lover armed her with the necessary explosives and instructions, and her husband drove her to the location of her death.[10]

In March 2004, Israel was able to stop two young Palestinian women from following in Al-Reyashi's footsteps. The terror group Tanzim had attempted to coerce these women into reclaiming their honor by killing themselves and as many Jews as possible. The first woman, Tehani Zaki Ali Halil, had committed adultery and was told to carry out a suicide attack in Tel Aviv as her penance. The second woman, a nineteen-year-old named Ramah Abed el-Majid Hasan Habaib, was accused of engaging in premarital sexual relations.[11] The two women were stopped, five days apart, at roadblocks near Nablus, where they told their stories to the Israeli officers.

Islamist clerics and terrorist groups have painted suicide bombings as the only way a Palestinian woman can achieve "equality." Islamic jihad, in other words, has now become "feminist" in the Muslim sense by adopting a "liberal" attitude toward female suicide bombing. Palestinian jihadi literature now contains statements like: "Our women are no longer the type of women who cry or weep. We have martyrdom women now."[12] And as will be demonstrated in Part IV, many Western leftist feminists are greatly attracted to female suicide bombers—seeing them as role models in the quest for power and dignity.

But before we explore the final part of our story, we must first finish the tale of Islamism's cravings for death with a delineation of its hatred of the Jews.

CHAPTER THIRTEEN

To Hate a Jew

"Behind the doctrine of atheistic materialism was a Jew; behind the doctrine of animalistic sexuality was a Jew; and behind the destruction of the family and the shattering of sacred relationships in society...was a Jew."

—Sayyid Qutb

The hatred of Jews serves as a central underpinning to the Islamist death cult—as it does to most death cults. Like its ideological cousins, fascism and communism, Islamism wages war against Jews in its effort to secure its own survival. Totalist ideologies detest modernity, individual freedom, and any value placed on individual human life—notions with which Jews are strongly identified. Jews also personify the enduring struggle to survive, rather than the impulse to destroy and perish. For Islamists—as for leftist believers, as delineated in the believer's diagnosis and documented throughout Part II—such a disposition is tantamount to a declaration of war.

In Islamists' eyes, not only are Jews guilty because, as a people, they are synonymous with liberty and the veneration of life on earth; they are also guilty for being the creators and inhabitants of the state of Israel—the very existence of which is an affront to Islam's quest for dominion over all the lands of the Middle East and, ultimately, the world. The fact that Israel is an ally of the United States only magnifies the "crimes" of the Jews. Consequently, the Jewish state serves as a nearby stand-in for the

West in general, and for America in particular. As Kenneth Timmerman notes, "much of today's anti-Semitism, while aimed at Jews, stems from a belief system that equally rejects America and indeed Western civilization as a whole."[1]

As will be demonstrated in this chapter, Islamist Jew hatred is, first and foremost, rooted in Islamic theology and culture. At the same time, it is important to stress that, as shown in chapter nine, since Islamism is partly an outgrowth of the European ideological virus that spawned communism and fascism, so too is its Jew hatred an outgrowth of those two death cults.

Many Muslim Arabs adored Hitler and were enchanted with his Final Solution. As mentioned in chapter nine, the Muslim Brotherhood's founder, Hassan al-Banna, was a devout admirer, and the Nazis helped create the organization as a weapon against the British in the Middle East.[2] By the end of World War II, the Muslim Brotherhood had a half million Arab Nazis as members.[3] The grand mufti of Jerusalem, Haj Amin al-Husseini, met with Hitler on November 28, 1941, to request German assistance in engendering a Middle Eastern Final Solution, and he offered to form an Arab army to help carry it out.[4] Al-Husseini became the Arabic voice of Nazi Germany in all of its broadcasts to the Arab world, exhorting Muslims to murder Jews.[5] Hitler's Palestinian disciple understood, however, that direct assistance could be provided only after the Führer had finished the job in Europe — an objective the Nazi dictator never achieved. Yasser Arafat was one of al-Husseini's most admiring disciples, even claiming that he was his nephew.[6]

Sayyid Qutb, meanwhile, helped frame the Jew hatred of the Islamic world in the modern era. For Qutb, the Jews represented the "eternal enemy" of Islam. Behind every evil, in Qutb's view, were the Jews: "Behind the doctrine of atheistic materialism was a Jew; behind the doctrine of animalistic sexuality was a Jew; and behind the destruction of the family and the shattering of sacred relationships in society...was a Jew."[7]

Al-Qaeda and all other Islamist terrorist organizations have emerged, clearly, from traditional political Islam. But they also have evolved from the Nazi-Arab World War II generation, through the connection with the Muslim Brotherhood, which remains the backbone of al-Qaeda and the parent of nearly every other Arab terrorist group.[8] As Timmerman has noted, "If today's Muslim anti-Semitism is like a tree with many branches, its roots feed directly off of Hitler's Third Reich."[9] *Mein Kampf* was and still is circulated widely in the Muslim world. It is, for instance, a bestseller among Palestinians and it has also recently been on the bestseller lists in Turkey.[10]

Just as it has Nazi-Fascist roots, so too the Islamist death cult has communist origins, as we saw in chapter nine, and the communist death cult was also rife with Jew hatred. The Soviet regime viciously persecuted its Jews, and newly discovered evidence indicates that Stalin was planning a second Great Terror, his own version of the Holocaust, to rid the Soviet Union of its remaining Jews.[11] Shortly before his death he authorized the construction of four large death camps for this purpose in Kazakhstan, Siberia, and the Arctic north.[12]

The Soviet regime consistently used its power and influence to channel Islamism's Jew hatred into a ferocious anti-Americanism.[13] Former Romanian intelligence general Mihai Pacepa has revealed how the Soviet-bloc espionage community's main objective was to transform Yasser Arafat's war against Israel and its main supporter, the United States, into a central doctrine throughout the whole Islamic world. Pacepa writes:

> According to KGB theorists, the Islamic world was a petri dish in which we could nurture a virulent strain of America-hate. Islamic cultures had a taste for nationalism, jingoism, and victimology. Their illiterate, oppressed mobs could be whipped up to a fever pitch. Terrorism and violence against America would flow naturally from their religious fervor. We had only to keep repeating, over and over, that the United States was a "Zionist country" bankrolled by rich Jews. Islam was obsessed with preventing the infidel's occupation of its territory, and it would be highly receptive to our dogma that American imperialism wanted to transform the rest of the world into a Jewish fiefdom.[14]

This explains why the Soviet bloc flooded the Islamic world with Arabic translations of the *Protocols of the Elders of Zion*, along with other "documentary" materials, "proving" that Jewish money governed the Zionist United States, whose aim was to extend its domination over the rest of the world.[15]

Soviet communism, therefore, fueled the energy and hate with which Islamism, its ideological cousin, would fight modern liberalism and freedom. The totalitarian virus was simply transported into a new theater. As Pacepa powerfully observes, "the hijacked airplane was launched into the world of contemporary terrorism by the KGB and its puppet Yasser Arafat, and it is significant that this became the weapon of choice for September 11, 2001."[16]

Islamism's Jew hatred also has numerous other sources. One significant ingredient is the humiliation phenomenon delineated in chapter eleven. Muslim Arabs experienced excruciating shame in losing three wars to the Israelis (1948, 1967, 1973) and in observing the success and prosperity of the Jewish civilization right in their midst. For generation after generation, Arabs in the Middle East have known nothing but backwardness, poverty, dictatorship, and cultural impotence. Yet they have had to witness a comparatively small number of European and American Jews migrate to a tiny stretch of desert a half century ago, to join the Jews already living there and, within a single generation, build the most powerful economic and industrial nation in the entire Middle East. This is an agonizing dose of reality for many Arabs, causing them to try to destroy the reminder of their own impotence—i.e., the Jews—rather than to acknowledge the flaws of their own civilization and admit that they might profit by learning something from the hated "infidels." In the Arab world, Israel's creation is *Nakba*—the Catastrophe.

But despite the Nazi and communist reinforcement, Islamist Jew hatred is primarily founded in Islamic sources, which will always take precedence for Muslims. And one of the key problems is that Muslims do not see Jews as merely *their* enemies; they see them as the enemies of God. The Koran attributes many negative characteristics to Jews, especially falsehood and distortion,[17] and it teaches that Allah, as well as David and Jesus, has cursed the

Jews.[18] In fact, Allah was so disgusted with Jews that he transformed them into apes and pigs.[19] The *hadiths* also contain many anti-Jewish teachings. A *hadith* collected in *Mishkat Al-Messabih*, for instance, says, "When judgment day arrives, Allah will give every Muslim a Jew or Christian to kill so that the Muslim will not enter into hell fire."[20]

It is important to point out, of course, that there are some Islamic leaders, such as Sheikh Abdul Hadi Palazzi, director of the Cultural Institute of the Italian Islamic community, who seek to abolish Jew hatred within Islam.[21] But they have a great struggle ahead of them.

The Prophet Muhammad taught Jew hatred explicitly *by example*. He commanded his followers: "Kill any Jew that falls into your power."[22] In his later years, Muhammad himself persecuted Jews and sanctioned the killing of the males of large Jewish tribes, notably in the brutal massacre of the Jewish tribe Banu Qurayza. Muhammad ratified a judgment that saw as many as nine hundred men from this tribe beheaded and their decapitated corpses buried in a pit while he looked on. The Muslims then sold most of the murdered men's wives and children into slavery, while distributing some of them as gifts among Muhammad's followers (Muhammad took one Qurayza woman, Rayhana, for his own pleasure).[23] In his 1895 biography of Muhammad, which relied entirely on the original Muslim sources, the scholar Sir William Muir observed: "The massacre of the Banu Coreiza was a barbarous deed which cannot be justified by any reason of political necessity…. [T]he indiscriminate slaughter of the whole tribe cannot be recognized otherwise than as an act of monstrous cruelty…"[24]

These crimes by Muhammad himself serve as a foundation for Muslim hatred and persecution of Jews throughout history. In AD 807, for instance, Harun al-Rashid, the caliph of Baghdad, enforced Muhammad's directive to humiliate Jews by mandating that they wear a yellow belt and dunce cap. If they failed to do so, they faced execution. In different periods of *dhimmitude*, Jews were also forced to wear the image of an ape on their clothes and to nail onto their front door a board bearing the sign of a monkey.[25] This was the inspiration for the yellow star later used by the Nazis.[26]

We get a clear picture of how Islam's ancient hatred of the Jews has fused with present-day resentments. Israel, like the United States, has become a symbol of modernity, freedom, corporate capitalism, and globalization—all things that are reviled by Muslim fundamentalists. And it is no coincidence that the Left despises modernity, freedom, corporate capitalism, and globalization as well. Jew hatred, therefore, serves as an indispensable element in the leftist-Islamist romance.

PART IV

ROMANCE WITH TERROR

CHAPTER FOURTEEN

Cheering for al-Qaeda

*"The Iraqis who have risen up against the occupation are not 'insurgents'
or 'terrorists' or 'The Enemy.' They are the REVOLUTION, the Minutemen,
and their numbers will grow—and they will win."*

—Michael Moore, April 14, 2004

W hen former U.S. President Jimmy Carter embarked on his Hamas
odyssey in April 2008 to embrace the leaders of that
Palestinian version of the Nazi Party, he brought the Left's—and his
own—long tradition of romancing America's totalitarian adversaries
to its most obvious fulfillment. Indeed, what could have symbolized
the Left's yearnings any better than Carter embracing an
organization whose life-purpose was to annihilate Jews and to
destroy every possible tenet connected to Western values—
including secular freedom and the individual pursuit of happiness?[1]

Noam Chomsky had set the tone well for Carter's Hamas
romance two years earlier—when he traveled to Lebanon in May
2006 to pay homage to Hezbollah, the world's largest terrorist
army. In this personal feat, Chomsky, like Carter, was merely
continuing his own dark tradition of reaching out to America's
vicious, sadistic, and despotic enemies. Meeting with the
secretary general, Sheikh Hassan Nasrallah, Chomsky echoed
Nasrallah's recent declaration that President Bush was the
world's top "terrorist," and called the United States one of the
"leading terrorist states."[2] Two prominent political observers

characterized this rendezvous between Chomsky and Nasrallah as "a meeting of murderous radical minds."[3]

It is obvious why Chomsky and the political Left he represents reach out to Hezbollah in the present-day terror war. Hezbollah has done all the right things to earn leftist veneration: Hezbollah calls for a Final Solution in the Middle East, while Nasrallah continues to reiterate that "Death to America" remains another of Hezbollah's top goals.[4]

On January 25, 2006, four months before Chomsky's pilgrimage, Hamas had defeated the Fatah Party in the Palestinian parliamentary elections. To be sure, the distinction between Hamas and Fatah is not all that great. Fatah was the creation of terrorist godfather Yasser Arafat, and although Fatah gives lip service to its professed desire to live peacefully alongside the Jews, it privately strives each day to bring about their extermination.[5] Hamas, by contrast, has never made an effort to conceal its guiding purpose: the annihilation of Israel and the slaughter of Jews everywhere. In its voracious lust for the blood of Jews, Hamas openly promotes suicide terrorism for its own children on its Web site.[6]

With the victory of Hamas, the Western Left's adulation for it rose correspondingly—and Carter's pilgrimage to meet Hamas leaders in Cairo and Damascus two years later served as the fitting culmination. The first sign of believers' excitement about Hamas's rise to power appeared in the determined attempt to avert any blockage of funds to the Palestinians' new governing party. When several pieces of legislation (e.g., the Ros-Lehtinen-Lantos Bill, HR 4681) were introduced in the U.S. Congress calling for a termination of aid to the Islamofascist party until it had renounced its commitment to destroying Israel and exterminating all Jews, the Left immediately opposed them.[7] The Jewish Left led by example. The behavior of the Brit Tzedek v'Shalom (Jewish Alliance for Justice and Peace) was typical. It published the names of 387 rabbis who had signed a petition demanding that the U.S. government not withhold aid to the new Hamas-controlled Palestinian Authority (PA) government.[8] These rabbis were ostensibly aware that they were in effect abetting the murder of their fellow Jews.

The Christian Left in Europe and in the United States likewise backed Hamas. The World Council of Churches (WCC), for instance, put pressure on the Council of the European Union to continue funding for a PA government led by Hamas, which the council was seriously considering terminating.[9] Like the rabbis of the Brit Tzedek v'Shalom, the WCC was entirely aware of the potential deadly consequences.[10] And when a suicide bomber killed nine people and wounded more than sixty in Tel Aviv on April 17, 2006, the Hamas government gave the attack its full blessing.[11] The Brit Tzedek v'Shalom and the WCC condemned neither the attack nor Hamas's support of it.

The rabbis and the WCC were merely following the party line of the Left in the terror war. The Hamas election victory came just six weeks after the Iraqi parliamentary elections, which, as we have seen, enraged the Left. The Western Left actually *outdid* the terrorists in Iraq, since even many of the Sunni terrorists cast their ballots and encouraged their neighbors to do so.

This makes perfect sense in the context of the Left's long dalliance with tyranny. Just as the Left yearned for America and the forces of freedom to lose the Cold War, and just as it worked for an American defeat by the forces of tyranny in Southeast Asia, it reaches out to the Islamist death cult that America is confronting today with a loyal commitment to its most cherished principles. The stakes are particularly high in Iraq, since bin Laden and other terrorist leaders have consistently made it clear that Iraq is the main battleground in the global terror war.[12]

The Left's romance with Islamism reached a high point, of course, in the tragedy of 9/11. But it had shown itself much earlier, in response to Khomeini's massacres and Palestinian celebrations over pools of Jewish blood.

As we saw in chapter nine, once Khomeini's regime proved itself to be a death cult that could perpetrate slaughter and destruction on a massive scale, believers around the world, led by progressive heroes such as Michel Foucault, heaped praise on the mullahs' reign of terror.[13]

For precisely the same reason, believers flocked to the Palestinian cause at *exactly the point* when its bloody excesses reached their climax. Once Arafat declared the al-Aqsa Intifada, the Palestinians became the Left's *cause célèbre*. The more mass death and suicide the Palestinians perpetrated, the guiltier Israel became in leftist eyes, and the greater the heroism the Left ascribed to the Palestinian cause.

The story of leftist reaction to 9/11 has been recounted in various works.[14] It would be well, however, for our purposes to briefly recreate the chilling scene.

Immediately following the 9/11 attack, leftist academics led with a drum roll. The very next day after the terrorist strike, Chomsky exonerated the terrorists, stating that the Clinton administration's bombing of the pharmaceutical plant in Sudan constituted a far more serious terrorist act, and warning that the United States would exploit 9/11 as an excuse to destroy Afghanistan.[15]

Leftist academics across the country echoed Chomsky's themes, lamenting the tragedy while cheering the terrorist acts— which they deemed a just retribution for America's transgressions. History professor Robin Kelley of New York University stated: "We need a civil war, class war, whatever to put an end to U.S. policies that endanger all of us." History professor Gerald Horne of the University of North Carolina asserted that "the bill has come due, the time of easy credit is up. It is time to pay." Professor Eric Foner of Columbia University, the renowned Marxist historian, expressed his personal confusion about "which is more frightening: the horror that engulfed New York City or the apocalyptic rhetoric emanating daily from the White House."[16] Barbara Foley, a professor of English at Rutgers University, felt 9/11 was a justified response to the "fascism" of U.S. foreign policy. Mark Lewis Taylor, a professor of theology and culture at Princeton Seminary, thought the WTC buildings were justifiable targets because they were a "symbol of today's wealth and trade." Robert Paul Churchill, a professor of philosophy at George Washington University, rationalized that the terrorist attack was justified because:

> What the terrorists despised and sought to defeat was our
> arrogance, our gluttonous way of life, our miserliness toward
> the poor and its starving; the expression of a soulless pop

culture...and a domineering attitude that insists on having
our own way no matter what the cost to others.[17]

Of course, the infamous Ward Churchill, as we have seen, outdid
all the others, blaming not only Bush and America but the "little
Eichmanns" themselves for the attacks.[18]

Churchill, Chomsky, and their kin on the academic Left were
joined by prominent figures in the progressive culture at large.
Norman Mailer stepped forward to opine that the suicide
hijackers were "brilliant."[19] In his view, the attack was completely
understandable, since "Everything wrong with America led to
the point where the country built that tower of Babel which
consequently had to be destroyed."[20] Oliver Stone affirmed that
he saw 9/11 as a "revolt," and compared the ensuing Palestinian
celebrations with those that had attended the French and Russian
Revolutions.[21] Susan Sontag held that the terrorist attack was the
result of "specific American alliances and actions."[22] Tony
Campolo, a leading Christian evangelist who served as one of
former President Clinton's "spiritual advisers," believed that 9/11
was a legitimate response to the Crusades.[23] Novelist Barbara
Kingsolver was incredulous that her daughter's kindergarten
teacher instructed the students to come to school the next day
dressed in red, white, and blue.[24] *Nation* columnist Katha Pollitt
had the same reaction regarding her teenage daughter's impulse
to fly an American flag outside the family home. Pollitt told her
that she could "buy a flag with her own money and fly it out her
bedroom window, because that's hers, but the living room is off-
limits." This was, Pollitt explained, because the American flag
stands for "jingoism and vengeance and war."[25]

Similar sentiments were heard throughout Europe as well.
The German composer Karlheinz Stockhausen described 9/11 as
"the greatest work of art for the whole cosmos."[26] Dario Fo, the
Italian Marxist who won the 1997 Nobel Prize for literature,
observed: "The great [Wall Street] speculators wallow in an
economy that every year kills tens of millions of people with
poverty, so what is twenty thousand dead in New York?"[27]

As the Twin Towers lay in ruins and America tried to come to
grips with an unspeakable act of evil, the Left's glee mutated into

a desperate feeling of compassion and protectiveness for the entity that had harbored the hijackers and facilitated their crime—the Islamofascist Taliban regime in Afghanistan. Some two hundred "antiwar" demonstrations took place in the United States and around the world before the end of September. On October 18, eleven days after U.S. forces invaded Afghanistan, Chomsky informed an MIT audience that the United States was the "greatest terrorist state" and was planning "a silent genocide" against the Afghans.[28] Leftists took their guru's lead and staged "peace vigils" and "teach-ins" on campuses across the country.[29]

The goal of America's action against the Taliban was to remove a regime that had hosted al-Qaeda, and thus to lessen the terrorists' ability to carry out a similar strike in the future. The Left was traumatized not only by its failure to prevent America from realizing this objective, but also by the fact that America's military success was achieved with minimal Afghan casualties—making a mockery of Chomsky's forecast of a U.S.-directed genocide. To make the developments even more excruciating, the United States succeeded in laying the groundwork for Afghanistan's democratization.

While the Left gnashed its teeth over this nightmare scenario in Afghanistan, it turned its sights toward Iraq, the next scene of confrontation in the terror war. As it had just done in Afghanistan, the Left reached out with affection to forces dedicated to the totalitarian tradition—in this case Saddam Hussein, whose brutality equaled Hitler's, Stalin's, and Pol Pot's. Saddam had also made his country a harbor for Islamist terrorists, to whom, the U.S. government feared, he might eventually transfer weapons of mass destruction.[30]

As the United States prepared its military objectives vis-à-vis Saddam, the Left gathered its forces. Mass "antiwar" demonstrations again broke out across America and Western Europe, organized and led by veteran activists who had rooted for the communists during the Cold War. This coalition welcomed all factions of the Left; it was composed of organizations that ranged from the Communist Party to the National Council of Churches to Muslim supporters of the terrorist jihad. Radical groups including International ANSWER (Act Now to Stop War and End Racism), a front group for the Workers World Party, a Marxist-Leninist sect aligned with Communist North Korea; Not in Our Name, a front created by the Revolutionary Communist Party, a Marxist-Leninist sect aligned with Communist China; United for Peace and Justice, an organization led by Leslie Cagan, a veteran 1960s leftist and a member of the Communist Party until after the fall of the Berlin Wall; and Code Pink, run by Medea Benjamin, head of the radical group Global Exchange organized the mobilizations.[31]

The antiwar demonstrations not only opposed American involvement in Iraq but also promoted Saddam's dictatorship and the Islamist terrorists. The behavior of Leslie Cagan and Medea Benjamin told the story best. These two "peace" leaders, joining forces, created a group called Occupation Watch and established a center in Baghdad. Pressing for an American defeat, the group encouraged American soldiers to defect, tried to discredit any American company attempting to rebuild Iraq, emphasized reports of American casualties (loyal to the leftist tradition of obsessing over body bags), and accused U.S. troops of committing horrific atrocities against Iraqis.[32]

The demonstrations themselves took on eerie and horrid manifestations. Leftists didn't *schmooze* just with the Islamofascists who supported the Ba'athists in Iraq, but also with Nazis who hated Jews and dreamed of future Final Solutions. Leftists marched side by side with Islamist fanatics who despised democracy, modernity, and individual freedom; practiced misogyny and homophobia; and supported theocracy and dictatorship. American "peace" protesters waved placards with pro-Islamist slogans and chanted "*Allahu Akbar*." It was typical of them that the only religious term these leftists would utter is the one cried out by Islamist suicide bombers before they blow themselves up alongside innocent people.[33]

Nicholas De Genova, a professor of anthropology at Columbia University, exemplifies this mentality perfectly. At a Columbia teach-in, he expressed the hope that America would lose in Iraq, arguing that the world's true heroes were those who would defeat the American military. He added that he yearned for "a million Mogadishus," referring to the grotesque 1993 incident in Somalia in which eighteen American soldiers died in an ambush carried out by an associate of al-Qaeda and one soldier was dragged through the streets in front of cheering crowds.[34]

Osama bin Laden himself understood very well what was happening. On February 12, 2003, just before the U.S. and British troops liberated Iraq, Al Jazeera TV aired a videotape in which the terror master declared: "The interests of Muslims and the interests of the socialists coincide in the war against the crusaders."

The Left did not disappoint bin Laden. As outlined in the introduction to this book, leftists like Tom Hayden, Naomi Klein, and "peace mom" Cindy Sheehan rushed to oppose President Bush and demand the evacuation of American forces from Iraq. But any politically conscious observer knew that such an evacuation would lead to a massive bloodbath—reminiscent of the carnage that the Left had spawned in Southeast Asia a generation earlier.

Hayden, Klein, and Sheehan are, of course, just a small fraction of the number of believers who came out in full-fledged support of the terrorists in Iraq. Michael Moore, as we have seen, had also pronounced his desire for the victory of jihad in Iraq. He produced his infamous propaganda film *Fahrenheit-9-11* which demonized the Bush administration by twisting every real fact about Iraq. Though authors such as Christopher Hitchens exposed the myriad of lies upon which the film was based,[35] the Left congratulated Moore from every corner.[36] Former President Jimmy Carter even honored Moore by inviting the propagandist to sit beside him at the Democratic National Convention in July 2004. Osama bin Laden also showed his appreciation, releasing a taped message shortly before the 2004 election clearly utilizing the main themes of Moore's film.[37]

Robert Jensen, meanwhile, a professor of journalism at the University of Texas, celebrated America's "defeat" in Iraq. As American Marines engaged Sunni terrorists in a fierce battle in Fallujah on December 3, 2004, the professor wrote:

> The United States has lost the war in Iraq, and that's a good thing.... I welcome the U.S. defeat, for a simple reason: It isn't the defeat of the United States—its people

or their ideals—but of that empire. And it's essential the
American empire be defeated and dismantled.[38]

Unfortunately for Jensen and for all believers, America would go
on to achieve its primary goals in Iraq. Part of the U.S. success
included the Sunni tribes aligning themselves with coalition
forces to flush out al-Qaeda (in what became known as the Anbar
Awakening in 2006) and the new American-trained Iraqi army
forcing Muqtada al Sadr's Mahdi Army to step down in Basra,
Baghdad, and other major cities. By the summer of 2008, the
success of the General David Petraeus-led surge—which Bush
had implemented in 2007 and the Democrats had vehemently
opposed—was clearly evident. The American military along with
Iraqi forces had routed al-Qaeda, significantly lowered sectarian
violence, and strengthened the democratic institutions of Iraq
with the immediate effect of improving Iraqis' lives.[39]

The Left mourned these developments. The Democratic
Party—whose leadership tilted more than ever to the radical
Left—began to realize that its war against the war had failed.[40]
The two Democratic leaders of Congress, Nancy Pelosi and Harry
Reid, who had proclaimed the Iraq War "lost," now had to
temper and dodge the fallout of their hasty and presumptuous
dismissal of General Petraeus's strategy.[41] Barack Obama, the
eventual president-elect, who had, in large part, based his
campaign during the Democratic primaries and caucuses on his
opposition to the Iraq War and the surge found himself in even
more dire straits, for he had now to explain his failed position to
the American people.

After Obama's trip to Iraq in July 2008—a trip that would
have been impossible if Obama had had his way in preventing
the surge—he conceded that progress had been made in Iraq and
that the surge had succeeded in bringing down the level of
violence. Here, one would have expected Obama to give some
credit to the Bush administration for the stunning turnaround in
Iraq. But Obama argued that the success of the surge was only
incidental, that the Iraqis themselves, especially those involved in
the Anbar Awakening, were the real cause of victory in Iraq.
Iraqis, of course, were flattered, although many patently

admitted that Obama's position was disingenuous and that U.S. forces had, indeed, achieved a major victory. Upon such shaky ground, moreover, Obama went as far as to affirm that if he could take time back, he would still oppose the surge.[42] In other words, if he had been president in 2007, knowing beforehand that the surge would be successful, Obama would still have abandoned the Iraqi theater of war, leaving the Iraqi government and people at the mercy of a ruthless and pitiless terrorist enemy.

Obama's about-face on Iraq was not very surprising or original. He is an individual who spent decades engaging in either political alliance or personal friendship with individuals who loathe this country. He held close company with the radical Left throughout his political career, including terrorist figures in the Weather Underground such as Bill Ayers and Bernardine Dohrn.[43] He sat for twenty years in the church of the socialist Reverend Wright whose antipathy towards the United States has become famous. These relationships and associations provide a window into Obama's politics—how he is perfectly at ease in the company of the hate-America Left and why even when confronted with the utter failure of his own world vision, such as in Iraq, he chose, during the campaign for president, to equivocate and avoid affirming America's ongoing struggle for democracy in the heart of the Middle East. His political opportunism has also, obviously, played a central role in this saga.[44]

Despite these realities, however, Obama has provided some grounds for hope that his administration will govern from the center right on foreign policy and will potentially avoid any significant influence from the anti-war Left on this realm. After becoming the president-elect, Obama formed a war cabinet that included would-be secretary of state Hillary Clinton; Bush administration defense secretary Robert Gates, who would retain his post; retired four-star general and soon to be national security advisor James Jones; and Arizona governor Janet Napolitano, Obama's nominee as secretary of the Department of Homeland Security.[45] These selections revealed that there would not necessarily be a sharp break with the Bush years on critical national security issues and that, to the distress of the Democratic Party's anti-war base, on foreign policy, there would be no left turns.[46]

Thus, while Obama has seemingly flip-flopped on foreign policy, dashing the hopes of the anti-war Left in his appointments for his war cabinet, much of the radical Left has obviously been much more brazen in its foreign policy impulses. Not only has it worked for an American defeat in Iraq, but it has struggled to create a solid Islamist-leftist alliance that will vanquish the forces of American democracy and capitalism. British leftist George Galloway is one of the prominent leftists who have frequently called for this alliance:

> Not only do I think it's possible [a Muslim-leftist alliance] but I think it is vitally necessary and I think it is happening already. It is possible because the progressive movement around the world and the Muslims have the same enemies. Their enemies are the Zionist occupation, American occupation, British occupation of poor countries, mainly Muslim countries. They have the same interest in opposing savage capitalist globalization, which is intent upon homogenizing the entire world, turning us basically into factory chickens which can be force fed the American diet of everything from food to Coca-Cola to movies and TV culture. And whose only role in life is to consume the things produced endlessly by the multinational corporations. And the progressive organizations and movements agree on that with the Muslims.[47]

While believers have continued to praise America's adversaries and to call for an alliance with the enemy, they have also faithfully engaged in their long tradition of fellow traveling. As has been shown, individuals such as Chomsky have led the way in this department. Foreshadowing his later Hezbollah political pilgrimage, for instance, he made sure, in the immediate aftermath of 9/11, to get as close as he could geographically to the Taliban and al-Qaeda in Afghanistan. Horowitz and Radosh describe Chomsky's bizarre odyssey:

> So, shortly after delivering his MIT remarks, and as the war in Afghanistan approached its climactic battles, he went off on a two-week tour of the Indian subcontinent,

adjacent to the war zone, and in particular to Islamabad—the capital city of Pakistan, a Muslim country and a nuclear power that was also the most dangerously volatile state in America's coalition to defeat the Taliban, and one that could easily tip the other way.[48]

Horowitz and Radosh explore the impulse behind Chomsky's new bout of fellow traveling: "The purpose of Chomsky's tour was to pursue what he thought was the best remedy: giving aid and comfort to America's terrorist enemies in the hope that they will win the war against us."[49]

On this tour, Chomsky spread his lies to millions of Muslims and Hindus. He talked about America's alleged aim to kill three to four million Afghans through starvation, called America the greatest terrorist state, and alleged that the United States was involved in something far worse than what the terrorists had perpetrated on 9/11.[50] But nothing that Chomsky said bore even the barest resemblance to reality. As Horowitz and Radosh have demonstrated, for instance, the Bush administration acted "to *prevent* the starvation of Afghan civilians at the very moment Noam Chomsky was claiming that it had begun a silent genocide." U.S. forces tried to bring in food and other needed items via truck convoys; it was the Taliban that attacked those convoys and stole the goods. But the United States persevered, and in the end, more food reached Afghans after the U.S. bombing than before it. The "U.S.-led military action in fact led to the *restoration* of food relief and lessened the danger of the mass starvation that might have followed under Taliban rule; that is, it may have *saved* millions of Afghan lives."[51] Chomsky refused to admit his errors when confronted about them, and even denied having ever articulated them.[52]

Al-Qaeda, meanwhile, showed its gratitude to the Left for its efforts. George Galloway was particularly singled out for his years of faithful support. In August 2006 American al-Qaeda operative Adam Yahiye Gadahn gave a broadcast in which he warned: "To Americans and the rest of Christendom we say, either repent [your] misguided ways and enter into the light of truth or keep your poison to yourself and suffer the consequences in this world and the next..."[53] In this broadcast, bin Laden's lieutenant thanked Galloway for his "admiration and respect for Islam" and specifically encouraged him to convert.[54]

The Islamist enemy would also show its appreciation to Hollywood's leftist elite, which has continued its long tradition of reaching out to America's despotic enemies. Few Hollywood stars represent liberal Hollywood better in this context than actor and director Sean Penn. A member of leftist anti-war organizations Not In Our Name and Artists United to Win Without War, and an avid supporter of MoveOn.org, Penn has been an outspoken critic of the Iraq war, a leader in fellow traveling, and a champion of jihadi terrorists.[55]

In December 2002, just prior to the U.S. liberation of Iraq, Penn embarked on a political pilgrimage to Baghdad with Medea Benjamin, a trip that was publicized as a "fact-finding" visit. It remains a mystery what "facts" Penn was looking for or even found, since the trip basically entailed him denouncing the approaching U.S. invasion and serving as a propaganda tool for Saddam.[56] Penn would continue his anti-war activism throughout the war and after, which included another trip he took to Iraq in late 2003, during which he demonized U.S. efforts to defeat the jihadists and bring stability to the country.[57] During that trip, U.S. soldiers had to rescue Penn when he conducted interviews in unsafe places.[58] Penn did not reflect, naturally, on whether he owed any gratitude to the U.S.—or on why he was being attacked in the first place and by whom. In other words, moral clarity eluded him even when his own nation saved him from those who hated him and wanted him dead.

Penn's anti-war activism continued unabated throughout the Iraq war, as the actor/director consistently called for an immediate U.S. withdrawal—despite the fact that such a premature withdrawal would lead to a terrorist victory in Iraq, embolden Islamofascists everywhere, and lead to a genocide.[59] In 2006, he joined congresswomen Cynthia McKinney and Lynn Woolsey, singer Willie Nelson, and actors Susan Sarandon, Danny Glover, and Ed Asner in staging a "Troops Home Fast" hunger strike to protest the

Iraq War. The effort was organized by Gold Star Families for Peace founder Cindy Sheehan and endorsed by Code Pink.[60]

Iraq was not the only target of Penn's totalitarian yearnings. Iran's despotism also served as a romantic attraction. And so in 2005, three years after his Iraq pilgrimage, Penn once again took on the role of fellow traveler, but this time traveling to Iran, acting as a correspondent for the *San Francisco Chronicle*. He attended Islamic prayer ceremonies in Tehran and interviewed Iranian political leaders. In his reporting for the *Chronicle*, he praised the mullahs for standing brave in the face of Bush calling Tehran a member of the "Axis of Evil."[61] He commended Iran for not (in his mind) pursuing uranium enrichment and he denounced the U.S. and Israeli positions, as well as any possible "reckless action" toward Iran that those countries might take. He did this despite the fact that the evidence had already confirmed that Iran was pursuing nuclear ambitions, a reality that subsequently forced the U.N. Security Council to pass a resolution ordering Iran to suspend its nuclear pursuits.[62]

Iran's mullahs and the jihadists fighting in Iraq weren't the only objects of Penn's affections. The Hollywood star has come to the defense of Castro's despotism while also nurturing a friendship with Venezuela's communist president Hugo Chavez, who has quoted from Penn's writings in some of his televised speeches.[63] Penn embarked on a political pilgrimage in August 2007 to embrace Chavez in person in Caracas, Venezuela. Not much interested in Chavez's tyrannical brutality, Penn called Chavez "a fascinating guy" who is "much more positive for Venezuela than he is negative." Chavez, in turn, praised Penn for advocating the impeachment of President Bush.[64]

Like Chavez, Islamists have shown their gratitude to Penn, cheering on the Hollywood star's statements about Iran, the Iraq war, and the war on terror and stressing that U.S. citizens should hearken to his message. The Al-Aqsa Martyrs Brigades terror group, which engages in suicide attacks, and has carried out hundreds of shootings and rocket attacks against Israeli citizens, including women and children, has expressed particular admiration for Penn. Ala Senakreh, the terror group's West Bank chief, affirmed that he had "deep respect" for Penn. Abu Hamed, northern Gaza Strip commander of the organization, invited Penn to officially represent his group's cause to the world media. Ramadan Adassi, the group's chief in the northern West Bank Anskar refugee camp, stated that Penn's words "express dignity" and a "deep humanitarian sense."[65]

Like Penn, CNN founder and media mogul Ted Turner is another of myriad prominent leftist U.S. figures who has made his contribution to supporting the enemies of the United States—and received their affection in return. Having given millions of dollars to leftist causes and political figures, he refers to himself as "a socialist at heart."[66] An admirer of Cuba's dictator Fidel Castro, Turner has called the communist despot "one hell of a guy." He told a class at Harvard Law School, "You'd like him. He has been the leader of Cuba for forty years. He's the most senior leader in the world, and most of the people that are still in Cuba like him."[67] Turner has also affirmed that it was Castro who inspired him to take CNN international, an inspiration that took place during Turner's political pilgrimage to Cuba in 1982, during which the media mogul embraced the dictator and drank alcohol and smoke cigars with him.[68]

Turner's passion for the war on terror has motivated him to call the 9/11 terrorists "brave," and to explain that "the reason that the World Trade Center got hit is because there are a lot of people living in abject poverty out there who don't have any hope for a better life."[69] He has accused Israel of engaging in "terrorism" and excused Palestinian suicide bombers for their homicidal acts because, according to him, they live in "poverty" and "desperation."[70]

Turner's philosophical worldview also involves Iran: despite the fact that the mullahs have vowed to obliterate Israel from the face of the earth if they acquire nuclear weapons, Turner has defended Iran's right to such weapons and has ridiculed President Bush for trying to stop Iran from doing so.[71] Turner has also refused to label the Saddam Hussein regime as "evil" and he has vehemently opposed the U.S. liberation of Iraq.[72] While the U.S. was clearly achieving its objectives in Iraq by early 2008, Turner was gleefully boasting in April 2008 that "we can't win in Iraq" and that "we're being beaten by insurgents who don't even have any tanks." The terrorists in Iraq, in his view, are "patriots."[73]

While believers like Turner and Penn have gone out of their way to weaken America abroad in the face of totalitarian enemies, so too they have been busy at home trying to make their own society vulnerable to attack—just as they had done during the Cold War. The usual suspects have been hard at work: the ACLU, the National Lawyers Guild, the Center for Constitutional Rights, United for Peace and Justice, MoveOn.org, and many others have been part of what David Horowitz has aptly termed the "unholy alliance" between the Left and radical Islam.

Particularly pernicious have been the efforts of the Legal Left—leftist lawyers who flock to defend terrorists. They have worked tirelessly to undermine America's ability to protect itself against another terrorist strike. In addition to defending individual terrorists, the Legal Left has taken aim at the Patriot Act, passed by Congress shortly after 9/11 in order to enhance homeland security and protect the nation from terrorism.

The Legal Left knew exactly what it was doing, of course. It understood very well that, for example, in the pre-Patriot Act era, it had taken fully seven years for Sami Al-Arian, a professor of computer sciences at the University of South Florida, to get arrested *after* the FBI began to investigate his work in funding terrorists.[74] As we saw in the case of the FBI agents being denied permission to confiscate Zacarias Moussaoui's computer, the wall the Clinton administration erected between criminal and intelligence investigations—which the Patriot Act broke down— had devastating effects. If the FBI agents had been allowed to act against Moussaoui, 9/11 could well have been averted.[75] This is precisely the scenario that the Left wants to avoid, and that is why it works for the destruction of the Patriot Act.[76]

Groups such as the National Lawyers Guild—which began as a Soviet front—have challenged every effort of the Department of Homeland Security to strengthen our borders.[77] The Legal Left's most effective tactic has been the canard that a "violation of civil liberties" is being perpetrated. Indeed, the Left charges that

America has entered a new era of "fascism" in its attempt to protect itself from further attacks.

The Center for Constitutional Rights and its president, Michael Ratner (a former president of the National Lawyers Guild), meanwhile, brought a lawsuit on behalf of two terrorist groups— the Kurdish Workers Party of Turkey and the Tamil Tigers of Sri Lanka—that had been responsible for mass murder.[78] In early 2004, a federal judge in Los Angeles agreed with the plaintiffs and struck down one of the Patriot Act's crucial provisions, which sought to block support for foreign terrorist groups.[79]

Not content to support the enemy via legal tactics, many believers, in the Julius and Ethel Rosenberg tradition, cross the line and betray their nation. A notable case is that of Lynne Stewart, the attorney for the "Blind Sheikh," Omar Abdel Rahman, the mastermind of the 1993 World Trade Center bombing. Despite Stewart's best efforts in court, Rahman was convicted in 1995 for his role in the bombing and sentenced to life in prison. But Stewart did not abandon her client. Indeed, while visiting him in prison, she assisted in conveying a message from the sheik to his followers in Egypt encouraging them to resume terrorist activities.[80] It is particularly telling that it was only *after* her indictment for abetting his terrorist plans that she was inundated with invitations to speak at universities, law schools, and other academic institutions. Convicted in February 2005, she has become an intellectual and political icon for the Left.[81]

Another notable case is that of Sami al-Arian. A prominent figure on the American Left, al-Arian helped to fund and organize the Palestinian Islamic Jihad.[82] This is one of the main terrorist groups in the Middle East, involved in suicide bombings that have killed more than a hundred people, including two Americans. As mentioned above, the FBI had been greatly hindered in its efforts to investigate al-Arian. But once the Patriot Act was passed, he ended up being arrested, indicted, and tried on terror-related charges. In December 2005, he was acquitted on eight of seventeen counts against him, but three months later he finally admitted his guilt in a deal with prosecutors, confessing, after years of denial, that he was in fact in league with the Islamic Jihad. He also agreed to accept deportation. The leftists who had defended him and maintained his innocence have never apologized.[83]

And so the new generation of believers found their own idols in the terror war. The romance with Islamism is just a logical continuation of the long leftist tradition of worshipping America's foes. In the next chapter we dig into the root causes of the new political romance with death.

CHAPTER FIFTEEN

Roots of a Romance

*"There is no way of knowing what really happened...
I should prefer to think that it was the Americans."*

—Mary McCarthy, referring to the communist massacre in Hué in 1968

As outlined earlier, the collapse of the Soviet Empire in 1989-91 robbed the Western Left of its central source of hope and object of veneration. Then came 9/11. Believers, who longed to worship a tyrannical enemy of their native society, looked upon this appalling catastrophe as a gift. Just as progressives had found new totalitarian models to worship throughout the twentieth century, from Stalin's Russia to Mao's China to the Sandinistas' Nicaragua, so they now discovered a new death cult through which they could express their destructive urges.

The Left clearly continues to cling to its undying Marxist conviction that capitalism is evil and that forces of revolution are rising to overthrow it—and must be supported. The violence coming from segments of the Third World—in this case, from Muslims, mainly in the Middle East—is regarded as a valiant form of "resistance" against American imperialism and oppression.

September 11 fulfilled the Left's key fantasy: the class enemy—the wealthy elite—was being eliminated because the poor, the oppressed, and the downtrodden had finally risen up. Thus we witnessed Ward Churchill's blessing of the 9/11 terrorists who had wiped out all those "little Eichmanns," and thus Noam Chomsky's glee that America had got what it deserved. As Horowitz observes:

> Their [the terrorists'] targets were the institutions of American power that Chomsky despises: Wall Street (the World Trade Center) and the Pentagon. On the day of the attacks, the Twin Towers were filled—as they normally would be—with bankers, brokers, international traders, and corporate lawyers, Chomsky's hated "ruling class"— the very people who (he believes) were running the "global order" so as to rob the poor in behalf of the rich.[1]

The Left also embraced the terror attack because the attack's victims represented the functionality of a society and a system that the Left hated. The victims served as symbols of two elements of democratic capitalism despised by Islamists and believers alike: success and diversity. As Horowitz puts it:

> New York is America's greatest population center, the portal through which immigrant generations of all colors and ethnicities have come in search of a better life. The World Trade Center is the Wall Street hub of the economy they enter; its victims were targeted for participating in the most productive, tolerant and generous society human beings have created.[2]

Among the victims of the terror attacks were people from eighty countries, representing the pluralism, diversity, tolerance, and inclusiveness of America, which Islamists and believers both revile. Just as Islamism rejects anything outside *sharia* law, the Left abhors all viewpoints incompatible with its Marxist vision. In the World Trade Center, both the Left and Islamism found the symbol of the Great Satan—a Satan that allows existence outside of the Party Line. This is precisely why President Bush stated, in his address to the nation on the evening of 9/11: "America was targeted for attack because we're the brightest beacon for freedom and opportunity in the world."[3]

An added ingredient in this equation is the Left's sacred cow of multiculturalism. The believer cannot accept the truth about Islamism or much of Islam, because he would then have to concede that not all cultures are equal, and that some cultures (e.g., America's, with its striving for equality) are superior to others (e.g., Islam's structure of gender apartheid). For the believer to retain his sense of purpose and to avoid the collapse of his identity and community, such thoughts must be suppressed at all cost. Because he seeks to nurture his self-identification as a victim and to lose himself inside a totalitarian collective whole, he must deny the truth about the object of his worship, as believers of previous generations denied the truth about Stalin's Russia, Mao's China, and other totalitarian societies.

Because of these factors, the believer clings to a rigid Marxist view of the terror war, no matter how much empirical evidence proves that Islamist violence has absolutely nothing to do with economic inequality, class oppression, or Western exploitation.[4] This is why, when Osama bin Laden and Abu Musab Al-Zarqawi justify their terror with references to the Koran, and when Zacarias Moussaoui casually explains in court that he was simply following the Koran's directive that Muslims make Islam the world's superpower, the believer always turns a deaf ear.[5]

This is a long tradition of the Left: progressives have always assumed that they understand the world much better than the people for whom they purport to speak. In terms of the terror war, there exists an obvious and profound racism in the believer's disposition, since the implication is that Muslims and Arabs are not bright enough to understand their own circumstances, and therefore their explanations of their own actions cannot be taken seriously.

So while the likes of bin Laden and Moussaoui may insist that the holy jihad is motivated by the desire to spread *sharia* throughout the world, to erase individual freedom, and to kill, convert, or subjugate infidels, the Western leftist is constrained to rationalize that they are saying such things only because they have been hurt by capitalism and American imperialism. As David Horowitz points out, the leftist holds the Marxist perspective that religion is nothing more than a thought structure rooted in suffering under capitalism.[6] Once the oppression stops, the believer assumes, the Islamist conceptions of Allah and jihad (which the believer privately considers ridiculous but would never dare say so in public) will simply disappear. Believers, therefore, inevitably deny the *Islamic* dimension that the terrorists themselves insist is their impetus for terror.

In reality, Islamic terror is not the result of American or Western-induced victimization and poverty, and, most importantly, *the terrorists themselves are not victims.* Indeed, Islamic fundamentalists, terrorists, and anti-Western zealots almost never originate from among the poor, the oppressed, and the downtrodden; many of them come from the most educated, prosperous, and Westernized elements in Islamic society.[7] And while some of these extremists wear beards and traditional turbans, they also use cutting-edge technology, and they often live decadent and hedonistic Western lifestyles—which as demonstrated in chapters eleven and twelve, leads to the self-hate that spawns suicidal and terrorist urges.

The private life of Khalid Shaikh Mohammed, the mastermind of the 9/11 hijackings, exemplifies this phenomenon perfectly. Growing up in Kuwait, he came from a privileged background and reveled in the Western lifestyle, drinking alcohol, womanizing, and engaging in other acts that Islam sternly forbids. It is now well documented that many of the hijackers he unleashed on 9/11 also partook of these pleasures.[8]

This social paradigm holds in much of the Middle East. Close to 60 percent of Palestinian suicide bombers have attended college; they are not the children of economic despair and hopelessness.[9] As Daniel Pipes affirms, "suicide bombers who hurl themselves against foreign enemies offer their lives not to protest financial deprivation but to change the world."[10] Contrary to the believer's vision, militant Islam finds its breeding ground in economic prosperity and Westernization—just as the socialist Left itself has never drawn its strength from actual poor people, but rather from intellectuals and other members of the privileged class that benefits most from capitalism and freedom. And believers and Islamists find common ground in feeling the need to purge themselves of the sense of shame they feel over their own affluence and privilege.

As the believer denies the true reasons for his support of Islamist terror, his outlook on the terror war is completely flawed. Moreover, his solution—alleviating poverty in the Middle East—would only aggravate the problem. While there is, of course, truth to the assertion that a better life will lessen desperation and hostility, in the case of militant Islam, one has to tread very carefully. As Pipes notes:

> Wealth does not resolve hatred; a prosperous enemy may simply be one more capable of making war…. Economic strength for Islamists represents not the good life but added strength to do battle against the West. Money serves to train *cadres* and buy weapons, not to buy a bigger house and late-model car. Wealth is a means, not an end.[11]

The believer shares yet another common denominator with the Islamic fundamentalist: hatred of the modern-day manifestation of capitalism: globalization.

The Western leftist sees "global capitalism" as spreading American-style democratic capitalism and liberal individualism worldwide. The Islamic militant, meanwhile, hates and fears global capitalism for the threat its poses to his closed world of tyranny and gender apartheid. The global spread of a system that values individual choice, women's freedom, and other Western values is a serious threat. It is no wonder, then, that the anti-globalization movement galvanizes the Left worldwide, serving as a unifying force in "antiwar" demonstrations and emphasizing themes that promote the Islamist enemy in the terror war.[12]

The self-styled socialist revolutionary Hugo Chávez, the president of Venezuela, perhaps best exemplifies the forging of a red-green alliance on the international stage. Chávez's unrelenting hatred of globalization and of America has led him to adopt the death cult in Iran as an energy partner, and to defend it against what he describes as "the most perverse, murderous, genocidal, immoral empire that this planet has known in one hundred centuries."[13] Unbeknownst to many, moreover, as journalist Christopher Brown reports, Iranian geologists "are working with a team of Chávez loyalists in the exploration for uranium deposits within Venezuela."[14] Such an alliance could very well lead to the emergence of a nuclear Islamist state, bent on destroying Israel and America. Chavez has also reached out in solidarity to Hezbollah, providing funds and refuge to the terrorist Islamist organization.[15]

In anti-globalization we once again find one of the most crucial commonalities between the Left and the Islamic fundamentalists: the hatred of individual freedom and of the individual himself. As shown throughout this work, there is a powerful yearning in both ideologies for the submergence of the individual in a collectivist totality. The Left and militant Islam also share a hatred of modernity. And America must bear the burden of being the generator, host, and symbol of modernity.[16]

In today's romance with Islamism, as in the twentieth century romances with communism and fascism, the believer must conceal his own malicious agenda from others—and from himself. Believers achieve the needed camouflage with a pattern of behavior that we have seen before and can accurately label: the denial-excuse-justification model.

As shown in Part II, believers consistently denied the communist regimes' mass crimes. When it became impossible, in the face of new information, to continue this denial, they admitted the reality of such atrocities but found excuses for them—excuses which always involved rationalizing the crimes (Stalin may have killed millions, but capitalism encircled him, and he had to industrialize the country; the Rosenbergs may have been spies, but someone had to give the Soviets the bomb to prevent America from holding a monopoly on nuclear weapons; and so on). These steps of first denying the crime, and then admitting it but explaining it away, are always followed by the actual justification of it.

The believers' favorite mode of justification is *the devil made them do it*. In this grotesque dynamic, leftists blame the devil (literally the "Great Satan"—the United States) for any and every crime perpetrated by its enemies.

The denial-excuse justification model is manifested most clearly in the behavior of Noam Chomsky. As we saw in chapter six, Chomsky denied the horrifying reports of the Khmer Rouge's killing fields that trickled out to the West. He defiantly questioned the validity of the accounts given by refugees and witnesses.[17] But finally, when the horror of Pol Pot's genocide could no longer be refuted, Chomsky turned to *the devil made them do it*. The Khmer Rouge's genocide, it turns out, was America's fault, because—according to Chomsky—the American bombing of Cambodia had driven the Jeffersonian reform-minded Khmer Rouge crazy, and had led them to slaughter three million of their fellow Cambodians. Chomsky's analysis ignored the fact that the Khmer Rouge were following the Marxist blueprint of wiping the slate clean in order to build a utopian society, and that they had meticulously planned their social engineering experiment long before the American bombing of Cambodia.[18]

As documented in Part II, the examples of believers using the denial-excuse justification model are endless. Each case takes its own particular twist. Mary McCarthy, for instance, refused to believe that the communists had perpetrated the Hué massacre— just as she couldn't believe the North Vietnamese would ever harm an American POW. In the case of Hué, where the communists had butchered approximately three thousand South Vietnamese men, women, and children, McCarthy preferred not only to deny it, but also to suggest that if a massacre did occur, the United States perpetrated it. She wrote, "There is no way of knowing what really happened.... I should prefer to think that it was the Americans."[19] This was reminiscent of William Kunstler, the radical lawyer, blaming the exodus of boat people from South Vietnam on the United States. The boat people fled, he explained, not because of the reign of terror that the communists had brought with them, but because U.S. imperialism had created a "massive upheaval."[20]

Chomsky and other believers have faithfully carried the denial-excuse justification model into the terror war. And some went even further than Chomsky, indulging in bizarre conspiracy theories maintaining that Jews and/or Americans rather than Islamists had carried out the 9/11 attacks. Typical of this is Scholars for 9/11 Truth, a group of leftist professors and college students who hold that the Bush administration "orchestrated" 9/11.[21]

Meanwhile, as David Horowitz notes, "In Chomsky's Manichean universe, America is the Evil Principle, responsible not only for its own crimes, but for the crimes of others as well—including those of the terrorists who struck the World Trade Center and the Pentagon on September 11, 2001."[22] For Chomsky, "the root cause of the attack on America was America's own crimes, and whatever atrocity has been committed against her, she has committed worse against others."[23]

Broadening the perspective, Paul Berman notes that, for Chomsky, there could be no "pathological or irrational movements, no movements that yearn to commit slaughters, no movements that yearn for death—and, if such movements do exist, it is because they have been conjured into existence by other forces."[24] Chomsky's rationalizations of 9/11 are simply an extension of his core ideology:

> [W]hen the 9/11 attacks took place, he did not need to collect his thoughts. He was unfazed. The entire purpose of his political outlook was to be unfazed, even by the worst of horrors. He knew exactly what to say. The notion that, in large parts of the world, a mass movement of radical Islamists had arisen, devoted to mad hatreds and conspiracy theories; the notion that radical Islamists were slaughtering people in one country after another for the purpose of slaughtering them; the notion that radical Islamists ought to be taken at their word and that *sharia* and the seventh century *caliphate* were their goals, and that Jews and Christians were demonic figures worthy of death; the notion that bin Laden had ordered random killings of Americans strictly for the purpose of killing Americans—all of this was, from Chomsky's perspective, not even worth discussing.[25]

Chomsky's is a typical case of a characteristic trait of the Left: the refusal to publicly accept that adversarial movements engage in mass murder and suicide simply for their own sake. However, as delineated in the believer's diagnosis, and as demonstrated in the histories of the communist odysseys in Part II, privately the believer knows precisely what motivates these adversarial mass movements, and he venerates them for this very reason: he and they share the notion of redemption through revolution. "The personal dream of every revolutionary," Horowitz writes, "is to be at the center of creation and the renewal of the world."[26] This process, of course, requires purification. As Horowitz explains: "The revolutionary mission is to cleanse the world of this corruption and its agents, and reverse the human Fall. The secular purification of the world has a name: *social justice*. It is the *sharia* of political faith."[27]

When Michael Moore states that the Iraqi terrorists are "the REVOLUTION," the "Minutemen," and that "they will win,"[28] he is simply articulating the essence of the progressive faith. Horowitz observes:

> In other words, Abu Musab al-Zarqawi, the beheader of Nicholas Berg, is not America's enemy, he is an Islamic reincarnation of Ethan Allen or Paul Revere, a harbinger of some new global freedom which can only be achieved by the overthrow of the Great American Satan. This obscene formulation is of course just an excessively vulgar version of the same Marxist fantasy that radicals like Moore were peddling in the 1960s about communist totalitarians like Ho Chi Minh.[29]

Self-anointed social redeemers, both believers and Islamists, must by necessity clear the ground in order to build the perfect world. And upon that ground stand flawed human beings who must be perfected or destroyed. As a result, human salvation *on earth*, orchestrated by human beings *alone*, necessarily "requires the damnation of those who do not want to be saved."[30] And as Horowitz observes about radical revolutionaries:

> They cannot live with themselves or the fault in creation, and therefore are at war with both. Because they are miserable themselves they cannot abide the happiness of others. To escape their suffering they seek judgement on all, the rectification that will take them home. If they do not believe in a God, they summon others to act as gods. If they believe in God, they do not trust His justice but arrange their own. In either case, the consequences of their passion is the same catastrophe. This is because the devil they hate is in themselves and their sword of vengeance is wielded by inhabitants of the very hell they wish to escape.[31]

The point about believers not being able to abide the happiness of others is crucial. For the believer, just as for the Islamist, the hatred of all earthly pleasure and desire is central. It leads directly to the instinct for death which unites the partners in this political romance. In the next chapter, we dig more deeply into the psychology of the death wish.

CHAPTER SIXTEEN

Cravings for Death

"Bit by bit, decorate it, arrange the details, find the ingredients, imagine it, choose it, get advice on it, shape it into a work without spectators, one which exists only for oneself, just for the shortest little moment of life."[1]

—Michel Foucault, describing the pleasure of
preparing oneself for suicide

Believers' longing for others' deaths is often accompanied by a longing for their own death, as we have seen again and again throughout this text. This is why martyrdom for *the idea* is a running theme in the history of the Left's unholy alliances.

This leftist tradition has, naturally, extended into the terror war. Its prototypes were the leftists who set out to serve as "human shields" for Saddam during the American liberation of Iraq. Many of them turned out to be cowards who ran away the moment they realized their lives were at risk. But many did not; their desire to put their own lives at risk for *the idea* animated them at least in part. This tradition has been carried on faithfully by the International Solidarity Movement (ISM), a leftist organization whose activists flock to the Palestinian territories to interfere, often violently, with Israeli military activities. They *intentionally* put themselves in harm's way in order to obstruct the efforts of Israeli soldiers to fight Palestinian terrorists.

ISM member Rachel Corrie became a poster child for the leftist pursuit of martyrdom. A twenty-three-year-old activist from

Olympia, Washington, she was accidentally crushed to death in March 2003 when she tried to obstruct the path of an Israeli bulldozer that was preparing to demolish the house in Rafah where she was lodging.[2] Like her ISM colleagues, she was knowingly abetting terrorists. (A few months earlier, when Palestinian militants seized the Church of the Nativity in Bethlehem, it was ISMers who smuggled food to them.) Many of the homes in Rafah rested atop a network of ninety tunnels that were used for smuggling weapons from the Egyptian border to Rafah. It was impossible for Corrie and her ISM comrades to have lived in Rafah and not witness the activity connected with these tunnels. That is why the bulldozer was in operation: the Israelis were trying to interrupt this tunnel activity.[3] Israeli professor and journalist Steven Plaut has explicitly called Corrie's death a suicide.[4]

The March 2006 death of American hostage Tom Fox is another disturbing example of this phenomenon. Fox was one of four members of the leftist Christian Peacemaker Teams (CPT) who were kidnapped in Iraq in November 2005. Aside from voicing support for the terrorists, one of the group's most powerfully articulated themes entailed the longing for death. Indeed, in the 1984 speech, "God's People Reconciling," which gave rise to the formation of the Christian Peacemaker Teams, Mennonite minister Ron Sider urged his listeners: "We must take up our cross and follow Jesus to Golgotha. We must be prepared to die by the thousands."[5] It is no coincidence that Fox died at the hands of the terrorists in whose dangerous path he yearned—and chose—to stand.

It is also unsurprising that when British and American troops rescued the other three CPT hostages and saved their lives, the freed captives refused to thank their liberators—who had risked their own lives participating in the rescue—or to cooperate in a critical debriefing session with intelligence officers.[6] Doug Pritchard, the co-chairman of CPT, went out of his way to tell the world that the kidnapping itself (and by implication Fox's murder) was *America's* fault, not the kidnappers' or the executioners'. "The illegal occupation of Iraq by multinational forces," he affirmed, was the "root cause" of the kidnappings.[7] In other words, *the devil made them do it.*

The freed captives resented the fact that the very forces they despised had liberated them. And the rescuers had robbed the remaining hostages of the idealized fate suffered by Fox. Jan Benvie, an Edinburgh teacher who was getting ready to go to Iraq with the group in the summer of 2006, learned the lesson well. She announced before her departure: "We make clear that if we are kidnapped we do not want there to be force or any form of violence used to release us."[8]

The believers' death wish also manifests itself in their desire to live vicariously through the tyranny and terror with which they associate themselves. The activism of the Legal Left--the likes of Lynne Stewart, Michael Ratner, Stanley Cohen, and Ramsey Clark, and the organizations with which they are involved, such as the National Lawyers Guild and the Center for Constitutional Rights— erfectly illustrates this phenomenon.[9] Legal Left lawyers view terrorists as victims of capitalist oppression and live vicariously through their terror by defending them.

We earlier looked briefly at Lynne Stewart, the attorney for the terrorist sheikh Omar Abdel Rahman. A protégée of radical lawyer William Kunstler, Stewart is filled with hatred for her own society. Indeed, she spent years openly championing "violence directed at the institutions which perpetuate capitalism, racism, and sexism."[10] In Stewart's calculus, the World Trade Center represented a legitimate target for violence, and the Islamist jihadists who struck on 9/11 were "forces of national liberation."[11] At the National Lawyers Guild's annual convention in 2004, Stewart condemned her nation for its "poisonous" imperialism and raised a glass to her heroes: "Ho and Mao and Lenin [and] Fidel..."[12] and of course Che Guevara, one of whose most famous lines she quoted with approval: "At the risk of seeming ridiculous, let me say that the true revolutionary is guided by a great feeling of love."[13]

For Stewart, this "great feeling of love" manifested itself in her affection for her client Rahman, the spiritual leader of the Islamic Group, an Egyptian terrorist organization with ties to al-Qaeda. Having masterminded the World Trade Center bombing in 1993, Rahman at the time of his arrest was making plans to bomb sites around New York City, including the Lincoln and Holland

Tunnels and the United Nations building. As Stewart familiarized herself with her new client, she began to regard him as "a fighter for national liberation on behalf of a people oppressed by dictatorship and American imperialism."[14] When the jury found Rahman guilty in 1995, Stewart wept.[15] And after Rahman was sentenced to life in prison, Stewart helped him to carry on his terrorist activities from his prison cell, illegally facilitating the delivery of his communications to his terrorist comrades in Egypt.[16] She outdid even Ward Churchill by actively abetting the terrorists' plans, instead of just cheering from the sidelines.

In an exclusive interview with journalist George Packer, Stewart opened a window into her treacherous mind. "My true goal," she explained, "was always to be on the right side of history." Since the United States was constantly at war around the world, she reasoned, it should not expect its terrible acts to go unanswered. The people in the towers "never knew what hit them," she said. "They had no idea that they could ever be a target for somebody's wrath, just by virtue of being American. They took it personally. And actually, it wasn't a personal thing." Asked about her view of the civilian deaths of 9/11, she responded: "I'm pretty inured to the notion that in a war or in an armed struggle, people die."[17]

Ron Kuby, a radical attorney who ended up having second thoughts, opined to Packer that "movement" lawyers—those who represent clients whose politics they champion—were cowards living vicariously through those clients. He said:

> In the best of cases we identify with their determination, with their courage, and we see the people that maybe we could have been had we the courage to do what they did. And as a result, if you're a good lawyer, you spend a lot of time doing gut checks. And because it's a profession that is so cowardly, enjoying the aura of being those people without ever taking the risks of being those people, it's easy to say: this is the right thing to do, I'm not hurting anyone, this is morally justified. I'm refusing to do it out of fear because I'm a coward, and I've got to change that. I can't succumb to that kind of fear, because if I'm afraid of the government here, I can't do this job.[18]

Author and *FrontPageMag* columnist Michael Tremoglie offers a profound interpretation of this phenomenon: "...lawyers like [Stanley] Cohen aspire to be terrorists and are terrorists in a manner of speaking. They explode the law instead of buildings. They exploit and manipulate the Constitution to dismantle and disrupt their own society's legal system and way of life."[19] At the root of the terrorist lawyers' vocation is, once again, the impulse for death and destruction that they share with all believers.

The believers' love affair with the Khomeini revolution in Iran serves as a revealing—and horrifying—example of this impulse. The French philosopher Michel Foucault was the poster boy for the Left's romance with Khomeini's killing machine—which Democratic President Jimmy Carter had helped spawn.[20] To be sure, Foucault's enchantment with death and destruction was nothing new in his life. Scholars Janet Afary and Kevin B. Anderson write:

> Throughout his life, Foucault's concept of authenticity meant looking at situations where people lived dangerously and flirted with death, the site where creativity originated. In the tradition of Friedrich Nietzsche and Georges Bataille, Foucault had embraced the artist who pushed the limits of rationality, and he wrote with great passion in defense of irrationalities that broke new boundaries. In 1978, Foucault found such transgressive powers in the revolutionary figure of Ayatollah Khomeini and the millions who faced death as they followed him in the course of the revolution. He knew that such "limit" experiences could lead to new forms of creativity, and he passionately lent his support.[21]

The "creativity" Foucault had in mind was the mass death that the Islamist revolution was sure to engender. Khomeini and the Islamist movement were unambiguous in their agenda; the teaching of Sayyid Qutb, with its emphasis on death and suicide, shaped their reality. It was evident that Khomeini was not planning to set up Jeffersonian institutions based on respect for individual liberty and the right to dissent. Khomeini's violent and intolerant attitude toward non-Muslim minorities (especially Baha'is and Jews), secularists, women, and all dissenters from the

Islamist line was no secret. The fate that would befall these groups when Khomeini came to power was preordained.

In his writing on the revolution, Foucault did not disguise his exhilaration at what Islamists would bring to Iran. Like most believers, he rejected and despised modernity and thus strongly endorsed the ayatollahs' staunch rejection of the Shah's plan of modernization and secularization and their goal of returning to an idealized, pre-modern past—the beginnings of Islam in the seventh century.[22] Foucault earnestly hoped that the Islamist movement's "insane" transgressive discourse would destroy the parameters of a "rational" modernity.[23]

We also see yet again, as over and over in the history of fellow travelers to communist despotisms, the desire of believers to shed their hated selves by blurring their individuality into a collective whole. Indeed, this yearning eerily manifested itself in Foucault's craving "to die liberated from every identity."[24] As Afary and Anderson explain:

> The Islamists and many others who joined the Iranian Revolution seemed to believe that by adopting an attitude of "freedom-toward-death," by recognizing and submitting to the finitude and limitation of their own insignificant human existence, and by aspiring to a cause greater than themselves, they could bring about the collective authentic existence of the Iranian community.[25]

The specter of Khomeini's terror inspired Foucault; he rejoiced over how "as an 'Islamic' movement, it can set the entire region afire, overturn the most unstable regimes, and disturb the most solid." With a hopeful exhilaration, he asked: "What would it be if this cause encompassed the dynamism of an Islamic movement, something much stronger than those with Marxist, Leninist, or Maoist character?"[26]

In his thirsting for a revolution that would purify the earth with human blood, it is by no means insignificant that, as biographer James Miller has meticulously demonstrated, fascination with pain, pleasure, sex, madness, suicide, and death dominated Foucault's life.[27] He celebrated the Marquis de Sade, and he practiced sado-masochism in his homosexual lifestyle.[28] He also made several suicide attempts in his early years—efforts that were connected, in the view of his French biographer, Didier Eribon, to his feelings of guilt over his homosexuality.[29] But the impulses toward suicide ended up forming the basis of a larger philosophy. To the end of his life, Foucault adamantly defended "everyone's right to kill himself"—as he told an interviewer in 1983.[30] Suicide, he wrote in a 1979 essay, was "the simplest of pleasures." One had to prepare for it:

> bit by bit, decorate it, arrange the details, find the ingredients, imagine it, choose it, get advice on it, shape it into a work without spectators, one which exists only for oneself, just for the shortest little moment of life.[31]

Foucault's attraction to the Iranian revolution's promise of death and destruction was also a logical extension of his general support for mob terror. In a debate with Noam Chomsky staged for Dutch television in November 1971, Foucault gleefully asserted that the most positive aspect of proletariat revolution was its violence. "The proletariat doesn't wage war against the ruling class because it considers such a war to be just," he told the MIT professor. He continued:

> The proletariat makes war with the ruling class because, for the first time in history, it wants to take power.... When the proletariat takes power, it may be quite possible that the proletariat will exert toward the classes over which it has triumphed, a violent, dictatorial, and even bloody power. I can't see what objection one could make to this.[32]

Foucault repeated this theme in his glorification of the bloodshed of the French Revolution. In February 1972, in a debate with Pierre Victor on the meaning of "popular justice" for a special issue of Sartre's magazine, *Les temps modernes*, he praised the September Massacres at the height of the French Revolution. As James Miller describes this period:

> [C]rowds of Parisian militants, inflamed by rumors of a royalist plot, had stormed the prisons and set upon suspected traitors. Those believed guilty—among them, a

number of prostitutes and ordinary criminals—were forced to run a gauntlet of clubs, pikes, axes, knives, sabers, even, in one instance, a carpenter's saw. After the victims had been bludgeoned to death and hacked to pieces, the lucky ones were thrown onto a bloody heap; the others had their body parts—decapitated heads, mutilated genitalia— mounted on pikes and triumphantly paraded through the streets of Paris. Before the orgy of killing was over, more than one thousand men and women had died.[33]

Foucault's main thesis in his support of the September Massacres was that popular justice would best be realized by opening up all the prisons and closing down all the courts.[34]

It becomes transparent what attracted Foucault to Khomeini, whom he regarded as a kind of a mythic "saint"[35]: the death and bloodshed of the revolution. As Afary and Anderson demonstrate, Foucault was fascinated by "the appropriation of Shi'ite myths of martyrdom and rituals of penitence by large parts of the revolutionary movement and their willingness to face death in their single-minded goal of overthrowing the Pahlavi regime."[36]

When Khomeini took power, he did not disappoint: the mass terror began immediately. Homosexuals were put in front of firing squads; adulterers (and alleged adulterers) were stoned to death; "enemies of the revolution" were imprisoned, tortured, and killed; women were segregated, forcibly veiled, and placed under a vicious and sadistic system of gender apartheid. And all the while, the killing machine began the mass extermination of Iranian citizens.

Critics who pressed Foucault to account for his position on the revolution confronted him in the French media. But he refused to make any retractions. All he had to say about the terror was his observation in one piece in *Le Monde*:

> Last summer the Iranians said, "We are ready to die by the thousands in order to get the Shah to go." Today it is the Ayatollah who says "Let Iran bleed so that the revolution may be strong." There is a strange echo between these phrases which links them to one another. Does the horror of the second condemn the rapture [*ivresse*] of the first?[37]

In another essay in 1979 ("Is It Useless to Revolt?"), Foucault acknowledged, in passing, the revolution's wrong turn but reaffirmed the principle of revolt and refused to condemn the terror or to apologize for what he had supported. It would be his final word on Iran—or on any issue, for after this he disengaged himself from the public arena and fell into silence.

For a person who had always been fascinated by death and its interconnections with sex, Foucault's life came to an eerie ending when he died of AIDS in 1984. Although many of the facts surrounding his death remain murky, the evidence suggests that Foucault consciously embraced, as Miller puts it, the "specter of death" in the San Francisco gay bathhouses in 1983.[38] It is significant that Foucault, who had attempted to kill himself several times out of guilt feelings regarding his homosexuality, ended up supporting a death cult that murdered homosexuals. As we shall see later in this chapter, many leftist homosexuals would follow this pattern of self-hate and a craving for death. This pathological behavior mirrors that of other leftist intellectuals supporting tyrannies that murder intellectuals—a reality documented throughout this work.

The Palestinian death cult became the next object of leftist veneration in the post-Cold War era. The Left's passion for the Palestinians did not begin only after the fall of communism, of course; it dated back to the 1960s. Believers had always adored Arafat—and he had earned their love. After all, the Soviets backed him, and not only did he oppose evil America, but he also dedicated his life to exterminating an American ally. Most of all, he won the Left's admiration for one particular feat: he created modern terrorism. As David Horowitz points out:

> With the help of the Castro dictatorship, which the American Left embraced for similar reasons, Arafat established the first terrorist training camps and launched the first international campaign of airline hijackings and hostage-takings. The attack of 9/11—whose weapon of choice was hijacked airlines loaded with hostages and whose targets were Wall Street and the Pentagon, the very symbols of American empire—was thus the juncture at which the two jihads finally met.[39]

In terms of being vicious and sadistic, Palestinian terrorists were never outmatched. And so, in terms of the Left's standards for romance, they met every requirement. The PLO's genocide against Lebanese Christians prior to the Israeli invasion of southern Lebanon in 1982 serves as a perfect example. One town priest relates a typical atrocity:

> An entire family had been killed, the Ca'an family, four children all dead and the mother, the father, and the grandfather. The mother was still hugging one of the children. And she was pregnant. The eyes of the children were gone and their limbs were cut off. No legs and no arms.... We buried them in the cemetery, under the shells of the PLO. And while I was burying them, more corpses were found in the street.[40]

Another typical crime:

> The PLO men killed Susan's father and her brother, and raped her mother, who suffered a hemorrhage and died. They raped Susan "many times." They cut off her breasts and shot her. Hours later she was found alive, but with all four of her limbs so badly broken and torn with gunshots that they had to be surgically amputated. She now has only the upper part of one arm.[41]

After Israel liberated Beirut from PLO terror in 1982, some Christian women put forth the idea of putting Susan's picture on a Lebanese stamp, feeling that her suffering symbolized the suffering of their country: "rape and dismemberment by the PLO."[42] But their idea was not actualized.

The victims of other grisly crimes were everywhere to be seen: a newspaper editor found with his fingers cut off joint by joint, his eyes gouged out, and his limbs hacked off; men castrated during torture sessions; men and women chopped to pieces with axes; a pregnant mother of eleven children murdered for no reason; a dead girl found with both hands severed and part of her head missing; a local religious leader forced to watch his daughter being raped and murdered, with her breasts torn away; a man whose limbs were chained to four vehicles which were then driven in opposite directions, tearing him to pieces.[43]

This was all part of the genocide that the PLO perpetrated in Lebanon, where it murdered some one hundred thousand civilians between 1975 and 1981.[44] These rituals of mass death earned the Palestinians a distinguished status in the eyes of the Left and put them next in line behind the communists for adulation. When the Cold War ended, the Palestinians assumed their place as the new barbaric deity to venerate.

Then, just as with the various communist regimes in the twentieth century, and as with Khomeini's bloody massacres, so too leftists flocked to the Palestinian cause at exactly the point when its mass death and suicide reached a pinnacle. As we saw in chapter nine, when Israeli prime minister Ehud Barak offered, at the Camp David talks in 2000, to give the Palestinians peace and their own nation, Arafat responded by rejecting the offer outright without even a counterproposal. It was clear that for the Godfather of Terror, peace with Israel would have ended his political career—and probably his life. It would also have negated the entire raison d'être of the Palestinian Authority: to pursue the mass murder of Jews via suicide.

Arafat launched the Al-Aqsa Intifada, and the American Left predictably took the side of the death cult. Paul Berman has noted how the more pathological the Palestinians became in their nihilistic quest for death, the more excited the Left became.[45] On American campuses from coast to coast, pro-Palestinian placards multiplied at left-wing demonstrations. The divestiture campaign increased its effort to persuade U.S. universities to boycott Israel. The Western European Left followed suit, and Israeli scholars were soon persona non grata at many European universities. The anti-globalization forces worldwide, meanwhile, adopted the Palestinian cause as their own. Berman recounts a typical scene: at the 2002 Socialist Scholars Conference, "a substantial crowd listened to an Egyptian novelist defend a young Palestinian woman who had just committed suicide and murder—and having heard the defense, the crowd broke into applause."[46]

Here again we see the model of *the devil made them do it*. With every violent act committed by Palestinians, the Left blamed Israel—while the United States served as a convenient demon in the background. As Berman notes, if Palestinian violence was monstrous, that surely meant, to the leftist psyche, that Israeli oppression of the Palestinians was monstrous. Israeli oppression was a form of apartheid; even better, from the Left's point of view, the Israelis were like Nazis—which became a standard accusation used to excuse any act of Palestinian violence.[47]

In the leftist vision, therefore, the more the Palestinians hurt the Jews, the more the Jews had obviously hurt the Palestinians. So when the suicide bombings escalated, the demonization of Israel escalated, and when the terror decreased, protests against Israel decreased. Berman explains:

> The protests against Israel, by putting the *onus* for suicide terror on Israeli shoulders, served a rather useful purpose, from this point of view. The protests explained the unexplainable. But when the Israeli response had grown sufficiently severe to stifle at least some of the suicide attacks, the need to defend the rationality of world events was no longer as great—and the impulse to drape Israel with images of Nazism, *apartheid*, and the hatefulness of Judaism consequently subsided.[48]

Once again Berman makes his central point: the Left cannot accept the notion that pathological mass movements exist and that they engage in murder for irrational and nihilistic purposes. But, once again, we must take the argument further: while the Left rationalizes and excuses ideological violence, the real reason it flew into euphoria during the height of the suicide bombings is that, as we have seen again and again, *it loves murderous nihilism and lives vicariously through its deadly manifestations*.

A striking example of the lust for death that burns in the heart of believers is the hatred for Israel among homosexual leftists. Israel is the only nation in the Middle East where homosexuals enjoy equality and rights and do not live in terror. Yet, like Michel Foucault worshipping the Iranian revolution, homosexual leftists support Israel's enemies—under whose rule they themselves would be tortured and killed.

Gay Palestinians live in perpetual fear of arrest, detention without trial, torture, and execution at the hands of Palestinian authorities or other terrorist groups and factions. Homosexual Palestinians are the victims of "honor" killings—otherwise reserved for women—by family members and vigilante mobs. Many Palestinian gays flee to Israel for protection, freedom, and acceptance. Yet leftist homosexuals in the West participate in efforts to assist Palestine in its war against Israel. The group QUIT!: Queers Undermining Israeli Terrorism illustrates this remarkable phenomenon. Their Web site proclaims: "As queers, we are part of an international movement for human rights that encompasses the movement for Palestinian liberation, and all other liberation movements. We are also part of the growing international movement seeking active ways to express our solidarity with the people of Palestine."[49]

Leftist gay groups actually attend "antiwar" and "peace" rallies to denounce Israel and support the Palestinians—only to be roughed up by those they support. In May 2004, in Trafalgar Square in London, Islamists attacked members of two British gay-rights groups, OutRage! and the Queer Youth Alliance, when they tried to participate in a rally for Palestinian rights. In the end, the Islamists forced members of those organizations to stand at the back of the assembled crowd. When the gay activists tried to speak, they were shouted down. They were called, among other things, "racists," "Zionists," "CIA and MI-5 agents," and "supporters of the Sharon government."[50] Gays supporting an adversarial culture that wishes to exterminate them is yet another dark reflection of the suicidal impulse in believers' hearts.

With this in mind, we must now delve into a related pathology: misogyny and the fear and hatred of women's sexuality. Contrary to its professed feminism at home, the Left finds Islamism's war on female freedom intoxicating.

CHAPTER SEVENTEEN

Loving the Burqa

Bring Najaf to New York

—Naomi Klein, the title of her August 26, 2004 article in *The Nation*

Just as the devotion to totalitarian puritanism played a central role in
the Left's solidarity with vicious communist regimes throughout
the twentieth century, so too it serves as a core component of the
Left's current romance with militant Islam.

As we have seen before, the Left's lust for totalitarian
puritanism does not mean, obviously, that believers are themselves
nonsexual. On the contrary: many of them are highly
promiscuous—and are passionate promoters of promiscuity.[1] The
key is that believers see sexual self-determination, like artistic and
intellectual freedom, as a hallmark of capitalist societies—the very
societies they aim to destroy via the transmutation of this right into
a weapon. In adversarial societies, where the road to utopia has
already been laid, such a right—and the emotional bonds that
might develop from it—must be rejected, since it threatens the
worship of the totality.

A death cult's attempt to purge human beings of their
capacity for personal love is invariably accompanied by an
assault on women and their freedom. Women's nature, and
especially their sexual qualities, are deeply subversive of a
totalitarian order, and so despotism will do everything it can to
stifle them. And believers will always cheer it on.

From what is ostensibly an entirely different perspective, Western leftists, and especially feminists, have long sought to prevent men from appreciating women's physical beauty. Labeling this appreciation the "objectification" and "exploitation" of the female body, believers have tried to prevent women from using their beauty and sexuality *as they see fit*. Just as believers such as Orville Schell, Claudie Broyelle, and Shirley MacLaine were enchanted with the enforced Maoist dress that attempted to desexualize Chinese citizens, so the new generation of believers genuflects before the Islamist *burqa*. The *burqa*, like the Maoist uniform, further attracts believers by virtue of the fact that women in Islamist societies have no say in whether or not they will wear it. Longing to submerge themselves in a totality where their own choices will be negated, believers are always drawn to a totalitarian ethos that forbids freedom of conscience.

We will now focus on Western feminists' solidarity with Islamist gender apartheid, a phenomenon, like Michel Foucault's death wish, that serves as a powerful demonstration of this work's central thesis.

One would think that upon examining the structure of Islamic gender apartheid, with its "honor" killings, mandatory veiling, forced segregation, forced marriage, female genital mutilation, and rape as punishment, a feminist would experience nothing less than horror and revulsion. But leftist feminists in the West have remained silent about the fate of women behind the Islamic Curtain, and their shameless but unsurprising disposition has been well documented.[2]

Leftist feminists' veneration of a death cult that hates and mutilates women demands a professional level of self-deception, and, as believers feminists have the Left's favorite model of denial-excuse justification readily available.[3]

The first step in dealing with Islam's gender apartheid, therefore, is denial. For decades, leftist feminists have howled with moral indignation about the "inequality" of women in their own society, yet when it comes to Islam's barbaric treatment of women, which has no parallel in the West, their reaction is silence. Author Kay S. Hymowitz comments on this phenomenon:

The weird fact is that, even after the excesses of the Taliban did more to forge an American consensus about women's rights than thirty years of speeches by Gloria Steinem, feminists refused to touch this subject. They have averted their eyes from the harsh, blatant oppression of millions of women, even while they have continued to stare into the Western patriarchal abyss, indignant over female executives who cannot join an exclusive golf club and college women who do not have their own lacrosse teams.[4]

Leftist feminists need to engage in this denial in order to pay allegiance to the party line of anti-Americanism, as well as to hold onto their self-created victim identity. If they conceded that adversarial regimes brutalize women in ways unlike anything that occurs in the home society they hate, then they would have to reconsider whether they themselves are in fact the victims they have always claimed to be. They would also have to question whether the community they desperately need to belong to—the worldwide community of the victims of capitalism and American imperialism—even exists. These realities are far too painful and threatening for most feminists to consider. A rare exception is author Elinor Burkett, a former leftist who changed her ideological views after traveling through the Muslim world. She observes:

> You're talking about people blinded by their own need to define themselves according to their own perceived oppression. They look around the world seeking "victims" to identify with to reinforce their own sense of victimization, to afford themselves the psychological and moral satisfaction of joining hands with the world's other oppressed. Unfortunately, since they're ultimately acting out of narcissism, they blunder into the most embarrassing possible contradictions without even seeing them. Then, when they're called on their inconsistency, they get the added benefit of feeling misunderstood and persecuted yet again.[5]

This phenomenon is at the core of the progressive faith: sacrificing others for the sake of one's own personal agenda. Kay Hymowitz delineates this perfectly: "The irony couldn't be darker: the very people protesting the imperialist exploitation of the 'Other' endorse that Other's repressive customs as a means of promoting their own uniquely Western agenda—subverting the heterosexual patriarchy."[6]

In order to keep their denial in place, leftist feminists employ myriad pathological strategies. Hymowitz notes how the exploitation of "gender feminism" is one of them.[7] Holding males to be inherently evil and violent, gender feminism excuses monsters like the Taliban because holding them up to real scrutiny might suggest that some men are worse than others and, more dangerous still, that it might actually be a progressive step for males in the U.S. military to liberate the abused women stuck in other men's primitive cultures. For gender feminists, this notion is unthinkable—especially since it also suggests that war, males' creation (according to gender feminism), might be justified in some cases.[8] Hymowitz writes:

> Too busy celebrating their own virtue and contemplating their own victimhood, gender feminists cannot address the suffering of their Muslim sisters realistically, as light years worse than their own petulant grievances. They are too intent on hating war to ask if unleashing its horrors might be worth it to overturn a brutal tyranny that, among its manifold inhumanities, treats women like animals. After all, hating war and *machismo* are evidence of the moral superiority that comes with being born female.[9]

Leftist feminists end up reasoning as follows: *Better to let women suffer under a vicious regime than to admit that there are cultures to which the West is superior.* Leftist feminists will go to extraordinary lengths to avoid acknowledging that the West may actually have something to teach non-Western societies.

When the empirical evidence begins to make it impossible for leftist feminists to deny the barbarity of Islamic gender apartheid, they switch to the second stage: excuse. Men perpetrate evil against women behind the Islamic Curtain because *the devil made them do it*. When confronted with the fact that, for instance, wife abuse is a widespread pathology in Palestinian culture, leftist feminists admit that Palestinian men are abusive, but argue they are so only because of the oppression and humiliation they experience under Israeli "occupation."[10] As feminist author Jan Goodwin argues, for example, if only American and Israeli oppression stopped, Palestinian men would no longer feel a need to beat their wives.[11]

Miriam Cooke, a Duke professor and head of the Association for Middle East Women's Studies, gives voice to another rationalization tactic. In an interview with Hymowitz, she explained that "When men are traumatized [by colonial rule], they tend to traumatize their own women.... Now there is a return of colonialism...in the context of globalization. What is driving Islamist men is globalization."[12] Cooke also praises female suicide bombers as strong women who manifest "agency" against colonial powers. Polygamy, meanwhile, can be "liberating and empowering." This is because, Cooke explains, "our norm is the Western, heterosexual, single couple. If we can imagine different forms that would allow us to be something other than a heterosexual couple, we might imagine polygamy working." She also argues that a woman may be relieved when her husband takes a new wife, because then he will make fewer demands on her—a utopian dream for the likes of radical feminist Andrea Dworkin, who, as we shall see later in this chapter, viewed sexual intercourse as oppression.[13] Or, Cooke argues, it may give these women the opportunity to take a lover. When Hymowitz asked how widespread this could be in a culture where women can be stoned to death for even the *rumor* of adultery, Cooke answers: "I don't know; I'm interested in discourse."[14]

Cooke perfectly exemplifies what Hymowitz describes as "postcolonial feminism." Postcolonial feminism holds that the "imperialist" history and legacy are so evil, oppressive, and destructive that no one in the West can ever, under any circumstances, make a legitimate criticism of *any* former colonial culture or people. No matter how bad they are, not only did we make them do it, *we are always worse.*

The entire "postcolonial" school is based on the Marxist notion that any barbarity committed in the Third World is the desperate backlash of those whose throats had been pinned down beneath the boots of the imperialist and capitalist West. Pressing forward with the revolution against capitalism, therefore, is much more important than worrying about the victims of the revolution itself.[15] Postcolonial feminism helps leftist feminists argue that the mutilation of their female counterparts in adversarial societies is unimportant, insignificant, and, ultimately, worthy of support.

Postcolonial feminism is intertwined with cultural relativism and multiculturalism: the West has no right to impose its values on non-Western societies, because no culture can be said to be better than any other (except that ours is always worse). To give Islamic leaders a pass on their persecution of women is, therefore, multiculturally sensitive. By following these steps, as Hymowitz notes, leftist feminists succeed in excusing the horrible crimes perpetrated against women under Islam as "an authentic, indigenous—and therefore appropriate—expression of Arab and Middle Eastern identity."[16]

The double standard in the Left's cultural relativism is transparent, since such relativism always dissipates when it comes time to scrutinize Western society. When the issue is enforced veiling and "honor" killings, for example, leftist feminists maintain that no one can say what is right and wrong. But if the issue is how women's bodies are "objectified" in Western advertising, cultural relativism immediately goes out the window. Such advertising is depicted as an immoral, loathsome emblem of the capitalist, patriarchal, heterosexist, homophobic power structure's attempt to marginalize women to spheres of powerlessness.[17]

The whole denial-excuse justification model is, of course, a cover for leftist feminists' inner celebration of the Islamist horror itself. Once again, as we have seen throughout this work, the denial-excuse justification tactic serves as a tool to keep the believer's vision intact while hiding his most powerful yearning: to venerate the death and destruction wreaked by the adversarial tyranny. In other words, leftist feminists give allegiance to woman haters like the Taliban and the Iranian mullahs not just because they hate America and worship the *the enemy of my enemy is my friend* paradigm, but also because, like Michel Foucault vis-à-vis Khomeini's revolution, or any number of intellectuals vis-à-vis the communist regimes, they thrill to what the Islamists do. Leftist feminists not only refuse to criticize the *burqa*, but romanticize and champion it, because they cherish the idea of a tyrannical force smothering the components of womanhood that they despise in their own societies and in themselves.

One of the underpinnings of leftist feminism is the rejection of female sexuality in the form in which it exists. Radical feminists, such as Andrea Dworkin and Catharine A. MacKinnon, argue that sexuality could be transformed because, in their view, it is a social construct of the capitalist/heterosexual world, rather than a constant in the human condition. This form of feminism despises the idea of women's bodies being appreciated in any way by males. Males' arousal by, and adoration of, the female physique is seen only negatively: as the objectification, exploitation, oppression, and devaluation of women. Dworkin, for instance, considered ordinary women's lives in the United States to be an "atrocity." By its very nature, sexual intercourse, in her view, was oppressive to women and a violation of their individuality.[18] This is why so many leftist feminists, like Dworkin herself, de-feminize and de-beautify themselves as a social statement. Thus, the concept of women having their femininity submerged and forcibly covered under an adversarial despotic regime is utopian. By contrast, the reality of women enjoying their own physical beauty and feeling and being empowered by it is anathema—at least as bad as anything the Taliban might do. Journalist Jill Nelson personifies this mentality. Writing about the Islamic riots that followed the Miss World pageant in Nigeria, she commented on MSNBC's Web site: "It's equally disrespectful and abusive to have women prancing around a stage in bathing suits for cash or walking the streets shrouded in *burqas* in order to survive."[19] Hymowitz reflects on this world view: "The utopian is less interested in freeing women to make their own choices than in engineering and imposing her own elite vision of a perfect society."[20]

The yearnings of leftist feminists reveal themselves throughout the "peace" demonstrations against the U.S. liberation of Iraq. At the "International Day of Emergency Protest" in San Francisco on June 5, 2004, for instance, some female antiwar protesters veiled themselves like Muslim women, while others dressed as terrorists. The next day, a birthday celebration for Israel—the "Israel in the

Ballpark" festival—took place at nearby SBC Park. The "peace movement" made sure to make its presence felt. Again, some of the women veiled themselves, while one woman wore a Saudi male head covering and high-heeled shoes.[21] It is worth noting that if any of these women attempted to act this way under the systems with which they were expressing solidarity, they would be imprisoned and tortured at least, and probably executed.

A prime example of this radical feminist psychology is Dr. Unni Wikan, a professor of social anthropology at the University of Oslo. Wikan's solution for the high incidence of Muslims raping Norwegian women stresses neither punishment of the perpetrators nor repudiation of the Islamic theology that legitimizes such abuse of women. Rather, Wikan recommends that Norwegian women should veil themselves. "I will not blame the rapes on Norwegian women," Wikan wrote. "But Norwegian women must understand that we live in a multicultural society and adapt themselves to it."[22]

It is clear, therefore, that the Western feminist who supports the *burqa* for others is attempting to rush the development in the external world that she has already initiated in her own internal world: the shattering of her own female persona and all the feminine qualities that she despises. And so it is no mystery at all why *Nation* columnist Naomi Klein calls out to "Bring Najaf to New York." In her account of the fighting in the Iraqi Shi'ite stronghold of Najaf, she urges leftists to join in solidarity with the Islamofascist terrorists headed by Muqtada al-Sadr and his Mahdi Army.[23] What would be the fate of women under a regime headed by Muqtada al-Sadr? Klein knows very well, just as Foucault understood the horrors that would befall homosexuals under Khomeini.

The *burqa* has a special place in the hearts of leftist feminists for the same reason that leftist Jews are attracted to Islamism, a haunting phenomenon that we explore in our final chapter. Nothing better crystallizes the lust for death and suicide that lurks in the heart of the progressive faith.

CHAPTER EIGHTEEN

The Bonds of Jew Hate

"Auschwitz meant that six million Jews were killed... for what they were: money Jews. Finance capital and the banks, the hard core of the system of imperialism and capitalism, had turned the hatred of men against money and exploitation and against the Jews...Anti-Semitism is really a hatred of capitalism."[1]

—Ulrike Meinhof, German leftist and PLO collaborator

When *Hezbollah terrorists* crossed into Israeli territory in July 2006, murdering three Israeli soldiers and kidnapping two, and then launched hundreds of rockets into Israeli cities and population centers, this was nothing new. Hezbollah had used southern Lebanon as a base of operations for years. This was in direct violation of UN Security Council Resolution 1559, which explicitly calls for the disarming of all militias in Lebanon and the reassertion of Lebanese government authority in the country's southern region.[2] The Iranian mullahs, however, have long used Hezbollah as a proxy to wage a terror war on Israel, and evidence suggests that they themselves ordered the July 2006 attacks.[3]

Israel responded to this Iranian-backed terror by launching first air strikes and then a ground assault against Hezbollah targets in Lebanon, in an effort to remove the terrorist army from the area and to disable the thousands of rockets it had acquired from Iran and from Syria.[4] However, while attempting to defend itself, Israel continued its long tradition of taking every precaution to avoid civilian casualties—and in so doing increased the risk of death and injury to its own soldiers. Hezbollah, on the other hand, engaged in *its* long tradition: targeting its rockets with the intention of killing as many Israeli civilians as possible, and positioning its bases in the midst of densely populated civilian areas so as to cause Lebanese civilian deaths, which could be exploited for propaganda purposes. The Qana "massacre" was typical: Israel was blamed for the deaths of Lebanese civilians in a building that collapsed after it was bombed, allegedly by Israeli troops. Hezbollah terrorists, however, had stationed themselves in the immediate vicinity of the building. Moreover, the bombing itself turned out to be a Hezbollah operation.[5] Yet the incident remained a propaganda coup against Israel, and the number of civilian deaths was exaggerated to blacken Israel's reputation even further.[6] Alongside these developments, the terror group Hamas—which, as we saw in chapter fourteen, represents the Palestinian version of the Nazi Party, and which now controls the Palestinian Parliament—also kidnapped an Israeli soldier, Gilad Shalit. This led Israel to attack Hamas headquarters in Gaza and to arrest Hamas leaders and officials, while once again doing its best to preserve innocent life.

In these dire circumstances, the Left carried on with its sacred tradition and extended a hand of solidarity to the usual suspects. *The Nation* led the way, excusing the terrorists and blaming their actions on Israel. Marwan Bishara's article "Israel on the Offensive" reflected the position of the magazine, painting Israel as the aggressor and refusing to condemn Hezbollah and Hamas. The terror groups, Bishara explained, are simply "a byproduct of an oppressive occupation, not the other way around."[7] In other words, *the devil made them do it.*

Bishara and *The Nation* weren't doing anything particularly new; their stance was simply a continuation of the Left's long romance with tyranny and terror. As David Horowitz noted: "The *Nation* is a fellow-traveler of the new Nazism, just as surely as it was a fellow-traveler of the old Stalinism." Horowitz continued:

> *The Nation*'s current apologetics for the terrorist bloc continue a nearly one-hundred-year tradition of its editors' support for the totalitarian enemies of America

and the West. For nearly one hundred years, the editors of *The Nation* explained and justified every communist tyrant from Stalin to Castro; when terrorists slaughtered the innocent on 9/11, *The Nation's* editors decried *American* jingoism and *America's* "empire;" they opposed the overthrow of Saddam Hussein; and they continue to attack the liberation of Iraq as an imperialist "occupation" and democratic America as a "terrorist state." [8]

Several strands of leftist ideology converge to make Jews and Israel the perfect objects of believers' hatred—even as they are intrinsically the objects of Islamists' hatred. First, as we saw in chapter thirteen, leftism, like Islamism, detests modernity, individual freedom, and any value placed on *individual* human life, notions with which Jews are strongly identified. Jewish values are most strongly represented by Israel, a tiny nation that refuses to be extinguished despite myriad attempts to drown it in violence and terror. Representing the triumph of the human spirit, Israel has come to symbolize all that is despised by Islamists and leftists alike.

In addition, Jews are seen as being synonymous with the oppressive structures of corporate capitalism and globalization,[9] and Israel is both the outpost of Western values in the Middle East and an ally of the United States in the terror war. While Islamists hate America, in part, for supporting Israel, leftists hate Israel for its alliance with the United States—and for sharing its principal values. This is why anti-Semitism has become so conveniently enmeshed with anti-Americanism, anti-capitalism, and anti-globalization.

Furthermore, since Palestinians are now the object of believers' worship, Jews have become the replacements for the "class enemy" of the communist era. In the vision of the believer, the existence of scapegoats is crucial in order to justify a continuous cycle of terror and death. With communism gone and the Palestinians serving as the new utopians, the Jews become the leading candidates for utopia's gulag.

In this context, we begin to understand more clearly why the Left so quickly rushed to the defense of Hamas and Hezbollah in the summer of 2006. American academia spearheaded the movement. One thousand leftist professors signed a petition that denounced Israel for its "brutal bombing and invasion of Gaza," and its "acts of Israeli state terrorism" in Lebanon. This petition included no denunciation of Hamas or Hezbollah, only a call for the immediate release of jailed terrorists (whom the petition described as "Palestinian and Lebanese political prisoners") and a condemnation of "Israel's destructive and expansionist policies," which the petition said were "primarily to blame for the seemingly perpetual 'Middle East crisis.'" In other words, once again: *the devil made them do it.* And the petition was not intended merely to criticize Israel; it also demanded that Israel immediately stop defending itself, but made no similar call for restraint by terrorist groups seeking Israel's annihilation.[10]

Three of the most prominent signatories of this Jew-hating petition were themselves of Jewish ancestry: leftist guru Noam Chomsky, Holocaust denier Norman Finkelstein, and terror-apologist Joel Beinin.[11] These leftist Jews perfectly represent the self-hate and instinct for death in which the believers' solidarity with the Islamist Jew-hating death cult is rooted.

Let us first consider Chomsky, who has dedicated much of his life to siding with those who perpetrate genocide against Jews. In Chomsky's view, Israel has committed the dual crimes of failing to pursue socialism and of being the cause of the entire conflict in the Middle East.[12] Chomsky's positions regarding Israel and Palestinians are not surprising. He casts no blame on Arafat's PLO even though it perpetrated genocide against Lebanese Christians. He maintains that the PLO left Lebanon in 1982 not because the Israelis forced it out, but for "humanitarian" reasons, to spare Beirut total destruction at the hands of the evil Israelis. Thus, he says, the terrorists left with an image of "heroism." Chomsky also believes that the PLO has been far more sincere and forthcoming than either Israel or the United States in trying to reach a peace agreement. And he often notes "points of similarity" between Israel and Nazi Germany.[13]

As is characteristic of believers, Chomsky's support for the Palestinians has always increased when their program of genocide against Israelis escalates. As we saw in chapter fourteen, when

Arafat punished Israel for offering the peace agreement at Camp David by unleashing the Second Intifada, Chomsky ecstatically took Arafat's side. Indeed, it was exactly at the height of the suicide bombings that Chomsky signed a petition demanding that universities withdraw their investments from Israel.[14]

Chomsky's romance with Islamic terror also involves a flirtation with Holocaust deniers and neo-Nazis. By denying the Holocaust, Jew haters attempt to erase historical memory and to increase the chances of another Holocaust taking place.[15] As sociologist Werner Cohn points out, Chomsky has dedicated himself to defending the freedom of speech of neo-Nazis. He has been a particularly passionate defender of the leaders of Holocaust "revisionism" in France.[16] Robert Faurisson, Europe's leading Holocaust revisionist scholar, and his followers have distinguished themselves primarily, as Cohn has noted, by their "relentless campaign of libel and slander—always couched in very personal terms—against the witnesses and the scholars of the Holocaust."[17]

Academic Norman Finkelstein is another example of a Jewish believer venerating those who seek to extinguish him. A Hamas and Hezbollah apologist, Finkelstein has made a career out of minimizing the magnitude of the Holocaust and of denouncing what he calls the Holocaust "industry," which he believes operates an "outright extortion racket."[18] In his book *The Holocaust Industry*, for instance, he alleges that Holocaust survivors were "cheats" who had made up their past to collect money. In Finkelstein's world, a global Zionist conspiracy exploits and exaggerates the Holocaust to extract reparations, gain a mantle of victimhood, and to legitimize the Israeli "oppression" of the Palestinians. It is the Jews, according to Finkelstein, who are to be blamed for anti-Semitism.[19] It is no great surprise that Finkelstein counts neo-Nazis among his staunchest defenders.[20]

Finkelstein has taken his Jew-hating show on the road. He regularly visits college campuses across the U.S., usually at the invitation of the Muslim Students Association, where he indulges in his favorite themes and embraces homicidal Palestinians. One of his most passionate themes is praising Hezbollah.[21] He honors the terror group for its "heroic resistance" and its "historic contributions."[22]

In January 2008, Finkelstein embarked on his own political pilgrimage, traveling to Lebanon to embrace Hezbollah in person. During this role of fellow traveler, he met with a senior Hezbollah official, Nabil Kaouk, in south Lebanon, in his office in the coastal city of Tyre and told reporters that "Hezbollah represents hope."[23] He also went on Lebanese television, expressing his "solidarity" with Hezbollah and calling Israel an "invader."[24]

Finkelstein's Hezbollah sojourn serves as a haunting mirror image of Chomsky's Hezbollah voyage in May 2006. Here, we see two leftist Jews embracing Jew-hating terrorist entities that seek to exterminate Jews—an eerie symbol of the continuation of the Left's dark tradition of political pilgrimages.

Chomsky and Finkelstein's love affairs with those who perpetrate genocide against Jews serve as a powerful reflection of the overall disposition of leftist Jews. As we saw in chapter fourteen, when Hamas won the Palestinian parliamentary elections of January 2006, the Brit Tzedek v'Shalom (Jewish Alliance for Justice and Peace) immediately published the names of 387 rabbis who had signed a petition demanding that the U.S. government not withhold aid to the new Hamas-controlled PA government. And these rabbis were fully cognizant of what Hamas is and what its key objectives are.[25]

This phenomenon is part of the same psychological virus that motivates leftist intellectuals to venerate adversarial tyrannies that exterminate intellectuals and that inspires leftist feminists to support totalisms that persecute women. Leftist Jews supporting Jew hatred is just another extension of the main death-wish impulse of believers.

And so we come to the end of our tale of the Left's romance with tyranny and terror. Just like the Western intellectuals who journeyed to Russia during and after the Bolshevik revolution, so too present-day Jewish, feminist, and homosexual believers continue the long tradition of members of the political faith in waging war on themselves and, ultimately, lusting for their own annihilation inside a totalitarian dream—and nightmare. This is the story of the Left: a long and horrifying journey into the heart of darkness, destruction, and death.

The image of Jimmy Carter embracing the leaders of Hamas, a terror organization that has spilled oceans of Jewish blood, speaks volumes of what dark desires and yearnings lurk in the heart of the American Left today. These are the desires and yearnings that have inspired the "progressive" feminist Naomi Klein and others of her ilk to pine and call for bringing "Najaf to New York." This would mean, of course, that the Iraqi Shi'ite stronghold, where Muqtada al-Sadr and his Mahdi Army at one time ran their torture chambers and sowed their terror, would be replicated on America's shores.

What could a Naomi Klein possibly see admirable in the vicious nihilistic terror of the Mahdi Army? Would she remain free and at large in a society under its tyrannical clutches? The dark answers to such questions lie in the fate of the believers who journeyed to Russia after the 1917 Bolshevik Revolution and in the fate of the leftist Iranians who returned to their country after the 1979 Iranian Revolution. These were the political pilgrims who came to help build the paradises in which they hoped to shed themselves of their own unwanted selves. They paid the ultimate price. And no lesser cost must be paid for the momentous transformation of sterilizing the unclean earth. For such disinfection can be made possible only by the purifying power of human blood—blood which, in the utopian enterprise, must, in the final chapter, become one's own.

NOTES

INTRODUCTION

1. Associated Press, "CBS's Wallace interviews Ahmadinejad," and Reuters, "What retirement? Mike Wallace gets scoop in Iran."
2. Laksin, "Carter's Terror Tour."
3. Rubin, "Carter's Hurrah?
4. Laksin, "Carter's Terror Tour."
5. Ibid.
6. Associated Press, "Former U.S. President Jimmy Carter calls for restoring aid to Palestinians."
7. Ignatius, "Beirut's Berlin Wall."
8. For an excellent account of the Left's reaction to the elections, see Ben Johnson, "Vindication," and Laksin, "The Antiwar Left's Conspiracy of Silence."
9. Ben Johnson, "Vindication."
10. Ibid.
11. Naomi Klein, "Bring Najaf to New York."
12. Kimball, "Hitchens, Galloway Clash."
13. Iraq New Network, "Galloway Calls for Global Unity." See Part IV of this book for a more detailed exposition.
14. Kovacs, "Cindy: Terrorists 'freedom fighters.'"
15. Laksin, "Tom Hayden's Iraqi Jihad."
16. MEMRI, "British MP George Galloway at Damascus University."
17. For an excellent analysis of the Left's position on Iraq in the context of its past Vietnam position, see Horowitz, "The McGovern Syndrome." For an analysis of how the Democratic Party itself wishes for an American defeat in Iraq, see Collier and Horowitz, "The Party of Retreat and Defeat."
18. Tom Hayden, "An Exit Strategy for Iraq Now."
19. Bishara, "Israel on the Offensive."
20. A fuller account of the Left's romance with Hezbollah is given in chapter eighteen.
21. Horowitz and Laksin, "Noam Chomsky's Love Affair with Nazis."
22. MEMRI, "U.S. Linguist Noam Chomsky Meets with Hizbullah Leaders" and Hussein, "Chomsky needs to learn a lot more about Lebanon."
23. MEMRI, "Hizbullah Leader Hassan Nasrallah: Death to America," and MEMRI, "Hizbullah Secretary-General Sheikh Hassan Nasrallah Threatens the U.S."
24. For an account of how Soros and other radicals have gained control of the Democratic Party and have stirred disunion and disloyalty in its ranks, see Horowitz and Poe, The Shadow Party.

25. Quoted in Horowitz and Johnson, *Party of Defeat*, 14. For an analysis of Soros' smear of Bush, see Ibid. 14-17.

26. Ibid, 17.

27. Ibid., 39-41.

28. For the best account of the damage the Left and the Democratic Party have inflicted, and continue to inflict, on American security in the face of Islamist terror, see Horowitz and Johnson, *Party of Defeat*. See also Horowitz, *Unholy Alliance* and Horowitz, "How the Left Undermined American Security before 9/11" for an account of how the Left influenced the Democratic Party's assault on America's national intelligence apparatus and military defenses. Bossie's *Intelligence Failure* demonstrates how the Clinton administration's devotion to leftist principles left America open to the 9/11 attacks. Paul Sperry exposes how the leftist agenda has allowed Islamist operatives to infiltrate American institutions—including law enforcement, the military, and the education system—in *Infiltration*. An excellent account of how President Jimmy Carter's leftist vision severely damaged America's security interests throughout the world is Steven Hayward's *The Real Jimmy Carter*.

CHAPTER ONE: THE ROOTS OF DENIAL

1. See *DiscoverTheNetworks.org*.

2. Kurt Nimmo, "David Horowitz's Smear Portal."

3. In an article on his Web site, Moore declares, "The Iraqis who have risen up against the occupation are not 'insurgents' or 'terrorists' or 'The Enemy.' They are the REVOLUTION, the Minutemen, and their numbers will grow—and they will win." See "Heads Up...from Michael Moore."

4. For examples of Nimmo's feelings of kindred connection with Islamist terrorists, see the collection of his essays for Alexander Cockburn's *CounterPunch.org* in Kurt Nimmo, *Another Day in the Empire*, and on his blog, *kurtnimmo.com*.

5. David Horowitz has done the best job of delineating the reasons why the Left can be labeled as it is and held accountable for complicity in the mass crimes of socialism. See his debate with Norm Geras and Nick Cohen in Glazov, "A New 'New Left'?" and his debate with Peter Beinart in Glazov, "Only Liberals Can Win the War on Terror?"

CHAPTER TWO: THE BELIEVER'S DIAGNOSIS

1. Davies, *Mission to Moscow*, 217.

2. Quoted in Fontova, *Fidel*, 11.

3. Berrigan, *Night Flight to Hanoi*, 125, 130.

4. Hoffer, *The True Believer*, 6.

5. For a comprehensive analysis of the how the leftist rejects his society for his own failure to find meaning in life, see Paul Hollander's masterpieces *Political Pilgrims* and *Anti-Americanism*.

6. See Horowitz's essay "The Religious Roots of Radicalism" in *The Politics of Bad Faith*.

7. Hoffer, *True Believer*, 12-13.

8. For a succinct compilation of communism's crimes and death toll in each country, see Courtois, et. al., *Black Book of Communism*.

9. For an excellent discussion of the Left's failure to deal with the historical meaning and future implications of communism's collapse, see Horowitz, *The Politics of Bad Faith*.

10. For one of the best works on how Marx's dark vision—and the morbid ingredients of his own personal life—laid the foundation for Marxist terror, see the chapter titled "Karl Marx: Howling Gigantic Curses," in Paul Johnson, *Intellectuals*, 52-82.

11. Quoted in Fontova, *Fidel*, 77.

12. The writers in *The God That Failed*—Arthur Koestler, Ignazio Silone, Richard Wright, André Gide, Louis Fischer, and Stephen Spender—represented the first generation that broke with the political faith and were dehumanized by their former comrades. See Crossman, *The God That Failed*. Yet while these individuals broke with communism, many of them did so by rejecting Stalinism while holding onto a belief in a "democratic socialism." David Horowitz and others, however, made a complete break with their past. Horowitz gives the most powerful testimony to the ordeal of breaking with the faith in his memoir, *Radical Son*.

13. See the compilation of Horowitz's best work in Horowitz, *Left Illusions*.

14. Horowitz, *Politics of Bad Faith*, 56.

15. The best works analyzing the Left's callous indifference to the victims of Communism are Hollander's *Political Pilgrims* and *Anti-Americanism*.

16. Potter, *History and American Society*, 307.

17. Hoffer, *True Believer*, 16.

18. Jerry Rubin, *Do It*, 22.

19. Ibid., 35-36.

20. The Christian Peacemaker Teams' Web site is www.cpt.org. See chapter sixteen for more details.

21. Potter, *History and American Society*, 381.

22. Hollander, *Anti-Americanism*, 468.

23. Hollander, *Political Pilgrims*, 8.

24. Inspired by her mentor, the leftist utopian Franz Boas, Mead embarked on her 1925-26 voyage to Samoa hungry to find a sexually liberated society where young people didn't go through the difficult phases of adolescent sexual adjustment characteristic of "repressed" Western youth. She "discovered" everything she sought: Samoans found romantic love silly and were nonchalant about infidelity, divorce, homosexuality, and so on. As common sense suggested and later evidence confirmed, Mead's "discoveries" were all false. The adolescent girls who were her informants made up the sorts of stories they sensed she wanted to hear. As anthropologist Derek Freeman concluded, Mead's work represents the worst example of "self-deception in the history of the behavioral sciences." See Freeman, *Margaret Mead and Samoa*.

25. Hollander, *Political Pilgrims*, 23.

26. Rubin, *Do It*, 7-8.

27. Hamilton, *Appeal of Fascism*. See also Griffiths, *Fellow Travellers of the Right*.

28. For an excellent essay on the modern Left's Fascist origins, see Ray, "Left-wing Fascism: An Intellectual Disorder." David Horowitz has shown how Nazi intellectuals, notably Martin Heidegger, have had an immense influence on the Left's vision. See Horowitz, "The Left after Communism," in *The Politics of Bad Faith*, 36-39. See also Robert Conquest's discussion of how fascist and communist totalitarianism blur into one another in *The Dragons of Expectation*, 11-21.

29. Berman, *Terror and Liberalism*, 45.

30. Quoted in Paul Johnson, *Modern Times*, 51.

31. Hollander, *Political Pilgrims*, 44-45.

32. Thoreau, *Walden*, 304.

33. For a succinct discussion of the Soviet anti-sexual revolution, see Pawel, "Sex under Socialism."

34. In Zamyatin's *We*, the earliest of these three novels, the despotic regime keeps human beings in line by giving them license for *regulated* sexual promiscuity, while private love is illegal. The hero breaks the rules with a woman who seduces him—not only into forbidden love but also into a counterrevolutionary struggle. In the end, the totality forces the hero, like the rest of the world's population, to undergo the Great Operation, which annihilates the part of the brain that gives life to passion and imagination, and therefore spawns the potential for love. In Orwell's *1984*, the main character ends up being tortured and broken at the Ministry of Love for having engaged in the outlawed behavior of unregulated love. In Huxley's *Brave New World*, promiscuity is encouraged—everyone has sex with everyone else under regime rules, but no one is allowed to make a deep and independent private connection.

35. Quoted in Collier and Horowitz, *Destructive Generation*, 85-86.

36. Ibid., 86-87.

37. Horowitz, "Religious Roots of Radicalism."

38. Horowitz, "V-Day, 2001," in *Left Illusions*, 315-318.

CHAPTER THREE: WORSHIPPING THE FIRST COMMUNIST DEATH CULT

1. The standard works on the fellow travelers are Paul Hollander's *Political Pilgrims* and *Anti-Americanism*. See also David Caute, *The Fellow-Travellers*.

2. Arthur Koestler provides a powerful description of the ideological "shock absorbers" that made him, and other believers, explain away what they saw. See Crossman, *The God That Failed*, 56-62.

3. Hollander, *Political Pilgrims*, 347-400.

4. The Potemkin villages get their name from Grigory Aleksandrovich Potemkin, who had entire fake villages built for the sole purpose of deceiving Catherine the Great on her visits to Ukraine and Crimea in the eighteenth century.

5. Quoted in Hollander, *Political Pilgrims*, 126.

6. Berman, *Terror and Liberalism*, 43.

7. Dmitri Volkogonov employed declassified KGB documents in the Soviet archives to confirm the Leninist roots of Stalinism. See Volkogonov, *Lenin: A New Biography*.

8. Quoted in Hollander, *Political Pilgrims*, 168.

9. Ibid.

10. Shaw, *Rationalization of Russia*, 18.

11. Conservative estimates place the number of deaths resulting from Stalin's purges and forced collectivization campaign at approximately twenty to twenty-five million. Directed primarily at farmers in the early 1930s, the official massacre by deportation and terror-famine dealt Ukraine the hardest blow: roughly five million Ukrainians (20 percent of the Ukrainian population) were executed or died from forced labor and officially inflicted starvation in 1932-33. The definitive accounts of Stalin's mass political purges and collectivization policies are Robert Conquest's *The Great Terror* and *The Harvest of Sorrow*. See also Walter Laqueur, *Stalin: The Glasnost Revelations* and Conquest, *The Great Terror: A Reassessment*. For one of the most authoritative and succinct accounts of Lenin's and Stalin's reigns of terror, see Nicolas Werth, "A State against Its People: Violence, Repression, and Terror in the Soviet Union," in Courtois et al., *Black Book of Communism*, 33-269.

12. Hollander, *Political Pilgrims*, 11.

13. Caute, *Fellow-Travellers*, 3.

14. Ibid., 107.

15. An excellent account of Duranty's life is Sally J. Taylor's biography, *Stalin's Apologist*.

16. Quoted in Berlau, "All the Lies Fit to Print."

17. Though it has been conclusively proven that Duranty was a willing accomplice to Stalin's mass murder, the *Times* still lists him in its annual list of *New York Times* Pulitzer Prize winners. This is no surprise, since the evidence demonstrates that the *Times* was complicit with Duranty in making sure his dispatches reflected the official position of the Stalin regime.

18. Taylor, *Stalin's Apologist*, 28-33.

19. Glazov, "A Blood-Stained Pulitzer."

20. Geduld's introduction to Shaw's *The Rationalization of Russia*.

21. Shaw, *Rationalization of Russia*, 91.

22. Strong, *This Soviet World*, 262.

23. Ibid., 250.

24. Caute, *Fellow-Travellers*, 4.

25. Klehr, review of *Right in Her Soul*.

26. Quoted in Caute, *Fellow-Travellers*, 4.

27. Ibid., 75.

28. Hollander, *Political Pilgrims*, 163.

29. Quoted in Johnson, *Intellectuals*, 190.

30. Ibid.

31. Ibid., 190-191.

32. Ibid., 190.

33. Ibid.

34. Caute, *Fellow-Travellers*, 13.

35. Davies, *Mission to Moscow*, 217.

36. Davis, *Behind Soviet Power*, 12.

37. Ibid., 10.

38. Ibid. 12.

39. Ibid.

40. Ibid., 13.

41. Quoted in Caute, *Fellow-Travellers*, 78.

42. See, for instance, John Earl Haynes and Harvey Klehr's appendix titled "The Invisible Dead: American Communists and Radicals Executed by Soviet Political Police and Buried at Sandarmokh," in *In Denial*, 235-249.

CHAPTER FOUR: THE "NEW LEFT": RENEWED INSTINCT FOR DESTRUCTION

1. See chapter three, page 38.

2. Available online at http://coursesa.matrix.msu.edu/~hst306/ documents/huron.html.

3. For all the mountains of socialist scholarship on the theme of how wealth will be distributed in the socialist paradise, not one socialist work sufficiently explains how socialism will create the wealth itself.

4. Johnson, *Intellectuals*, 52-82.

5. Hollander provides a comprehensive analysis of the self-imposed torments of the sixties leftists in chapter five, "The Rejection of Western Society in the 1960s and 70s," in *Political Pilgrims*, 177-222.

6. Ibid., 179.

7. Ronald Radosh, *Commies*, 131.

8. Collier and Horowitz, *Destructive Generation*, 100.

9. Ibid.

10. Marcuse, *One-Dimensional Man*.

11. For a good example of this Chomskyan theme, see Chomsky and Herman, *Manufacturing Consent*. Theodor Adorno also helpfully provided believers with the fantasy that entertainment and comfort under capitalism distracts people from how truly oppressed and miserable they are. See Adorno, *Culture Industry*.

12. Hollander, *Political Pilgrims*, 177-222.

13. Rubin, *Do It*, 29.

14. Quoted in David Horowitz, *Hating Whitey*, 24.

15. For an excellent essay on the Weather Underground, see chapter two, "The Rise and Fall of the Weather Underground: Doing It," in Collier and Horowitz, *Destructive Generation*, 67-120. For a discussion of Panther crimes, see David Horowitz's account of what he witnessed first-hand during his own Panther experience in his memoir, *Radical Son*.

16. Rubin, *Do It*, 25.

17. Hollander, *Political Pilgrims*, 264.

CHAPTER FIVE: CASTRO'S SLAVE CAMPS: AFFECTION FOR NEW KILLING FIELDS

1. Raul Castro served the Cuban tyranny faithfully and was just as vicious—if not more so—as Fidel. For an account of Raul's career as executioner and hardliner in Fidel's despotism, see Fontova, "Cuba's New and Improved Tyrant."

2. For one of the best accounts of the brutality of the Castro regime, see Pascal Fontaine, "Cuba: Interminable Totalitarianism in the Tropics," in Courtois et al., *Black Book of Communism*, 647-665.

3. Ibid., 657.

4. Valladares, *Against All Hope*, 137.

5. Ibid., 379.

6. For China's case, see chapter seven of this book; for Cambodia's, see Perazzo, "Left-Wing Monster: Pol Pot."

7. Valladares, *Against All Hope*, 378.

8. Rochester and Frederick, chapter nineteen, "The Zoo, 1967-1969: The Cuban Program and Other Atrocities," in *Honor Bound*.

9. Fontova, *Fidel*, 141-142.

10. Rochester and Kiley, *Honor Bound*, 400.

11. Ibid., 404.

12. Fontova, *Fidel*, 88.

13. Ibid., 14-15, 49.

14. Ibid., 8, 56-57.

15. Ibid., 157-163.

16. For a comprehensive account of the Left's adoration of Castro's Cuba, see Hollander, *Political Pilgrims*, 223-267.

17. Huberman and Sweezy, *Cuba: Anatomy of a Revolution*, 176.

18. Ibid.

19. Ibid., 177.

20. Rubin, *Do It*, 20. In fact, Rubin did return to the "political bullshit in the United States." He ended up earning a private fortune working on Wall Street and becoming a business entrepreneur, something that the victims of Vietnamese and Cuban tyranny had no opportunity to do.

21. Quoted in Collier and Horowitz, *Destructive Generation*, 272.

22. Sontag, "Some Thoughts."

23. Ibid., 14.

24. Ibid., 10.

25. Ibid.

26. For discussions of Castro's persecution of homosexuals, see Valladares's *Against All Hope*; Fontaine, "Cuba," 656, and the memoir *Before Night Falls* by the Cuban gay writer Reinaldo Arenas.

27. Hollander, *Political Pilgrims*, 261. In recent years persecution of homosexuals has softened in Cuba, due, in part, to the communist regime's having to "moderate" its tyranny in several areas to retain power.

28. Collier and Horowitz, *Destructive Generation*, 246-247.
29. Fontova, *Fidel*, 11.
30. Ibid., 154.

CHAPTER SIX: IN LOVE WITH HANOI'S BUTCHERS

1. Jean-Louis Margolin, "Vietnam and Laos: The Impasse of War Communism," in Courtois et al., *Black Book of Communism*, 565-575.
2. Steven Morris, "Whitewashing Dictatorship in Communist Vietnam and Cambodia," in Collier and Horowitz, *Anti-Chomsky Reader*, 5-6.
3. Rubin, *Do It*, 105.
4. Hollander, *Political Pilgrims*, 198.
5. Sontag, *Trip to Hanoi*, 87.
6. Rubin, *Do It*, 246.
7. Margolin, "Vietnam and Laos," 572.
8. Sontag, *Trip to Hanoi*, 27.
9. Ibid., 28.
10. Ibid., 33.
11. Ibid., 34.
12. McCarthy, *Hanoi*, 7.
13. Ibid., 13-14.
14. Ibid., 14, 30-31.
15. Ibid., 53.
16. Sontag, *Trip to Hanoi*, 36, 69.
17. Ibid., 48.
18. Ibid., 71.
19. Ibid., 72, 77.
20. McCarthy, *Hanoi*, 90, 126-127.
21. Ibid., 27.
22. Sontag, *Trip to Hanoi*, 31.
23. Ibid., 86, 87, 90.
24. Ibid., 76.
25. McCarthy, *Hanoi*, 115-116.
26. Ibid., 130.
27. Quoted in Peter Collier, "Introduction," in Collier and Horowitz, *Anti-Chomsky Reader*, ix.
28. Morris, "Whitewashing Dictatorship," 7.
29. For the best account of Jane Fonda's pilgrimage to North Vietnam, see Holzer and Holzer, *"Aid and Comfort."*
30. Horowitz, "An Open Letter to the 'Anti-War' Demonstrators."
31. For an authoritative account of the bloodbath in South Vietnam and Laos, see Margolin, "Vietnam and Laos," 565-576. For a comprehensive discussion of Pol Pot's killing fields in Cambodia, see Margolin, "Cambodia: The Country of Disconcerting Crimes," in Courtois et al., *Black Book of Communism*, 576-635.

32. "Vietnam: A Time for Healing and Compassion," advertisement, *New York Times*, January 30, 1977.

33. For an excellent account of Chomsky's denial of Pol Pot's genocide, see Morris, "Whitewashing Dictatorship," 1-35.

34. Quoted in McCarthy, *Hanoi*, ix-xii.

CHAPTER SEVEN: FLIRTING WITH MAO'S EXECUTIONERS

1. For a succinct and comprehensive account of Mao's reign of terror, see Jean-Louis Margolin, "China: A Long March into Night," in Courtois et al., *Black Book of Communism*, 463-547.

2. Chang and Halliday, *Mao*, 438.

3. Margolin, "China," 492-494.

4. Chang and Halliday, *Mao*, 438.

5. Ibid.

6. Paul Johnson, *Modern Times*, 556-557.

7. Margolin, "China," 520.

8. Wu, *Laogai: The Chinese Gulag*.

9. Ruo-Wang and Chelminski, *Prisoner of Mao*.

10. Margolin, "China," 498-500.

11. Chang and Halliday, *Mao*, 3.

12. Ibid., 15.

13. Ibid.

14. Ibid., 439.

15. Ibid.

16. Hollander has documented the Left's travels to Mao's China in chapter seven, "Pilgrimage to China," in *Political Pilgrims*, 278-346. See also Caute, chapter eleven, "Into China," in *Fellow-Travellers*, 361-380.

17. Hollander, *Political Pilgrims*, 299.

18. Ibid., 292-293.

19. Klehr, review of *Right in Her Soul*.

20. Johnson, *Intellectuals*, 225-252.

21. De Beauvoir, *The Long March*, 286.

22. Chang and Halliday, *Mao*, 460.

23. Caute, *Fellow-Travellers*, 376.

24. Ibid.

25. MacLaine, *You Can Get There*, 159.

26. Ibid., 124.

27. Horn, *Away with All Pests*, 31-32.

28. MacLaine, *You Can Get There*, 146.

29. Caute, *Fellow-Travellers*, 368.

30. Ibid., 375-376.

31. Robinson, *Cultural Revolution in China*, 26.

32. Hollander, *Political Pilgrims*, 311.

33. Schell, *In the People's Republic*, 21-22.

34. Chang and Halliday, *Mao*, 247.

35. MacLaine, *You Can Get There*, 206.

36. Ibid., 234.

37. It appears that Karen never acted on this intense desire. There is no record of her requesting the Chinese authorities to let her remain in the country, or of her ever attempting to return to China.

38. MacLaine, *You Can Get There*, 152-153.

39. Ibid., 206-207.

40. Ibid., 204.

41. Ibid., 213.

42. Cameron, *Mandarin Red*, 95-99.

43. Quoted in Caute, *Fellow-Travellers*, 370.

44. MacLaine, *You Can Get There*, 215.

45. Ibid., 216.

46. Ibid.

47. Schell, *In the People's Republic*, 21-22.

48. Ibid., 94.

49. Ibid., 97.

50. Hewlett Johnson, *China's New Creative Age*, 94-95.

51. MacLaine, *You Can Get There*, 175, 183-184.

52. Broyelle, *Women's Liberation in China*, 150.

53. Ibid., 153.

54. Ibid., 154.

55. MacLaine, *You Can Get There*, 183.

56. Ibid., 232.

57. Johnson, *China's New Creative Age*, 146.

58. Ibid., 146-147.

59. Ibid., 138-139.

60. Topping, *Dawn Wakes in the East*, 42.

61. MacLaine, *You Can Get There*, 228.

62. Ibid., 246, 248.

CHAPTER EIGHT: NICARAGUA: THE LAST COMMUNIST HOPE

1. For a comprehensive account of the Sandinista reign of terror, see Pascal Fontaine, "Nicaragua: The Failure of a Totalitarian Project," in Courtois et al., *The Black Book of Communism*, 665-675.

2. Kriele, *Nicaragua*, 41-42.

3. For a succinct analysis of how the Sandinistas destroyed Nicaragua's economy, see Kriele, *Nicaragua*, 11-36.

4. Fontaine, "Nicaragua," 668-669. For a concise account of the Sandinistas' genocidal program against the Miskito Indians, see Humberto Belli, chapter nine, "The Miskitos: An Ethnic Tragedy," in *Breaking Faith*, 106-117.

5. Documents declassified from the Soviet archives in the 1990s revealed that an even greater number of Poles was executed than had been thought. A March 1940 Soviet memorandum, for instance, showed Beria requesting Stalin's approval for shooting 25,700 Polish captives. See "Bulletin," From the Russian Archives, issue 3, 74. For the definitive studies of Katyn, Allen, *Katyn*, and Abarinov, *Murderers of Katyn*.

6. Fontaine, "Nicaragua," 671.

7. Dillon, *Commandos*, 159-160.

8. Waller, "Tropical Chekists."

9. For a discussion of the Sandinistas' alignment with the Soviets and Cubans and the increased presence of Soviet-bloc personnel in the country, see Belli, *Breaking Faith*, 71-78.

10. For a comprehensive account documenting how the Contras were a genuine grassroots peasant movement, far from the mercenaries that the American liberal media depicted them to be, see Dillon's *Commandos*.

11. Hollander, *Anti-Americanism*, 268.

12. Hollander has best documented Hollywood leftists' dalliance with the Sandinistas in *Anti-Americanism*, 259-306. For accounts of the fellow travelers' own personal observations in Nicaragua, see David Horowitz's reflections in Collier and Horowitz, *Destructive Generation*, 333-344, and Ronald Radosh's chapter "Adventures in Sandinista Land," in *Commies*, 173-196.

13. Hollander, *Anti-Americanism*, 264.

14. Quoted in Hollander, *Anti-Americanism*, 279.

15. In the summer of 2006, Grass confessed he had been a member of Hitler's notorious Waffen SS in the final months of World War II—yet another chilling reminder of the Left's close association with fascism. See Brown and Laksin, "SS Man of the Left."

16. Grass, "Epilogue: America's Backyard," 247.

17. Hollander, *Anti-Americanism*, 285.

18. Belli, *Breaking Faith*, 127.

19. Ridenour, *Yankee Sandinistas*, 98.

20. Hollander, *Anti-Americanism*, 287.

21. Radosh, *Commies*, 175.

22. The LeoGrande-Borosage-Bendana planning session was witnessed by Ronald Radosh, Nina Shea, and Devon Gaffney on their trip to Managua in 1983. See Collier and Horowitz, *Destructive Generation*, 340.

23. Ridenour, *Yankee Sandinistas*, 124.

24. Kriele, *Nicaragua*, 17-18.

25. For an excellent analysis of why the Sandinistas lost the February 1990 election, see Cruz and Falcoff, "Who Won Nicaragua?"

26. There remained the problem of Sandinista influence within the new government. For example, Mrs. Chamorro accepted ex-President Carter's advice regarding "national reconciliation" and allowed Humberto Ortega (Daniel Ortega's brother) to remain head of the army. For an excellent discussion of the limitations on

Nicaragua's liberation due to ongoing Sandinista participation, see Elliott Abrams, "Who Won Nicaragua?"

27. Collier and Horowitz, *Destructive Generation*, 335.

28. Radosh, *Commies*, 108-109. Scheer has yet to account for the logic in his veneration of Kim Il Sung's regime.

CHAPTER NINE: YEARNINGS FOR DEATH AND SUICIDE

1. Berman, *Terror and Liberalism*, 60.

2. The Muslim Brotherhood was the first modern mass movement of political Islam. Its purpose was to annihilate secularism and Western liberalism. It yearns for a return to the supposedly pure form of Islam practiced by Muhammad and his earliest followers.

3. Loftus, "The Muslim Brotherhood." For a discussion of Islamism's fascist roots, see Wonder.

4. Robert Spencer, "Islamo-Fascism Denial."

5. Akyol, "Bolshevism in a Headdress."

6. Spencer, *Onward Muslim Soldiers*, 237-244.

7. For a comprehensive account of the KGB's propaganda activity in the Middle East and its influence on Islamic-Arab anti-Americanism, see Andrew and Mitrokhin, *The World Was Going Our Way*.

8. Jafary and Anderson, *Foucault and the Iranian Revolution*, 60.

9. Horowitz, *Unholy Alliance*, 124-125.

10. Great Satan and Little Satan are traditional Islamic terms referring to pillars in Mecca at which pilgrims throw stones.

11. Horowitz, *Unholy Alliance*, 125.

12. For a succinct analysis of Qutb's promotion of violent jihad and the Islamic roots with which he justified it, see Spencer, *Onward Muslim Soldiers*, 226-237.

13. Berman, *Terror and Liberalism*, 99-100.

14. Peter Raddatz, interview with author, February 5, 2006.

15. Murawiec, *The Mind of Jihad*, 8. This is also the title of chapter seven of Amir Taheri's *Holy Terror*, 90-103.

16. Murawiec, *Mind of Jihad*, 8-9.

17. Ibid., 16.

18. Ibid.

19. Ibid., 18-19.

20. Ibid., 18-27.

21. Quoted in Berman, *Terror and Liberalism*, 68.

22. Ibid., 120.

23. Brooks, "Among the Bourgeoisophobes."

24. For a brief but concrete discussion of the Camp David talks, see Alan Dershowitz, *The Case for Israel*, 109-122. For an account of Arafat's malicious intent from the moment the Oslo Accords were signed in 1993, see Efraim Karsh, *Arafat's War*.

25. Typical is the interview with Umm Nidal, a Palestinian mother who rejoiced that her young son Muhammad Farhat had died in a martyrdom operation on March 20, 2002. She boasted that she encouraged all her sons to die a martyr's death (she received another part of her wish a year later when her second son, Nidal, was killed by Israeli forces), and that she wished the same thing for herself. See MEMRI, "Umm Nidal: 'The Mother of the *Shahids*'."

26. For a discussion of Carter's betrayal of the Shah and his facilitation of Khomeini's bloodbath, see Horowitz and Johnson, *Party of Defeat*, 28-30.

27. Berman, *Terror and Liberalism*, 108. Iran's Islamist tyranny is powerfully illuminated in Azar Nafisi, *Reading Lolita in Tehran*, and Roya Hakakian, *Journey from the Land of No*. See also Freidoune Sahebjam, *The Stoning of Soraya M*.

28. Taheri, *Holy Terror*, 114.

29. Peter Raddatz interview, February 5, 2006.

30. For an account of the monstrosities perpetrated by the Taliban, see Rashid, *Taliban*.

31. Pipes, "[The Issue of Compulsion in Religion:]".

32. Ibid.

33. Akyol, "Bolshevism in a Headdress."

34. Wahhabism seeks to restore what it deems the "purity" of Islam by rejecting any progress that occurred after the third Islamic century (around 950). It declares all non-Wahhabi Muslims apostates and wages jihad against them. It is the majority sect in Saudi Arabia, and its teachings are dispersed around the world via mosques and schools generously bankrolled by the Saudis. While Wahhabism plays a major role in Islamist terrorism, it is important to keep in mind that many Islamic groups that the Wahhabis condemn as apostates are just as adamant about jihad against unbelievers. See Robert Spencer, *Islam Unveiled*, 12, 169.

35. Osama bin Laden, "Declaration of War against the Americans Occupying the Land of the Two Holy Places," August 23, 1996, available at http://www.outpost-of-freedom.com/opf980830a.htm.

36. Lewis, *Crisis of Islam*, xxix.

37. *Sahih Muslim*, book 19, no. 4,366.

38. This teaching complements Islam's concrete division of the world into two spheres: the House of Peace *(Dar al-Islam)*, which is Islamic, and the House of War *(Dar al-Harb)*, which is non-Islamic (Lewis, *Crisis of Islam*, 31). World peace, according to Islam, is achieved only when *Dar al-Islam* rules throughout the world. Waging war to subjugate non-Muslims, therefore, is a common-sense application of Islam's view of the world.

39. For a comprehensive analysis of how jihad is rooted in Islamic literature, see Spencer's *Onward Muslim Soldiers*, 115-147. There are critics who argue that Islam's teachings about the duty of violence against unbelievers were meant for a certain time and place. The problem is that, unlike Christians and Jews, who believe that their holy books were written by human beings inspired by God, Muslims believe the Koran to be the *literal* word of Allah. The belief, which is a central tenet of the Islamic faith, is that Allah *dictated every word* to Muhammad

through the Angel Gabriel (Ibid., 127). These words are timeless, apply to all eternity, and are sealed in heaven. As Bernard Lewis notes, according to Islamic doctrine, "the Qur'an itself is uncreated and eternal, divine and immutable" (Lewis, *Crisis in Islam*, 8). This is one of the key obstacles facing Muslim reformers.

40. Sura 9:29.

41. For a comprehensive history of Islam's oppression of Jews and Christians under its reign, see Bat Ye'or, *Islam and Dhimmitude*.

42. Sura 48:29.

43. Pryce-Jones, *Closed Circle*, 17.

44. Quoted in Spencer, *Onward Muslim Soldiers*, 93-94.

45. Lal, *Legacy of Muslim Rule in India*, 307.

46. Hitti, *The Arabs: A Short History*, 205.

47. Lal, *Legacy of Muslim Rule in India*, 306-307.

48. Ibid., 176.

49. Ibid., 43.

50. Pipes, "What Is Jihad?"

51. Spencer, *Onward Muslim Soldiers*, 43.

CHAPTER TEN: TO HATE A WOMAN

1. Islamism's demonization of homosexuality does have its own unique Islamic roots. However, there remains a great contradiction in that, as we shall see in chapter eleven, Islamic societies are rife with homosexual behavior that is considered a social norm—but discussion of it remains taboo.

2. While Turkey and Jordan, for instance, are obviously more liberal in terms of women's rights than places like Saudi Arabia and Pakistan, vicious institutions of violence against women continue to prevail there. "Honor" killings remain a frequent occurrence in Turkey and Jordan despite those countries' "modernity." This is precisely because Islamic principles have not been relaxed in the societies at large.

3. Mernissi, *The Veil and the Male Elite*.

4. Manji, *The Trouble with Islam Today*.

5. Coleman, "Women, Islam, and the New Iraq."

6. Sura 2:28, for instance, affirms that men are superior to women. Al-Bukhari's *hadith* in volume 3:826 of the *Sahih Al-Bukhari* quotes Muhammad as saying that women are deficient in mind and religion. Sura 4:11, meanwhile, instructs that in matters of inheritance, women should only be given half of what their brothers receive. For a discussion of Islamic sources that legitimize misogyny, see Spencer, *Islam Unveiled*, 73-93.

7. Pryce-Jones, *Closed Circle*, 124.

8. Saadawi, *Hidden Face of Eve*, 10.

9. Souad, *Burned Alive*, 20. When a young neighbor seduced and impregnated Souad, he knew full well he had delivered her a death sentence. Her family subsequently planned out her murder, and her brother-in-law was assigned the heroic

task. He doused Souad with gasoline and set her aflame. Ninety percent of the girl's body was burned, and she was left to die in a local hospital—where the staff refused to treat her. Souad's mother showed up at the hospital and tried to make her drink a glass of poison. Because of the courageous intervention of a Swiss-based humanitarian worker ("Jacqueline"), Souad survived and was flown to Europe—where she lives today under a secret identity. If her family discovered her new whereabouts, they would still come to murder her.

10. Ibid.

11. Saadawi, *Hidden Face of Eve*, 12.

12. *Economist*, "Arab Women; Out of the Shadows, into the World."

13. Souad, *Burned Alive*, 17.

14. Mernissi, *Beyond the Veil*, 31.

15. Ibid., 45.

16. Sabbah, *Woman in the Muslim Unconscious*, 98-117. Imam Ibn al-Jawzi, for instance, wrote, in his text *Dhamm al-hawa*, that the "beauty of women is one of the poisoned arrows of the devil." The notion that hell is largely populated by women is also to be found in Islamic texts. According to a *hadith* in Imam Bukhari's *Al-Sahih*, for instance, the Prophet Muhammad states that, as he stood at the gate of hell, he observed that "most of those who entered there were women."

17. Mernissi, *Beyond the Veil*, 113.

18. Quoted in Pryce-Jones, *Closed Circle*, 131.

19. Mernissi, *Beyond the Veil*, 54.

20. The year 622, the *hijra*, is considered the first year of Islam—year one of civilization. Ibid., 46.

21. Ibid., 85.

22. Ibid., 107.

23. Pryce-Jones, *Closed Circle*, 126.

24. For further details, which include the couple having to look away from Mecca so that the antagonism between Allah and the woman is clear, see Mernissi, *Beyond the Veil*, 113-114.

25. Ibid., 115-120.

26. Ibid., 132, 135.

27. Saadawi, *Hidden Face of Eve*, 23.

28. Associated Press, "Dukhtaran-e-Millat activists burn Valentine's Day cards."

29. Pipes, "Hating Valentine's Day in the Third World."

30. BBC News, "Hindu and Muslim anger at Valentine's."

31. Peter Raddatz, interview, with author, April 28, 2006.

32. Saadawi, *Hidden Face of Eve*, 33.

33. For a fuller account of FGM in the Muslim-Arab world, see Saadawi's chapter "Circumcision of Girls." (Ibid., 33-43.)

34. Ibid., 9.

35. Ibid., 8.

36. Quoted in Spencer, *Islam Unveiled*, 88.

37. *Umdat al-Salik* (translated into English as *Reliance of the Traveler*), e4.3.

38. Chernitsky, "Egyptian Controversy over Circumcising Girls."
39. Ibid.
40. Quoted in Spencer, *Politically Incorrect Guide to Islam*, 76.
41. Chernitsky, "Egyptian Controversy."
42. Spencer, *Islam Unveiled*, 88.
43. Saadawi, *Hidden Face of Eve*, 26.
44. Ibid., 28.
45. Sura 24:31. Again, hope remains that Muslim reformers can eliminate the tyranny of forced veiling through reinterpretation *within* an Islamic framework. For instance, Irshad Manji argues, "While the Koran requires the Prophet's wives to veil, it never decrees such a practice for all women. Why, indeed, should it?" (Manji, *The Trouble with Islam Today*, 140.) It should, perhaps, because Muhammad is recorded in other texts as having said that when a woman reaches the age of menstruation, she should not show anything in public except her face and hands. (Abu Dawud, book 32, no. 4,092.) Still, this issue has the potential to be debated, and the practice to be changed, by Muslims themselves.
46. Spencer, *Politically Incorrect Guide*, 68.
47. For a brief, horrifying account of "honor" killings in the Muslim world, see Phyllis Chesler, *The Death of Feminism*, 10-13.
48. Hymowitz, "Feminist Fog."
49 Sura 4:34. There are numerous legitimizations of woman beating in the *hadiths*. In his *hadith* in volume 3:826 of the *Sahih Al-Bukhari*, for instance, Imam Al-Bukhari quotes Muhammad's order to the husband regarding his wife: "Hang up your scourge where your wife can see it." The Prophet Muhammad himself recommended that beatings take place in the privacy of one's own home. He commanded that "you shall not slap her on the face, nor revile her, nor desert her except within the house." (Imam Kitab al-Nikah's *hadith* no. 1,850 in *The Book of Marriage*.)
50. BBC, "Imam rapped for wife-beating book."
51. Stalinsky and Yehoshua, "Muslim Clerics on the Religious Rulings Regarding Wife-Beating."
52. Spencer, *Politically Incorrect Guide*, 70.
53. Souad, *Burned Alive*, 13.
54. Sura 4:3.
55. In her unpublished book, *The Sheikh's New Clothes*, Kobrin shows how, by internalizing their culture's hatred of women, Islamic Arab males open themselves up to a set of dynamics that spawn the urge for death and suicide.
56. Sabbah, *Woman in the Muslim Unconscious*, 96.

CHAPTER ELEVEN: THE SEEDS OF DEATH

1. Pryce-Jones, *Closed Circle*, 13.
2. Statement aired on Al Jazeera TV after the U.S. bombing of Afghanistan began.
3. Lewis, *Crisis of Islam*, xv-xvii.
4. Pryce-Jones, *Closed Circle*, 50, 57.

5. Abul A'la Maududi, *Towards Understanding the Qur'an*, 202.

6. M. H. Abrams, *The Mirror and the Lamp*, 42.

7. Pryce-Jones, *Closed Circle*, xiii.

8. Ibid., 53.

9. Theodore Dalrymple, "The Suicide Bombers among Us."

10. Quoted in Pryce-Jones, *Closed Circle*, 131.

11. Ibid., 128.

12. Dunne, "Power and Sexuality."

13. For a discussion of the widespread homosexuality among men in Muslim societies in North Africa and South Asia, see Arno Schmitt and Jehoeda Sofer, *Sexuality and Eroticism among Males in Moslem Societies*.

14. Dunne, "Power and Sexuality."

15. Chesler, *Death of Feminism*, 144.

16. Ibid.

17. See Saadawi, *Hidden Face of Eve*, 12-24. While it is obvious that this abuse, like the abuse of young boys, is connected to the unavailability of women in the culture at large, Chesler notes that the abuse of female children "is one of the main ways of traumatizing and shaming girls into obedience and rendering them less capable of rebellion or resistance when they grow up." (Chesler, *Death of Feminism*, 145.)

18. Ibid., 88, 144.

19. Dunne, "Power and Sexuality."

20. Gutmann, "Symposium: Purifying Allah's Soil."

21. Chesler, *Death of Feminism*, 187-188.

22. Pryce-Jones, *Closed Circle*, 130.

23. Lapkin, "Muslim Gang Rapes and the Aussie Riots."

24. Sura 4:23-24.

25. Fjordman, "Immigrant Rape Wave in Sweden."

26. Quoted in Pryce-Jones, *Closed Circle*, 128.

27. Part of Qutb's *Milestones* was translated and published in John Calvert, "'The World Is an Undutiful Boy!': Qutb's "American Experience." Translations of *Milestones* can also be found on several Muslim students' Web sites. See, for instance, http://www.youngmuslims.ca/online_library/books/milestones/.

28. Calvert, "'The World Is an Undutiful Boy!'" 97.

29. Ibid.

30. Quoted in Spencer, *Politically Incorrect Guide*, 88.

31. Ibid., 117.

32. Ibid.

33. Quoted in *Time*, "The Mystic Who Lit the Fires of Hatred."

34. Quoted in Spencer, *Islam Unveiled*, 118.

35. Saadawi, *Hidden Face of Eve*, 10.

36. Souad, *Burned Alive*, 158.

37. Steven Vincent, *In the Red Zone,* was kidnapped and killed by terrorists in Basra, Iraq, on August 3, 2006. He was a friend of the author and is greatly missed. See his chapter eight, "Beneath the Veil," 160-183.

38. Ibid., 181.

39. Glazov, "In the Red Zone."

40. Pryce-Jones, *Closed Circle,* 134.

41. See, for instance, "Arab Kids Play Beheading Game," http://inhonor.net/videos/uped/fl_video.php?f_num=74500.

CHAPTER TWELVE: KILLING AND DYING FOR PURITY

1. Dalrymple, "The Suicide Bombers among Us."

2. Spencer, *Onward Muslim Soldiers,* 154-155.

3. For promises regarding virgins, see Suras 78:31, 37:40-48, and 44:51-55; for the pre-pubescent boys, see Suras 52:24, 56:17, and 76:19.

4. Rehov, "What Paradise?"

5. Sura 33:50.

6. Sura 47:15.

7. Cochran, interview with Pierre Rehov.

8. Kobrin, *Sheikh's New Clothes.*

9. Ibid.

10. Newman, "The Worst Exploitation."

11. Ibid.

12. Ibid.

CHAPTER THIRTEEN: TO HATE A JEW

1. Timmerman, *Preachers of Hate,* 2.

2. Loftus, "The Muslim Brotherhood."

3. *DiscovertheNetworks.org,* Hassan al-Banna profile.

4. Robert Spencer, "Islamo-Fascism Denial."

5. For an excellent account of the al-Husseini story, see Chuck Morse, *The Nazi Connection to Islamic Terrorism.*

6. See Kenneth Timmerman's comments in Jamie Glazov, "Symposium: Islamic Anti-Semitism."

7. Quoted in Timmerman, *Preachers of Hate,* 122.

8. Loftus, "Muslim Brotherhood."

9. Ibid., 104.

10. Pryce-Jones, "Their *Kampf.*"

11. Scholars have comprehensively documented the brutal realities of Soviet Jew hatred. See Elie Wiesel, *The Jews of Silence;* Theodore Freedman, ed., *Anti-Semitism in the Soviet Union;* and Ronald I. Rubin, ed., *The Unredeemed.*

12. Brent and Naumov, *Stalin's Last Crime.*

13. For a comprehensive account of the KGB's propaganda activity in the Middle East and its influence on Islamic anti-Americanism, see Andrew and Mitrokhin, *The World Was Going Our Way*.

14. Ion Mihai Pacepa's comment in "Symposium: The Terror War: How We Can Win," *FrontPageMag.com*, November 15, 2004.

15. Ibid.

16. Ibid.

17 Suras 3:71 and 4:46.

18. Suras 2:61–58 and 5:78–82.

19. Suras 5:60-65, 2:65, and 7:166.

20. *Mishkat Al-Messabih*, vol. 2, no. 5,552.

21. Glazov, "The Anti-Terror, Pro-Israel Sheikh."

22. Muhammad, as quoted in Ibn Ishaq, *Sirat Rasul Allah*, 369.

23. Bostom, "Muhammad, the Qurayza Massacre, and PBS."

24. Ibid.

25. Christians were forced to wear the image of a pig. See Bat Ye'or, *The Dhimmi*, 186-187, 420, 440.

26. Timmerman, *Preachers of Hate*, 99.

CHAPTER FOURTEEN: CHEERING FOR AL-QAEDA

1. For an account of Carter's Hamas romance, see 7-9.

2. See MEMRI, "U.S. Linguist Noam Chomsky Meets with Hizbullah Leaders in Lebanon," and Ali Hussein, "Chomsky needs to learn a lot more about Lebanon."

3. Horowitz and Laksin, "Noam Chomsky's Love Affair with Nazis."

4. See MEMRI TV clips "Hizbullah Leader Hassan Nasrallah: Death to America," and "Hizbullah Secretary-General Sheikh Hassan Nasrallah Threatens the U.S."

5. See Jonathan Schanzer, *Hamas vs. Fatah*.

6. Marcus and Crook, "Suicide terror for children glorified on Hamas children's Web site."

7. David Meir-Levi, "My Brother's Keeper?"

8. Ibid.

9. Ibid.

10. Conger, "Christian Left Rejects Hamas Boycott."

11. "Hamas' Defense of Terror," *HonestReporting.com*, April 23, 2006.

12. Typical of this theme is bin Laden's audiotaped message released on Al Jazeera in late April 2006. See Dinan, "Bush: Iraq win is 'blow' to al Qaeda."

13. Afary and Anderson, *Foucault and the Iranian Revolution*.

14. David Horowitz's *Unholy Alliance* remains the best work on the subject.

15. The Clinton administration suspected the pharmaceutical plant of being a factory which produced chemical weapons for terrorists. The attack on the plant was a response to the Islamist blowing up of two American embassies in Africa, which killed hundreds of people, most of them African civilians. While

the terrorist attacks' main objective was to kill as many people as possible, the Clinton administration's attack tried to minimize the taking of human life, which is why it occurred at night, when the building would be unoccupied. (Horowitz, *Unholy Alliance*, 183.)

16. Daniel Pipes, "The Left's Dream."

17. All of the statements quoted in this pargraph are now on the public record. Paul Hollander has an excellent sampling of them in *Understanding Anti-Americanism*, 24-27. For a wide selection of academics who verbalized similar praise of the 9/11 attacks, see Horowitz, *The Professors*.

18. Ward Churchill profile, *DiscoverTheNetworks.org*.

19. Quoted in Pipes, "The Left's Dream."

20. Norman Mailer profile, *DiscoverTheNetworks.org*.

21. Hollander, ed., *Understanding Anti-Americanism*, 24.

22. Ibid., 25.

23. Ibid., 27.

24. Horowitz, *Unholy Alliance*, 13.

25. Pollitt, "Put Out No Flags."

26. Quoted in Pipes, "The Left's Dream."

27. Ibid.

28. For an account of Chomsky's response to 9/11, see Horowitz and Radosh, "Chomsky and 9/11," in Collier and Horowitz, *The Anti-Chomsky Reader*, 161-181.

29. Horowitz, *Unholy Alliance*, 11.

30. Documents captured from the fallen Iraqi regime confirm Saddam's links to al-Qaeda as well as the fact that he had WMDs. See Jamie Glazov, "Saddam and Osama: The New Revelations." See also Stephen F. Hayes, *The Connection*.

31. See the profiles on all these groups on *DiscoverTheNetworks.org*.

32. Horowitz, *Unholy Alliance*, 31-37 and 165-176.

33. The Left's double standard is embodied most clearly in its position on prayer in public school. The Left maintains its vehement opposition to such prayer when it is *Christian*. However, there is a deafening silence in leftist ranks in response to Muslim trainers teaching American public school children about Islam. This Islamic education includes homework that has seventh graders wear a Muslim robe, adopt a Muslim name, stage a personal "jihad," memorize Koranic verses, pray aloud "in the name of Allah, the Compassionate, the Merciful," and chant "Praise to Allah, Lord of Creation." See WorldNetDaily, "Brave New Schools: Islam Studies Required in California District Course."

34. Horowitz, "Neo-Communism."

35. Hitchens, "Unfairenheit 9/11."

36. For a discussion of the Left's and the Democratic Party's enthusiasm for Moore's film, see Horowitz and Johnson, *Party of Defeat*, 109-110.

37. Ibid., 110.

38. Jensen, "A Defeat for an Empire."

39. Taheri, "O's Tour De Farce." See also Shaidle, "Obama's Surge Purge."

40. For the best account of the how the Democratic Party intentionally tried to undermine Bush's war policy for the sake of destroying his presidency, see Horowitz and Johnson.

41. Horowitz and Johnson, *Party of Defeat*.

42. Laksin, "Obama's Muddle over Iraq" and Dickerson, "What Did Obama Learn in Iraq?" See also Taheri and Shaidle.

43. For a discussion of Obama's ties to extremist anti-American figures throughout his political career, see Laksin's "Obama's World." See also the *DiscovertheNetworks.org* feature, "Barack's World," which explores more than fifty of Obama's connections to radicals over the years. http://www.discoverthenetworks.org/viewSubCategory.asp?id=800.

44. See Laksin's "Obama's World."

45. Laksin, "No Left Turns on the War?"

46. Ibid.

47. Iraq News Network, "Galloway Calls for Global Unity."

48. Horowitz and Radosh, "Chomsky and 9/11," in *Anti-Chomksy Reader*, 179-180.

49. Ibid., 180.

50. Ibid., 162.

51. Ibid., 164-169.

52. Collier, Introduction, *Anti-Chomsky Reader*, xiv.

53. Quoted by Michelle Malkin at http://michellemalkin.com/2006/09/02/convert-or-die/.

54. See Walid Phares, "'Azzam': The Domestic *Jihad*."

55. Sean Penn profile, *DiscovertheNetworks.org*, http://www.discoverthenetworks.org/individualProfile.asp?indid=1086.

56. Ibid.

57. Ben Johnson, "Sean Penn's Baghdad Homecoming."

58. James Hirsen, "Fasting for Peace, Hollywood-Style."

59. For an account of Islamist ethnic-cleansing in Iraq, and how a premature U.S. withdrawal would make religious minorities more vulnerable to genocide, see Jamie Glazov, "Islamist Ethnic-Cleansing of Assyrians in Iraq."

60. Ibid.

61. Sean Penn profile.

62. Ibid. See also Zand-Bonazzi and Bonazzi, "Sean Penn: Our Man in Tehran."

63. Sean Penn profile.

64. Ibid.

65. Aaron Klein, *Schmoozing With Terrorists*, 96-98.

66. Ted Turner profile, *DiscovertheNetworks.org*. http://www.discoverthenetworks.org/individualProfile.asp?indid=2004.

67. Ibid.

68. Burns, "'Commie Dictator' Castro Inspired CNN, Ted Turner Admits."

69. Burns, "Ted Turner Says September 11 Terrorists Were Brave Men."

70. Shuman, "CNN founder accuses Israel of terror."

71. Ted Turner profile.

72. Ibid

73. Media Research Center, "Turner: Iraqi Insurgents 'Patriots,' Warming Inaction: Cannibalism."

74. Horowitz, *Unholy Alliance*, 189-190.

75. See 18-19.

76. Horowitz, *Unholy Alliance*, 177-204.

77. Ibid., 183-186.

78. Horowitz, "Unholy Alliance, How the Left Supports Terrorists at Home."

79. Horowitz, *Unholy Alliance*, 177-204.

80. Lynne Stewart profile, *DiscoverTheNetworks.org*.

81. For a succinct account of the campus promotion of Lynne Stewart, see Horowitz and Johnson, *Campus Support for Terrorism*.

82. Sami al-Arian profile, *DiscoverTheNetworks.org*.

83. Robert Spencer, "Guilty as Charged," *FrontPageMag.com*, April 20, 2006. See also Horowitz's discussion of Al-Arian in *Unholy Alliance*, 188-199. *DiscoverTheNetworks.org*, Lynne Stewart profile.

CHAPTER FIFTEEN: ROOTS OF A ROMANCE

1. Horowitz, "Noam Chomsky's Anti-American Obsession," in Collier and Horowitz, *Anti-Chomsky Reader*, 186.

2. Horowitz, "How the Left Undermined America's Security before 9/11."

3. White House New Release, "Statement by the President in His Address to the Nation."

4. For one of the best works showing that Islamic terrorism is an outgrowth of Islam's millenarian imperial tradition, and is in no way a response to outside aggression or oppression, see Efraim Karsh, *Islamic Imperialism*.

5. Spencer, "Sympathy for the Devil."

6. Horowitz, *Unholy Alliance*, 129-130.

7. See chapter 5, "Does Poverty Cause Militant Islam?" in Pipes, *Militant Islam Reaches America*, 52-63.

8. Like most leaders and active "doers" of extreme puritanical organizations, these individuals felt themselves exempt from their own religion's values and rules because, in part, they saw themselves as paying a high price in their duties for the cause. They saw themselves as a vanguard—Lenin's great invention—and as such they were above the rules. Furthermore, it is explicit in the Islamist's calculus that the guilt incurred by such activity can be washed away by engaging in jihad warfare.

9. Pipes, *Militant Islam*, x.

10. Ibid., 56.

11. Ibid., 60, 62.

12. David Horowitz provides a comprehensive account of the anti-globalization Left in *Unholy Alliance*, 155-161.

13. Stakelbeck, "Dangerous Brotherhood."
14. Brown, "The Other Iranian Nuclear Crisis."
15. Arostegui, "U.S. ties Caracas to Hezbollah aid."
16. Hollander, *Understanding Anti-Americanism*, 12.
17. Morris, "Whitewashing Dictatorship."
18. Ibid., 26-28.
19. Quoted in Joan Colebrook, "Prisoners of War."
20. Quoted in Paul Hollander, *Political Pilgrims*, 68.
21. See Scholars for 9/11 Truth profile, *DiscoverTheNetworks.org*.
22. Horowitz, "Noam Chomsky's Anti-American Obsession," in Collier and Horowitz, *Anti-Chomsky Reader*, 181.
23. Ibid.
24. Berman, *Terror and Liberalism*, 151.
25. Ibid., 149.
26. Horowitz, *End of Time*, 119.
27. Ibid., 101.
28. Moore, "Heads Up...from Michael Moore."
29. Horowitz, "Where Have All the Democrats Gone?"
30. Horowitz, *End of Time*, 90.
31. Ibid., 105-106.

CHAPTER SIXTEEN: CRAVINGS FOR DEATH

1. Quoted in Miller, *Passion of Michel Foucault*, 55.
2. Ticker, "The Case against Rachel Corrie."
3. Ibid.
4. Plaut, "Anniversary of Rachel Corrie's Suicide on Behalf of Terrorists."
5. http://www.cpt.org/publications/sider.php.
6. Rayment, "Rescued hostage rations his thanks."
7. After being faced with international anger and disbelief, one of the freed activists, Norman Kember, uttered a few words of qualified thanks. See Rayment, "Rescued hostage rations his thanks."
8. Ibid.
9. Horowitz, *Unholy Alliance*, 177-204.
10. David Horowitz, "Lynne Stewart; The Left on Trial."
11. Ibid.
12. Ibid.
13. Ibid.
14. Packer, "Terrorist Lawyer."
15. Ibid. See also Perazzo, "CCR: Fifth Column Law Factory."
16. Lynne Stewart profile, *DiscoverTheNetworks.org*.
17. Packer, "Terrorist Lawyer."
18. Ibid.
19. Tremoglie, "Stanley Cohen: Terrorist Mouthpiece."

20. For a discussion of Carter's betrayal of the Shah and his facilitation of Khomeini's bloodbath, see Horowitz and Johnson, *Party of Defeat,* 28-30.

21. Afary and Anderson, *Foucault and the Iranian Revolution,* 2.

22. Ibid., 35-36.

23. Ibid., 105.

24. Quoted in Miller, *Passion of Michel Foucault,* 55.

25. Afary and Anderson, *Foucault and the Iranian Revolution,* 36.

26. Ibid., 4.

27. Miller, *Passion of Michel Foucault.*

28. Ibid., Chapter 8, "The Will to Know," 245-284.

29. Ibid., 55.

30. Ibid., 54.

31. Ibid., 55.

32. Ibid., 201-203.

33. Ibid., 204-205.

34. Ibid., 205.

35. Ibid., 309.

36. Afary and Anderson, *Foucault and the Iranian Revolution,* 4.

37. Miller, *Passion of Michel Foucault,* 312-313.

38. Ibid., 55.

39. Horowitz, *Unholy Alliance,* 145.

40. Quoted in "Chomsky's War against Israel," in Collier and Horowitz, *The Anti-Chomsky Reader,* 95.

41. Ibid.

42. Ibid.

43. Ibid.

44. Ibid., 96.

45. Berman, *Terror and Liberalism,* 129-131.

46. Ibid., 131.

47. Ibid., 142-143.

48. Ibid., 143.

49. See QUIT!'s Web site, *QuitPalestine.org.*

50. Peter Moore, "Gays Attacked at Palestinian Protest." See also Richard J. Rosendall, "The Queer Left's Palestinian Folly."

CHAPTER SEVENTEEN: LOVING THE BURQA

1. One of the best works examining the sexual promiscuity of believers, and the philosophy that spawns it, is Michael Jones's *Degenerate Moderns.* Theodore Dalrymple also provides a profound discussion of how revolutionaries pursue totalitarian ends through utopian sexual agendas in his essay, "All Sex, All the Time," in his book *Our Culture, What's Left of It,* 234-250.

2. The best work on leftist feminists' betrayal of Muslim women is Phyllis Chesler's *Death of Feminism*. See also Horowitz and Spencer, "A Response to Feminists."

3. See Ch. 15, 211-213.

4. Hymowitz, "Why Feminism Is AWOL."

5. Glazov, "Symposium: Feminist Anti-Semitism."

6. Hymowitz, "Why Feminism Is AWOL."

7. Ibid.

8. Ibid.

9. Ibid.

10. It remains debatable how the end of Israel's "occupation" of Palestine would negate Koranic verses that devalue women and legitimize their beating, or cancel out all the intrinsic pathologies within Islamic culture (outlined in chapter ten) that spawn the hatred of women.

11. For an excellent deconstruction of leftist feminists', including Goodwin's, tactics of blaming Israel in order to exonerate Palestinian wife abusers, see Chesler, *Death of Feminism*, 114-120.

12. Hymowitz, "Why Feminism Is AWOL."

13. Ibid.

14. Ibid.

15. Ibid.

16. Ibid.

17. The leftist feminists' double standard is examined by Cathy Young in her essay "The Feminist Hostility toward American Society," in Hollander, *Understanding Anti-Americanism*, 279-300.

18. Ibid., 286.

19. Hymowitz, "Why Feminism Is AWOL."

20. Ibid.

21. *FrontPageMag.com*, The American Peace Movement."

22. Lapkin, "Western Muslims' Racist Rape Spree."

23. Naomi Klein, "Bring Najaf to New York."

CHAPTER EIGHTEEN: THE BONDS OF JEW HATE

1. Quoted in Benjamin Kerstein, "Here There is No Why?"

2. Avineri, "Ending the Lebanon Crisis."

3. Timmerman, "Iran's War."

4. Rothfeld, "Ignoring Hezbollah a Costly Error."

5. Robert Spencer, "Stage-Managed Massacre."

6. *Haaretz* "Number of casualties from Qana air strike is 28, not 52."

7. Bishara, "Israel on the Offensive."

8. Horowitz, "Fellow Travelers."

9. Horowitz gives an account of the anti-globalization movement in *Unholy Alliance*, 155-161.

10. For an excellent analysis of this petition and *exposé* of the anti-Jewish views of its signers, see Laksin, "Petition for Genocide."

11. For an account of Joel Beinin's romance with terror, see his profile on *DiscoverTheNetworks.org*.

12. For an excellent analysis of Chomsky's hatred of Israel, see "Chomsky's War against Israel," in Collier and Horowitz, *The Anti-Chomsky Reader*, 87-117.

13. Ibid.

14. Ibid., 106.

15. The exact same instincts motivate believers' Gulag denial. See Jamie Glazov, "Cold War Revelations and 'Progressive' Holocaust Denial."

16. For a succinct analysis of Chomsky's association with neo-Nazis and support for Holocaust denial, see Werner Cohn, "Chomsky and Holocaust Denial," in Collier and Horowitz, *The Anti-Chomsky Reader*, 117-158.

17. Ibid.

18. Cravatts, "Answering Israel's Campus Critics."

19. See Cravatts, "Answering Israel's Campus Critics" and Laksin, "What Lies Beyond *Chutzpah*?"

20. Laksin, "What Lies Beyond *Chutzpah*?"

21. Cravatts, "Answering Israel's Campus Critics."

22. Ibid.

23. Associated Press, "U.S. academic Finkelstein meets top Hezbollah official in Lebanon."

24. See the video clip at Memri, http://www.memritv.org/clip/en/1676.htm.

25. David Meir-Levi, "My Brother's Keeper?"

Abarinov, Vladimir. *The Murderers of Katyn*. New York: Hippocrene Books, 1992.

Abrams, Elliot. "Who Won Nicaragua?" *Commentary* (July 1991).

Abrams, M. H. *The Mirror and the Lamp: Romantic Theory and the Critical Tradition*. New York: W. W. Norton, 1958.

Abul A'la Maududi, Sayyid. *Towards Understanding the Qur'an*. Rev. ed. Translated and edited by Zafar Ishaq Ansari. Vol. 3. Leicester, UK: The Islamic Foundation, 1999.

Adorno, Theodor W. *The Culture Industry: Selected Essays on Mass Culture*. Edited by J. M. Bernstein. London: Routledge, 1991.

Afary, Janet and Kevin B. Anderson. *Foucault and the Iranian Revolution: Gender and the Seductions of Islamism*. Chicago: University of Chicago Press, 2005.

Akyol, Mustafa. "Bolshevism in a Headdress." *American Enterprise*, April-May 2005.

Allen, Paul. *Katyn: The Untold Story of Stalin's Polish Massacre*. New York: Scribner's, 1991.

Andrew, Christopher and Vasili Mitrokhin. *The World Was Going Our Way: The KGB and the Battle for the Third World*. New York: Basic Books, 2005.

Arenas, Reinaldo. *Before Night Falls*. Translated by Dolores M. Koch. New York: Viking, 1993.

Arostegui, Martin. "U.S. ties Caracas to Hezbollah aid." *Washington Times*, July 7, 2008.

Associated Press. "CBS's Wallace interviews Ahmadinejad." *Washington Post*, August 9, 2006.

― ― ―. "Dukhtaran-e-Millat activists burn Valentine's Day cards in Kashmir." February 10, 2006.

― ― ―. "Former U.S. President Jimmy Carter calls for restoring aid to Palestinians." *Haaretz.com*, July 10, 2006.

― ― ―. "U.S. academic Finkelstein meets top Hezbollah official in Lebanon." January 8, 2008.

Avineri, Shlomo. "Ending the Lebanon Crisis." *FrontPageMag.com*, August 1, 2006.

BBC News. "Hindu and Muslim anger at Valentine's." February 11, 2003.

― ― ―. "Imam rapped for wife-beating book." January 14, 2004.

Belli, Humberto. *Breaking Faith—The Sandinista Revolution and Its Impact on Freedom and Christian Faith in Nicaragua*. Westchester, Ill.: Crossway Books, 1985.

Berlau, John. "All the Lies Fit to Print: Jayson Blair Scandal Nothing New at *N.Y. Times*?" *WorldNetDaily.com*, July 10, 2003.

Berman, Paul. *Terror and Liberalism*. New York: W. W. Norton, 2003.

Berrigan, Daniel. *Night Flight to Hanoi*. New York: Macmillan, 1968.

Bishara, Marwan. "Israel on the Offensive." *The Nation*, July 5, 2006.

Bossie, David N. *Intelligence Failure: How Clinton's National Security Policy Set the Stage for 9/11*. Nashville: Thomas Nelson, 2004.

Bostom, Andrew G. "Muhammad, the Qurayza Massacre, and PBS." *FrontPageMag.com*, December 20, 2002.

Brent, Jonathan and Vladimir Naumov. *Stalin's Last Crime: The Plot against the Jewish Doctors, 1948-1953.* New York: HarperCollins, 2003.

Brooks, David. "Among the Bourgeoisophobes: Why the Europeans and Arabs, each in their own way, hate America and Israel." *Weekly Standard,* April 15, 2002.

Brown, Christopher. "The Other Iranian Nuclear Crisis." *FrontPageMag.com,* March 22, 2006.

Brown, Stephen and Jacob Laksin. "SS Man of the Left." *FrontPageMag.com,* August 28, 2006.

Broyelle, Claudie. *Women's Liberation in China.* Translated by Michèle Cohen and Gary Herman. Atlantic Highlands, N.J.: Humanities Press, 1977.

Burns, Jim. "'Commie Dictator' Castro Inspired CNN, Ted Turner Admits." *CNSNews.com,* November 30, 2001.

———. "Ted Turner Says September 11 Terrorists Were Brave Men." *CNSNews.com,* February 12, 2002.

Calvert, John. "'The World Is an Undutiful Boy!'" *Islam and Christian-Muslim Relations* 11, no. 1 (March 2000): 87-103.

Cameron, James. *Mandarin Red: A Journey behind the "Bamboo Curtain."* London: M. Joseph, 1955.

Caute, David. *The Fellow-Travellers: A Postscript to the Enlightenment.* London: Weidenfeld and Nicolson, 1973.

Chang, Jung and Jon Halliday. *Mao: The Unknown Story.* New York: Knopf, 2005.

Chesler, Phyllis. *The Death of Feminism: What's Next in the Struggle for Women's Freedom.* New York: Palgrave Macmillan, 2005.

Chernitsky, B. "The Egyptian Controversy over Circumcising Girls." MEMRI, no. 152, (November 7, 2003).

Chomsky, Noam and Edward S. Herman. *Manufacturing Consent.* New York: Pantheon, 1988.

Cochran, Andrew. "Interview with Pierre Rehov." *The Counterterrorism Blog,* July 27, 2005, counterterror.typepad.com.

Colebrook, Joan. "Prisoners of War." *Commentary* (January 1974).

Coleman, Isobel. "Women, Islam, and the New Iraq." *Foreign Affairs* (January-February 2006): 32-33.

Collier, Peter and David Horowitz, eds. *The Anti-Chomsky Reader.* San Francisco: Encounter Books, 2004.

Collier, Peter and David Horowitz. *Destructive Generation: Second Thoughts about the Sixties.* New York: Free Press, 1996.

———. "The Party of Retreat and Defeat." *FrontPageMag.com,* June 19, 2006.

Conger, George. "Christian Left Rejects Hamas Boycott." *Jerusalem Post,* April 14, 2006.

Conquest, Robert. *The Dragons of Expectation: Reality and Delusion in the Course of History.* New York: W. W. Norton, 2005.

———. *The Great Terror: A Reassessment.* New York: Oxford University Press, 1990.

———. *The Great Terror: Stalin's Purge of the Thirties.* London: Macmillan, 1968.

———. *The Harvest of Sorrow: Soviet Collectivization and the Terror-Famine.* Edmonton: University of Alberta Press, 1986.

Courtois, Stéphane, and Nicolas Werth, Jean-Louis Panné, Andrzej Paczkowski, Karel Bartosek, Jean-Louis Margolin, Sylvain Boulougue, Pascal Fontaine, Rémi Kauffer, Pierre Rigoulet, and Yves Santamaria. *The Black Book of Communism: Crimes, Terror, Repression*. Translated by Jonathan Murphy and Mark Kramer. Cambridge, Mass., and London: Harvard University Press, 1999.

Cravatts, Richard L. "Answering Israel's Campus Critics." *FrontPageMag.com*, Monday, July 14, 2008, http://frontpagemag.com/Articles/Printable.aspx?GUID= BE16E2C2-A686-4E22-9E50-11FD936026F1.

Crossman, Richard., ed. *The God That Failed*. New York: Harper and Row, 1963.

Cruz, Arturo J., Jr. and Mark Falcoff. "Who Won Nicaragua?" *Commentary* (May 1990): 31-38.

Dalrymple, Theodore. *Our Culture, What's Left of It*. Chicago: Ivan R. Dee, 2005.

― ― ―. "The Suicide Bombers among Us." *City Journal* (Autumn 2005).

Davies, Joseph E. *Mission to Moscow*. New York: Simon and Schuster, 1941.

Davis, Jerome. *Behind Soviet Power: Stalin and the Russians*. New York: Reader's Press, 1946.

De Beauvoir, Simone. *The Long March*. Translated by Austryn Wainhouse. New York: World Publishing, 1958.

Dershowitz, Alan. *The Case for Israel*. Hoboken, N.J.: John Wiley, 2003.

Dickerson, John. "What Did Obama Learn in Iraq?" *Slate.com*, July 25, 2008.

Dillon, Sam. *Commandos: The CIA and Nicaragua's Contra Rebels*. New York: Henry Holt, 1991.

Dinan, Stephen. "Bush: Iraq win is 'blow' to al Qaeda." *Washington Times*, April 25, 2006.

Dunne, Bruce. "Power and Sexuality in the Middle East." *Middle East Report* (Spring 1998).

Economist. "Arab Women; Out of the Shadows, into the World." June 17, 2004.

El Saadawi, Nawal. *The Hidden Face of Eve: Women in the Arab World*. Translated and edited by Sherif Hetata. London: Zed Books, 2002.

Fjordman. "Immigrant Rape Wave in Sweden." *fjordman.blogspot.com*, December 12, 2005.

Fontova, Humberto. "Cuba's New and Improved Tyrant." *FrontPageMag.com*, February 27, 2008.

― ― ―. *Fidel: Hollywood's Favorite Tyrant*. Washington, D.C.: Regnery, 2005.

Freedman, Theodore, ed. *Anti-Semitism in the Soviet Union: Its Roots and Consequences*. New York: Freedom Library Press of the New York Anti-Defamation League of B'nai B'rith, 1984.

Freeman, Derek. *Margaret Mead and Samoa: The Making and Unmaking of an Anthropological Myth*. Cambridge, Mass.: Harvard University Press, 1983.

FrontPageMag.com. "The American Peace Movement." June 15, 2004.

Glazov, Jamie. "A Blood-Stained Pulitzer." *FrontPageMag.com*, November 17, 2005.

― ― ―. "A New `New Left'?" *FrontPageMag.com*, July 14, 2006.

― ― ―. "The Anti-Terror, Pro-Israel Sheikh." *FrontPageMag.com*, September 12, 2005.

― ― ―. "Cold War Revelations and 'Progressive' Holocaust Denial." *FrontPageMag.com*, October 28, 1999.

― ― ―. "In the Red Zone." *FrontPageMag.com*, December 9, 2004.

― ― ―. "Islamist Ethnic-Cleansing of Assyrians in Iraq." *FrontPageMag.com*, August 13, 2008.

————. "Only Liberals Can Win the War on Terror?" *FrontPageMag.com*, July 4, 2006.

————. "Saddam and Osama: The New Revelations." *FrontPageMag.com*, April 18, 2006.

————. "Symposium: Feminist Anti-Semitism." *FrontPageMag.com*, August 27, 2004, http://www.frontpagemag.com/Articles/Read.aspx?GUID= A3F38FA2-9E4A-43F1-9694-54D544AB4820.

————. "Symposium: Islamic Anti-Semitism." *FrontPageMag.com*, October 31, 2003.

————. "Symposium: The Terror War: How We Can Win." *FrontPageMag.com*, November 15, 2004.

Grass, Günter. "Epilogue: America's Backyard." In *Trouble in Our Backyard: Central America and the United States in the Eighties*, edited by Martin Diskin. New York: Pantheon, 1983.

Griffiths, Richard M. *Fellow Travellers of the Right: British Enthusiasts for Nazi Germany, 1933-1939*. London: Constable, 1980.

Gutmann, David. "Symposium: Purifying Allah's Soil." *FrontPageMag.com*, January 27, 2006.

Haaretz. "Lebanese hospital: Number of casualties from Qana air strike is 28, not 52." August 3, 2006.

Hakakian, Roya. *Journey from the Land of No: A Girlhood Caught in Revolutionary Iran*. New York: Crown, 2004.

Hamilton, Alastair. *The Appeal of Fascism: A Study of Intellectuals and Fascism, 1919-1945*. London: A. Blond, 1971.

Hayden, Tom, "An Exit Strategy for Iraq Now." *Los Angeles Times*, August 16, 2005.

Hayes, Stephen F. *The Connection: How al Qaeda's Collaboration with Saddam Hussein Has Endangered America*. New York: HarperCollins, 2004.

Haynes, John Earl and Harvey Klehr. *In Denial: Historians, Communism and Espionage*. San Fransisco: Encounter Books, 2005.

Hayward, Steven. *The Real Jimmy Carter*. Washington, D.C.: Regnery, 2004.

Hirsen, James. "Fasting for Peace, Hollywood-Style." *DiscovertheNetworks.org*, July 5, 2006.

Hitchens, Christopher. "Unfairenheit 9/11: The lies of Michael Moore." *Slate.com*, June 21, 2004.

Hitti, Philip K. *The Arabs: A Short History*. rev. ed. Washington, D.C.: Regnery, 1970.

Hoffer, Eric. *The True Believer: Thoughts on the Nature of Mass Movements*. New York: Harper and Row, 1951.

Hollander, Paul. *Anti-Americanism: Critiques at Home & Abroad, 1965-1990*. New York: Oxford University Press, 1992.

————. *Political Pilgrims: Travels of Western Intellectuals to the Soviet Union, China, & Cuba 1928-1978*. New York: Oxford University Press, 1981.

————. *Understanding Anti-Americanism: Its Origins and Impact at Home and Abroad*. Chicago: Ivan R. Dee, 2004.

Holzer, Henry Mark and Erika Holzer. *"Aid and Comfort": Jane Fonda in North Vietnam*. Jefferson, N.C.: McFarland, 2002.

HonestReporting.com. "Hamas's Defense of Terror." April 23, 2006, http://www.honestreporting.com/articles/45884734/critiques/

Hamas_Defense_of_Terror.asp.

Horn, Joshua. *Away with All Pests: An English Surgeon in People's China, 1954-1969.* New York: Hamlyn, 1969.

Horowitz, David. "An Open Letter to the 'Anti-War' Demonstrators: Think Twice Before You Bring the War Home." *FrontPageMag.com,* September 27, 2001.

– – –. *The End of Time.* San Francisco: Encounter Books, 2005.

– – –. "Fellow Travelers." *FrontPageMag.com,* July 18, 2006.

– – –. *Hating Whitey: And Other Progressive Causes.* Dallas: Spence, 1999.

– – –. "How the Left Undermined American Security before 9/11." *FrontPageMag.com,* September 10, 2004.

– – –. *Left Illusions: An Intellectual Odyssey.* Dallas: Spence, 2003.

– – –. "Lynne Stewart: The Left on Trial." *FrontPageMag.com,* January 10, 2005.

– – –. "The McGovern Syndrome." *FrontPageMag.com,* December 27, 2004.

– – –. "Neo-Communism." *FrontPageMag.com,* April 22, 2003.

– – –. *The Politics of Bad Faith: The Radical Assault on America's Future.* New York: Free Press, 2000.

– – –. *The Professors: The 101 Most Dangerous Academics in America.* Washington, D.C.: Regnery, 2006.

– – –. *Radical Son: A Generational Odyssey.* New York: Free Press, 1997.

– – –. "Unholy Alliance, How the Left Supports Terrorists at Home." *FrontPageMag.com,* September 24, 2004.

– – –. *Unholy Alliance: Radical Islam and the American Left.* Washington, D.C.: Regnery, 2004.

– – –. "Where Have All the Democrats Gone?" *FrontPageMag.com,* June 28, 2004.

Horowitz, David and Ben Johnson, eds., *Campus Support for Terrorism.* Los Angeles: Center for the Study of Popular Culture, 2004.

Horowitz, David and Ben Johnson. *Party of Defeat.* Dallas: Spence, 2008.

Horowitz, David and Jacob Laksin. "Noam Chomsky's Love Affair with Nazis." *FrontPageMag.com,* May 15, 2006.

Horowitz, David and Richard Poe. *The Shadow Party.* Nashville: Thomas Nelson, 2006.

Horowitz, David and Robert Spencer. "A Response to Feminists on the Violent Oppression of Women in Islam." *FrontPageMag.com,* January 24, 2008.

Huberman Leo and Paul Sweezy. *Cuba: Anatomy of a Revolution.* New York: Monthly Review Press, 1961.

Hussein, Ali. "Chomsky needs to learn a lot more about Lebanon." *YaLibnan.com,* May 13, 2006.

Hymowitz, Kay. S. "Feminist Fog." *New York Post,* February 9, 2003.

– – –. "Why Feminism Is AWOL on Islam." *City Journal* (Winter 2003).

Ignatius, David. "Beirut's Berlin Wall." *Washington Post,* February 23, 2005.

Iraq New Network. "Galloway Calls for Global Unity between Islamic and Leftist forces." April 25, 2005.

Ishaq, Ibn. *Sirat Rasul Allah.* Translated by A. Guillaume as *The Life of Muhammad.* Oxford and New York: Oxford University Press, 1967.

Jensen, Robert. "A Defeat for an Empire." *Fort Worth Star-Telegram,* December 9, 2004.

Johnson, Ben. "Sean Penn's Baghdad Homecoming." *FrontPageMag.com*, January 21, 2004.

— — —. "Vindication." *FrontPageMag.com*, December 20, 2005.

Johnson, Hewlett. *China's New Creative Age*. Westport, Conn.: Greenwood Press, 1953.

Johnson, Paul. *Intellectuals*. London: Weidenfeld and Nicolson, 1988.

— — —. *Modern Times: The World from the Twenties to the Eighties*. London: Weidenfeld and Nicolson, 1983.

Jones, Michael. *Degenerate Moderns: Modernity as Rationalized Sexual Misbehavior*. San Francisco: Ignatius, 1993.

Karsh, Efraim. *Arafat's War: The Man and His Battle for Israeli Conquest*. New York: Grove Press, 2003.

— — —. *Islamic Imperialism: A History*. New Haven: Yale University Press, 2006.

Kerstein, Benjamin. "Here There is No Why?" August 2004, http://www.discoverthenetworks.org/Articles/Here%20There%20is%20No%20Why.htm.

Kimball, Roger. "Hitchens, Galloway Clash in Heated Debate on Iraq War." *New York Sun*, September 16, 2005.

Klehr, Harvey. Review of *Right in Her Soul: The Life of Anna Louise Strong. The New Republic*, March 19, 1984.

Klein, Aaron. *Schmoozing With Terrorists*. Los Angeles: WND Books, 2007.

Klein, Naomi. "Bring Najaf to New York." *The Nation*, August 26, 2004.

Kobrin, Nancy. *The Sheikh's New Clothes: Al Qaeda's Suicide Terrorism and What It's All About*. Unpublished manuscript.

Kovacs, Joe. "Cindy: Terrorists 'freedom fighters.'" *WorldNetDaily.com*, August 23, 2005.

Kriele, Martin. *Nicaragua—Das blutende Herz Amerikas*. Mainz, Germany: Hase & Koehler, 1985.

Laksin, Jacob. "The Antiwar Left's Conspiracy of Silence." *FrontPageMag.com*, December 20, 2005.

— — —. "Carter's Terror Tour." *FrontPageMag.com*, April 14, 2008, http://www.frontpagemag.com/Articles/Read.aspx?GUID=E3C3EA75-A7ED-4EC2-AB68-ECB514358AE1.

— — —. "No Left Turns on the War?" *FrontPageMag.com*, December 5, 2008.

— — —. "Obama's Muddle over Iraq." *FrontPageMag.com*, July 22, 2008.

— — —. "Obama's World." *FrontPageMag.com*, Wednesday, May 07, 2008.

— — —. "Petition for Genocide." *FrontPageMag.com*, July 28, 2006.

— — —. "Tom Hayden's Iraqi Jihad." *FrontPageMag.com*, October 25, 2005.

— — —. "What Lies Beyond *Chutzpah*?" *FrontPageMag.com*, October 4, 2005, http://www.frontpagemag.com/Articles/Read.aspx?GUID=63E08152-CDEC-44BB-9EBE-E6B6C7F55CC8.

Lal, K.S. *The Legacy of Muslim Rule in India*. New Delhi: Aditya Prakashan, 1992.

Lapkin, Sharon. "Muslim Gang Rapes and the Aussie Riots." *FrontPageMag.com*, December 15, 2005.

— — —. "Western Muslims' Racist Rape Spree." *FrontPageMag.com*, December 27, 2005.

Laqueur, Walter. *Stalin: The Glasnost Revelations*. New York: Scribner's, 1990.

Lewis, Bernard. *The Crisis of Islam*. New York: Random House, 2003.

Loftus, John. "The Muslim Brotherhood, Nazis, and al-Qaeda." *Jewish Community News*, October 10, 2006.

———. "The Muslim Brotherhood, the Nazis and Al-Qa'ida." *Nexus* 12, no. 6 (October-November 2005).

MacLaine, Shirley. *You Can Get There from Here*. New York: W. W. Norton, 1975.

Manji, Irshad. *The Trouble with Islam Today: A Muslim's Call for Reform in Her Faith*. New York: St. Martin's Griffin, 2005.

Marcus, Itamar and Barbara Crook. "Suicide terror for children glorified on Hamas children's Web site." Palestinian Media Watch (*www.pmw.org*), March 16, 2006.

Marcuse, Herbert. *One-Dimensional Man: Studies in the Ideology of Advanced Industrial Society*. Boston: Beacon, 1964.

McCarthy, Mary. *Hanoi*. New York: Harcourt, Brace, and World, 1968.

Media Research Center. "Turner: Iraqi Insurgents 'Patriots,' Warming Inaction: Cannibalism." April 2, 2008.

Meir-Levi, David. "My Brother's Keeper?" *FrontPageMag.com*, March 13, 2006.

MEMRI (Middle East Media Research Institute). "British MP George Galloway at Damascus University to Support Bashar Al-Assad." Special Dispatch Series, no. 1,024, November 17, 2005.

———. TV clip no. 566. "Hizbullah Leader Hassan Nasrallah: Death to America." http://www.memritv.org/search.asp?ACT=S9&P1=566; and MEMRI. TV clip no. 74. "Hizbullah Secretary-General Sheikh Hassan Nasrallah Threatens the U.S." http://www.memritv.org/search.asp?ACT=S9&P1=74.

———. "Umm Nidal: 'The Mother of the *Shahids*.'" Special Dispatch Series, no. 673, March 4, 2004.

———. "U.S. Linguist Noam Chomsky Meets with Hizbullah Leaders in Lebanon." Special Dispatch Series, no. 1,165, May 16, 2006.

Mernissi, Fatima. *Beyond the Veil: Male-Female Dynamics in Modern Muslim Society*. Bloomington: Indiana University Press, 1987.

———. *The Veil and the Male Elite: A Feminist Interpretation of Women's Rights in Islam*. Translated by Mary Jo Lakeland. New York: Addison-Wesley, 1987.

Miller, James. *The Passion of Michel Foucault*. Cambridge, Mass.: Harvard University Press, 2000.

Moore, Michael. "Heads Up...from Michael Moore." *MichaelMoore.com*, April 14, 2004, http://www.michaelmoore.com/words/message/ index.php?messageDate=2004-04-14.

Moore, Peter. "Gays Attacked at Palestinian Protest." *FrontPageMag.com*, May 16, 2004.

Morse, Chuck. *The Nazi Connection to Islamic Terrorism: Adolf Hitler and Haj Amin al-Husseini*. Lincoln, Neb.: iUniverse, 2003.

Murawiec, Laurent. *The Mind of Jihad*. Washington, D.C.: Hudson Institute, 2005.

Nafisi, Azar. *Reading Lolita in Tehran: A Memoir in Books*. New York: Random House, 2003.

Newman, Hillel. "The Worst Exploitation." *Boston Globe*, June 7, 2004.

Nimmo, Kurt. *Another Day in the Empire: Life in Neoconservative America.* Tempe, Ariz.: Dandelion Books, 2003.

— — —. "DiscoverTheNetwork: David Horowitz's Smear Portal." *PressAction.com,* February 15, 2005, http://www.pressaction.com/news/ weblog/full_article/nimmo02152005/.

Packer, George. "Terrorist Lawyer." *New York Times,* September 23, 2002.

Pawel, Ernst. "Sex under Socialism" *Commentary* (September 1965): 90-95.

Perazzo, John. "CCR: Fifth Column Law Factory." *FrontPageMag.com,* July 31, 2002.

— — —. "Left-Wing Monster: Pol Pot." *FrontPageMag.com,* August 8, 2005.

Phares, Walid. "'Azzam': The Domestic Jihad." *CounterTerrorismBlog.org,* September 5, 2006.

Pipes, Daniel. "Hating Valentine's Day in the Third World." *FrontPageMag.com,* February 17, 2004.

— — —. "[The Issue of Compulsion in Religion:] Islam Is What Its Followers Make of It." *New York Sun,* September 28, 2004.

— — —. "The Left's Dream." *CNSNews.com,* March 18, 2003.

— — —. *Militant Islam Reaches America.* New York: W. W. Norton, 2002.

— — —. "What Is Jihad?" *New York Post,* December 31, 2002.

Plaut, Steven. "The Anniversary of Rachel Corrie's Suicide on Behalf of Terrorists." *ChronWatch.com,* March 16, 2005.

Potter, David. *History and American Society.* New York: Oxford University Press, 1973.

Pryce-Jones, David. *The Closed Circle: An Interpretation of the Arabs.* Chicago: Irvin R. Dee, 2002.

— — —. "Their *Kampf:* Hitler's Book in Arab Hands." *National Review,* July 29, 2002.

Qutb, Sayyid. "American Experience." *Islam and Christian-Muslim Relations* 11, no. 1 (2000).

Radosh, Ronald. *Commies: A Journey through the Old Left, the New Left, and the Leftover Left.* San Francisco: Encounter Books, 2001.

Rashid, Ahmed. *Taliban: Militant Islam, Oil and Fundamentalism in Central Asia.* New Haven: Yale University Press, 2001.

Ray, John. "Left-wing Fascism: An Intellectual Disorder." *FrontPageMag.com,* October 22, 2002.

Rayment, Sean. "Rescued hostage rations his thanks." *Sunday Telegraph* (London), March 26, 2006.

Rehov, Pierre. "What Paradise?" *FrontPageMag.com,* November 16, 2005.

Reuters. "What retirement? Mike Wallace gets scoop in Iran." *RedOrbit.com,* August 10, 2006.

Ridenour, Ron. *Yankee Sandinistas: Interviews with North Americans Living and Working in the New Nicaragua.* Willimantic, Conn.: Curbstone Press, 1986..

Robinson, Joan. *The Cultural Revolution in China.* London: Penguin, 1969.

Rochester, Stuart I. and Frederick Kiley. *Honor Bound: American Prisoners of War in Southeast Asia 1961-1973.* Annapolis: Naval Institute Press, 1999.

Rosendall, Richard J. "The Queer Left's Palestinian Folly." *FrontPageMag.com,* February 2, 2006.

Rothfeld, Michael. "Ignoring Hezbollah a Costly Error." *Newsday.com,* August 8, 2006.

Rubin, Jerry. *Do It: Scenarios of the Revolution.* New York: Simon & Schuster, 1970.

Rubin, Neil, "Carter's Hurrah?" *JewishTimes.com*, April 25, 2008.

Rubin, Ronald I., ed., *The Unredeemed: Anti-Semitism in the Soviet Union.* Chicago: Quadrangle, 1968.

Ruo-Wang, Bao and Rudolph Chelminski. *Prisoner of Mao.* New York: Coward, McCann & Geoghegan, 1973.

Saadawi, Nawal El. *The Hidden Face of Eve.* Translated and edited by Sherif Hetata. London: Zed Books, 2002.

Sabbah, Fatna Aït. *Woman in the Muslim Unconscious.* Translated by Mary Jo Lakeland. New York: Pergamon Press, 1984.

Sahebjam, Freidoune. *The Stoning of Soraya M.: A True Story.* New York: Arcade Publishing, 1994.

Schanzer, Jonathan. *Hamas vs. Fatah: The Struggle for Palestine.* Palgrave Macmillan, 2008.

Schell, Orville. *In the People's Republic: An American's First Hand View of Living and Working in China.* New York: Random House, 1977.

Schmitt, Arno and Jehoeda Sofer, eds. *Sexuality and Eroticism among Males in Moslem Societies.* New York: Haworth Press, 1991.

Shaidle, Kathy. "Obama's Surge Purge." *FrontPageMag.com*, July 30, 2008.

Shaw, George Bernard. *The Rationalization of Russia* Edited by Harry M. Geduld. Bloomington: University of Indiana Press, 1964.

Shuman, Ellis. "CNN founder accuses Israel of terror." *Israel Insider*, June 18, 2002.

Sontag, Susan. "Some Thoughts on the Right Way (for Us) to Love the Cuban Revolution." *Ramparts* (April 1969).

———. *Trip to Hanoi.* New York: Farrar, Straus, and Giroux, 1968.

Souad. *Burned Alive: A Victim of the Law of Men.* New York: Warner Books, 2003.

Spencer, Robert. "Guilty as Charged." *FrontPageMag.com*, April 20, 2006.

———. *Islam Unveiled: Disturbing Questions about the World's Fastest-Growing Faith.* San Francisco: Encounter Books, 2002.

———. "Islamo-Fascism Denial." *Frontpagemag.com*, October 23, 2007, http://www.frontpagemag.com/Articles/Read.aspx?GUID= FDD13E54-41C7-4C89-A482-58159E9435A5.

———. *Onward Muslim Soldiers: How Jihad Still Threatens America and the West.* Washington, D.C.: Regnery, 2003.

———. *The Politically Incorrect Guide to Islam (and the Crusades).* Washington, D.C.: Regnery, 2005.

———. "Stage-Managed Massacre." *FrontPageMag.com*, August 2, 2006, http://www.frontpagemag.com/Articles/Read.aspx?GUID= 3CF1C090-E95B-4FF0-9514-8DE6706EA586.

———. "Sympathy for the Devil." *FrontPageMag.com*, May 4, 2006.

Sperry, Paul. *Infiltration: How Muslim Spies and Subversives Have Penetrated Washington.* Nashville: Thomas Nelson, 2005.

Stakelbeck, Jr., Frederick W. "Dangerous Brotherhood." *FrontPageMag.com*, June 6, 2006.

Stalinsky, Steven and Y. Yehoshua. "Muslim Clerics on the Religious Rulings Regarding Wife-Beating." MEMRI, no. 27, March 22, 2004.

Strong, Anna Louise. *This Soviet World*. New York: H. Holt, 1936.

Taheri, Amir. *Holy Terror: The Inside Story of Islamic Terrorism*. London: Sphere Books, 1987.

— — —. "O's Tour De Farce." *New York Post*, July 29, 2008.

Taylor, Sally J. *Stalin's Apologist: Walter Duranty: The* New York Times's *Man in Moscow*. New York: Oxford University Press, 1990.

Thoreau, Henry David. *Walden and on the Duty of Civil Disobedience*. 1961 ed. New York: Holt, Rinehart, and Winston, 1854.

Ticker, Bruce. "The Case against Rachel Corrie." *IsraelNationalNews.com*, June 1, 2004.

Time. "The Mystic Who Lit the Fires of Hatred" in "Man of the Year: Ayatullah Khomeini," January 7, 1980.

Timmerman, Kenneth R. "Iran's War." *FrontPageMag.com*, July 27, 2006.

— — —. *Preachers of Hate: Islam and the War on America*. New York: Crown Forum, 2003.

Topping, Audrey. *Dawn Wakes in the East*. New York: Harper and Row, 1972.

Tremoglie, Michael. "Stanley Cohen: Terrorist Mouthpiece." *FrontPageMag.com*, December 17, 2002.

Valladares, Armando. *Against All Hope: A Memoir of Life in Castro's Gulag*. Translated by Andrew Hurley. San Francisco: Encounter Books, 2001.

Vincent, Steven. *In the Red Zone: A Journey into the Soul of Iraq*. Dallas: Spence, 2004.

Volkogonov, Dmitri. *Lenin: A New Biography*. Translated and edited by Harold Shukman. New York: The Free Press, 1994.

Waller, J. Michael. "Tropical Chekists: The Sandinista Secret Police Legacy in Nicaragua." *Demokratizatsiya: The Journal of Post-Soviet Democratization* (Summer 2004).

White House News Release. "Statement by the President in His Address to the Nation." September 11, 2001, http://www.whitehouse.gov/news/ releases/2001/09/20010911-16.html.

Wiesel, Elie. *The Jews of Silence: A Personal Report on Soviet Jewry*. Translated by Neal Kozodoy. New York: Holt, Rinehart, and Winston, 1966.

Wonder, Terri. "Re-Islamization in Higher Education from Above and Below: The University of South Florida and Its Global Contexts." PhD diss. available online at http://council.smallwarsjournal.com/showthread.php?t=1247.

WorldNetDaily, "Brave New Schools: Islam Studies Required in California District Course Has 7th-Graders Memorizing Koran Verses, Praying to Allah." *WorldNetDaily.com*, January 11, 2002.

Wu, Harry Hongda. *Laogai: The Chinese Gulag*. Translated by Ted Slingerland. Boulder, Colorado: Westview Press, 1992.

Ye'or, Bat. *The Dhimmi: Jews and Christians under Islam*. Translated by David Maisel, Paul Fenton, and David Littman. Rutherford, N.J.: Fairleigh Dickinson University Press, 1985.

— — —. *Islam and Dhimmitude: Where Civilizations Collide*. Translated by Miriam Kochan and David Littman. Madison, N.J.: Fairleigh Dickinson University Press, 2002.

Zand-Bonazzi, Banafsheh and Elio Bonazzi. "Sean Penn: Our Man in Tehran." *FrontPageMag.com*, June 16, 2005.